My Laughable Life with Garfield

My Laughable Life with Garfield

The Jon Arbuckle Chronicles

by
Jim "**Dorkmeister**" Davis
with his geeky gang

Mark "**Spacey**" Acey

Brett "**Dummkopf**" Koth

Scott "**Nerdnik**" Nickel

Thomas "**Bonehead**" Howard

BALLANTINE BOOKS • NEW YORK

A Ballantine Books Trade Paperback Original

Published in the United States by Ballantine Books, an imprint of
The Random House Publishing Group, a division of Random House, Inc., New York.

ISBN 978-0-345-52591-8

www.ballantinebooks.com
www.garfield.com

9 8 7 6 5 4 3 2 1

Credits

EDITORIAL

Mark Acey, Scott Nickel, Brett Koth

ILLUSTRATION

Brett Koth, Lynette Nuding, Lori Barker, Larry Fentz

DESIGN

Thomas Howard

PRODUCTION

Brad Hill, Kenny Goetzinger

Introduction

They say every dork has his day, and I guess this is Jon's. He's finally getting a book of his own. I'm just surprised it's not a coloring book.

I've known Jon Arbuckle since I was just a kitten. In fact, Jon was my first scratching post. I shredded his ugly polyester pants when I was only a few weeks old.

Jon's always had an atrocious fashion sense. His wardrobe is straight out of Geeks "R" Us. Jon makes circus clowns look like tasteful dressers. And he's the only guy I know who thinks wearing a powder-blue tuxedo with a ruffled lavender shirt is chic.

The only thing more pathetic than Jon's clothes is his love life. He's dated the weirdest women. There was Kimmy, who was raised by wolves; Loretta Gnish, who had a third nostril; Big Bertha, who made a hippo seem petite; and, of course, who could forget Cindy Krovitz, *Barbershop Digest* cover model? (She had a great handlebar mustache!)

After years of striking out, Jon's finally in a relationship with Liz, the veterinarian. I have to question her taste in men, along with her sanity.

Sure I diss the dweeb, but it's all in fun. Deep down I know I need Jon. After all, who else is going to pay the pizza delivery guy?

 Garfield

THE GENESIS OF JON

That darn cat. He always got the funny lines.

In the mid-1970s while working as an assistant on *Tumbleweeds*, Jim Davis started developing his own strip, which featured a bachelor cartoonist (very much like Jim himself) and a big fat cat. Jim sent samples of the comic strip to several syndicate editors and received encouraging responses. They especially liked the cat.

"The more I worked on the strip," Davis recalled, "the more obvious it became that Garfield was the real star."

True to his nature, the tubby tabby hogged the spotlight. Jim did some reworking, renamed the strip, and a comics legend was born.

But Jon Arbuckle, the bumbling bachelor cartoonist, remained an integral part of *Garfield*, appearing in more than 8,000 strips by 2012.

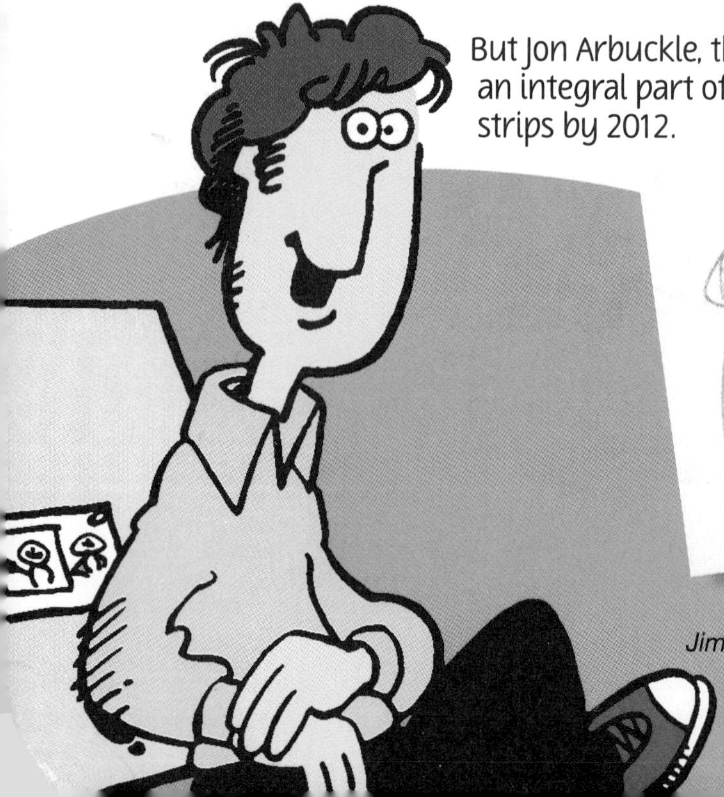

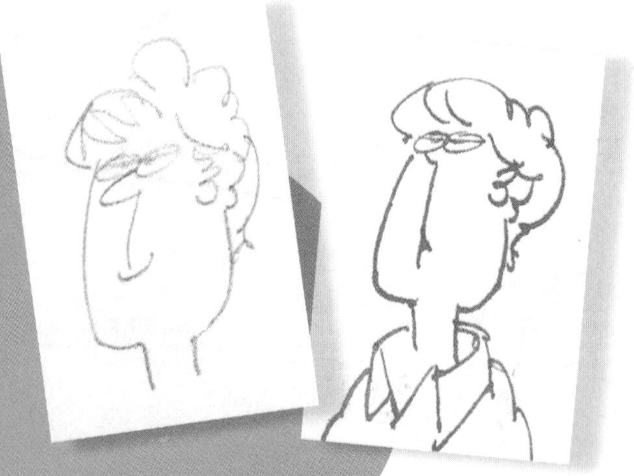

Jim Davis' early sketches of Jon, circa 1976.

THIS IS IT GARFIELD. THE LATE-LATE MOVIE WITH BRIGITTE BARDOT
GOT OUR SODA POP. GOT OUR POPCORN. WE'RE SET
JIM DAVIS
ZZZZZZ
ZZZZ

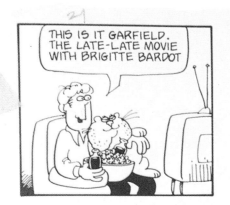

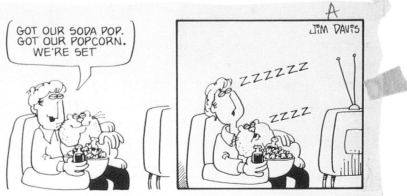

The name Jon Arbuckle came from an old coffee commercial that Jim remembered. He also used the name as an "expert source" to add "credibility" to speeches during college debates.

RELEASE MY HAND, GARFIELD
YOU RELEASE HAMBURGER, I RELEASE HAND

When Jim was creating the characters, the name Jon Arbuckle just seemed to fit the kind of poor sap who would get stuck with a cranky cat with an overactive appetite.

JIM DAVIS
5-5
© 1983 PAWS, INC. All Rights Reserved.
RELEASE MY HAND, GARFIELD
YOU RELEASE HAMBURGER, I RELEASE HAND

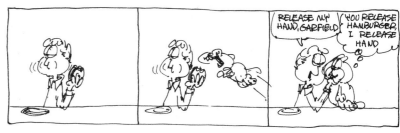

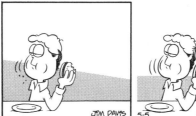

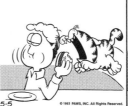

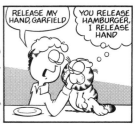

TOP: Sample from an early syndication submission.

ABOVE: A rough from the 1980s and the finished strip.

Like Garfield, Jon has changed over the years. His eyes got rounder (and geekier), but he's still hopelessly unhip—the same bungling, boring nerd who provides love, food, and shelter, while his playful pets, Garfield and Odie, provide the laughs.

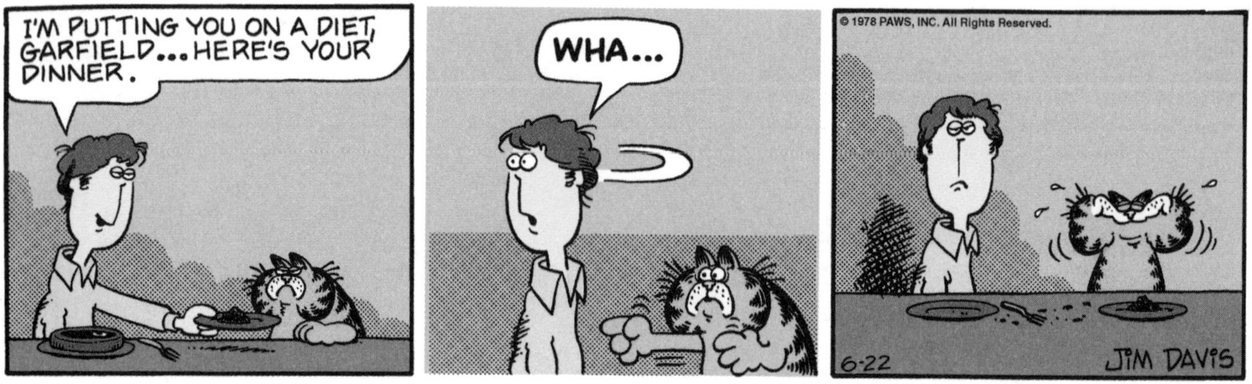
I'M PUTTING YOU ON A DIET, GARFIELD... HERE'S YOUR DINNER.
WHA...
© 1978 PAWS, INC. All Rights Reserved.
6-22
JIM DAVIS

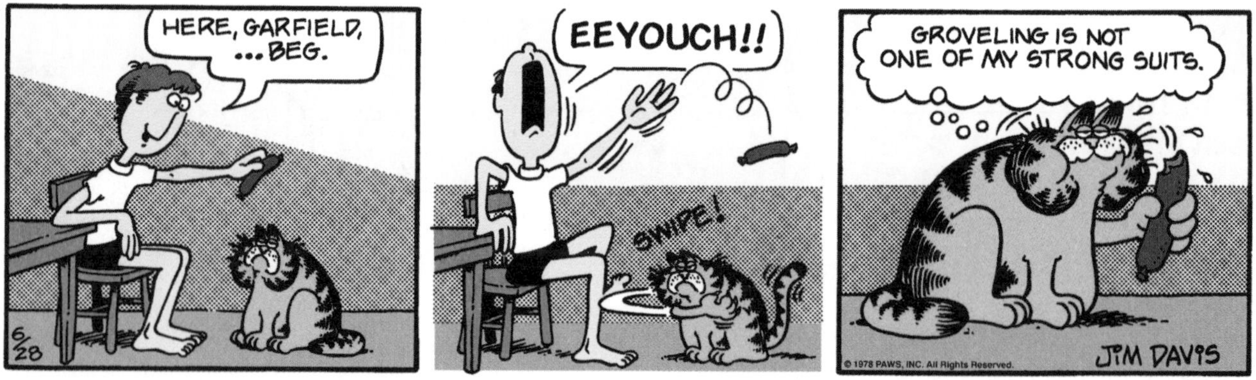
HERE, GARFIELD, ...BEG.
6/28
EEYOUCH!!
SWIPE!
GROVELING IS NOT ONE OF MY STRONG SUITS.
© 1978 PAWS, INC. All Rights Reserved.
JIM DAVIS

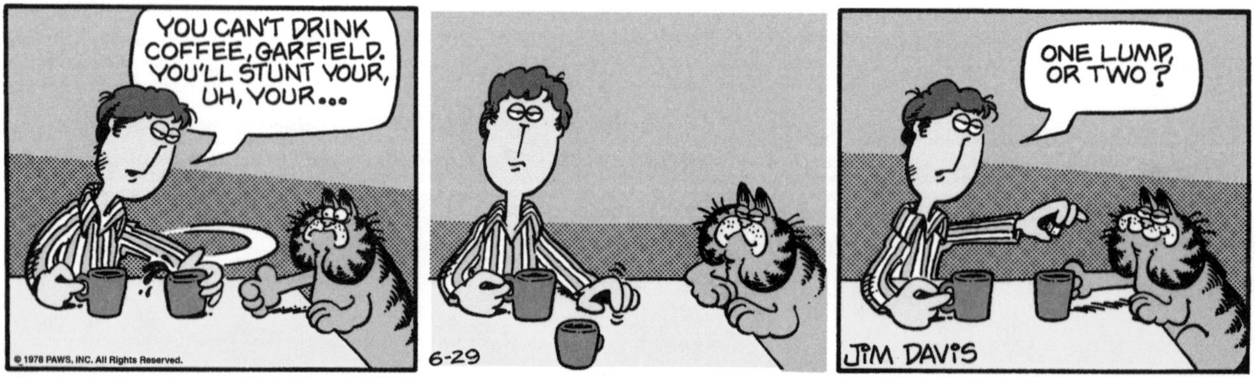
YOU CAN'T DRINK COFFEE, GARFIELD. YOU'LL STUNT YOUR, UH, YOUR...
© 1978 PAWS, INC. All Rights Reserved.
6-29
ONE LUMP, OR TWO ?
JIM DAVIS

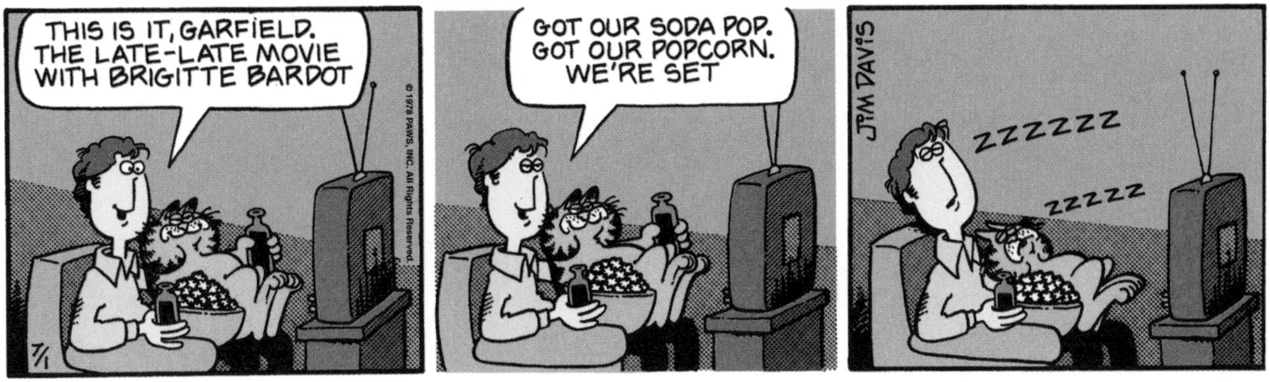

THIS IS IT, GARFIELD. THE LATE-LATE MOVIE WITH BRIGITTE BARDOT
© 1978 PAWS, INC. All Rights Reserved
7/1
GOT OUR SODA POP. GOT OUR POPCORN. WE'RE SET
JIM DAVIS
ZZZZZZ
ZZZZZ

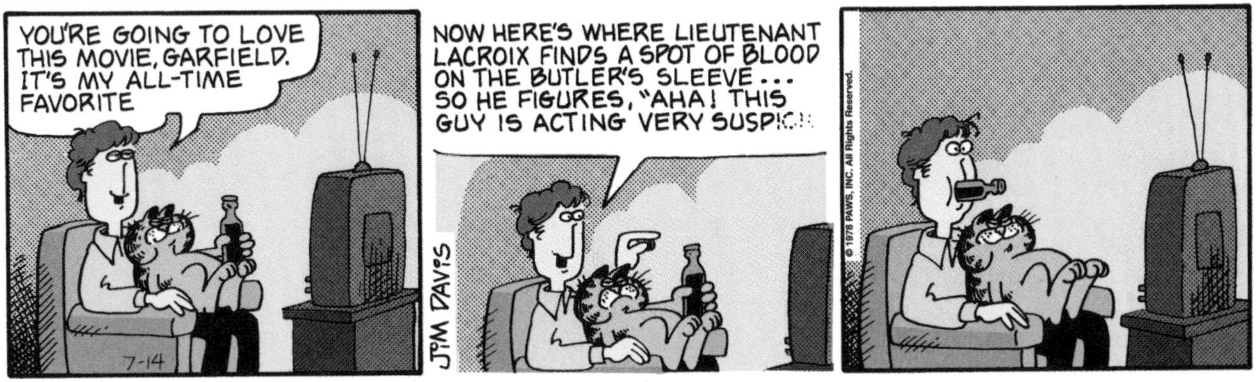

YOU'RE GOING TO LOVE THIS MOVIE, GARFIELD. IT'S MY ALL-TIME FAVORITE
7-14
NOW HERE'S WHERE LIEUTENANT LACROIX FINDS A SPOT OF BLOOD ON THE BUTLER'S SLEEVE... SO HE FIGURES, "AHA! THIS GUY IS ACTING VERY SUSPIC
JIM DAVIS
© 1978 PAWS, INC. All Rights Reserved.

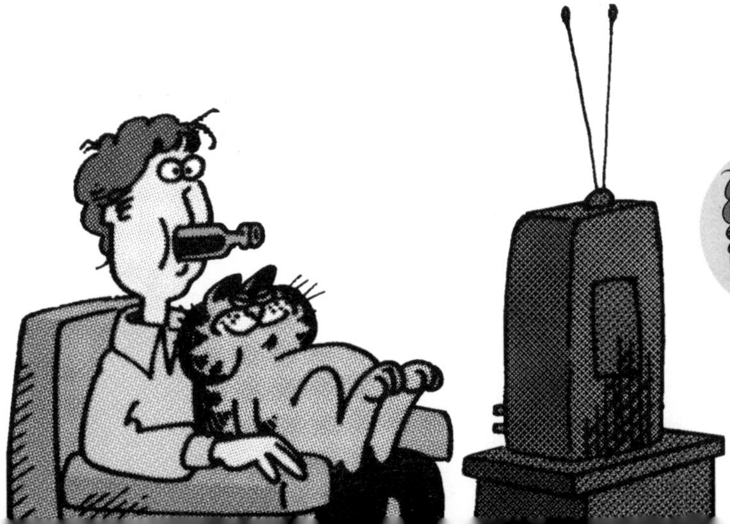

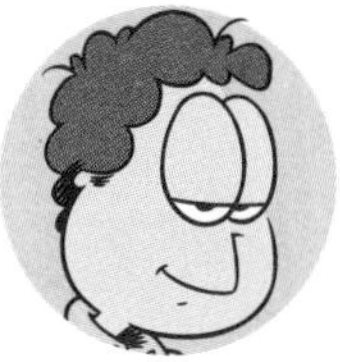

"Garfield's always been a real handful. And sometimes a mouthful."

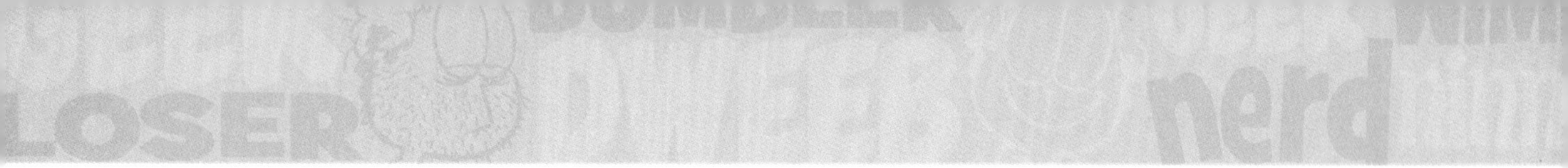
LOSER
nerd

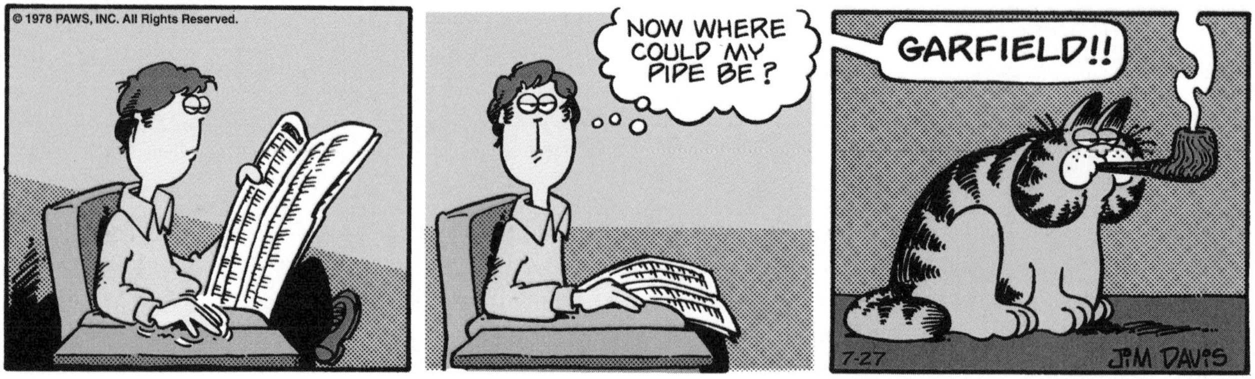
© 1978 PAWS, INC. All Rights Reserved.
NOW WHERE COULD MY PIPE BE?
GARFIELD!!
7-27
JIM DAVIS

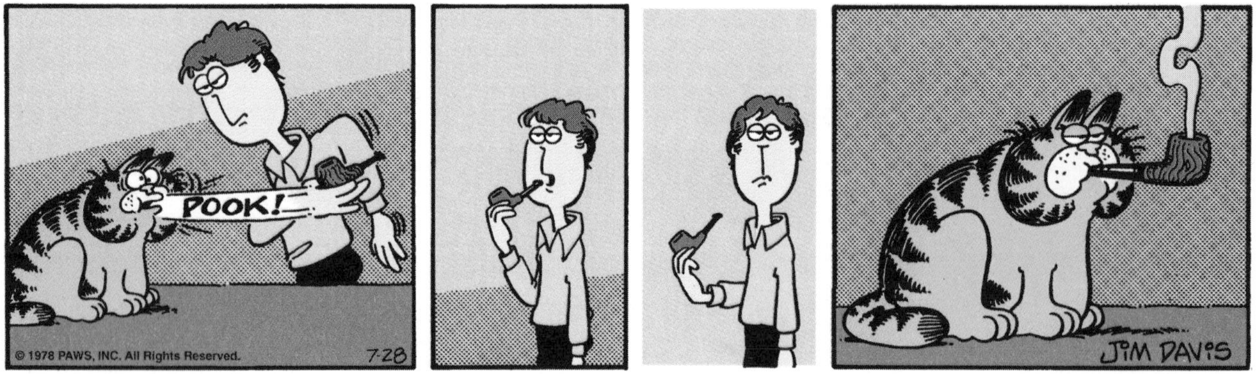
POOK!
© 1978 PAWS, INC. All Rights Reserved.
7-28
JIM DAVIS

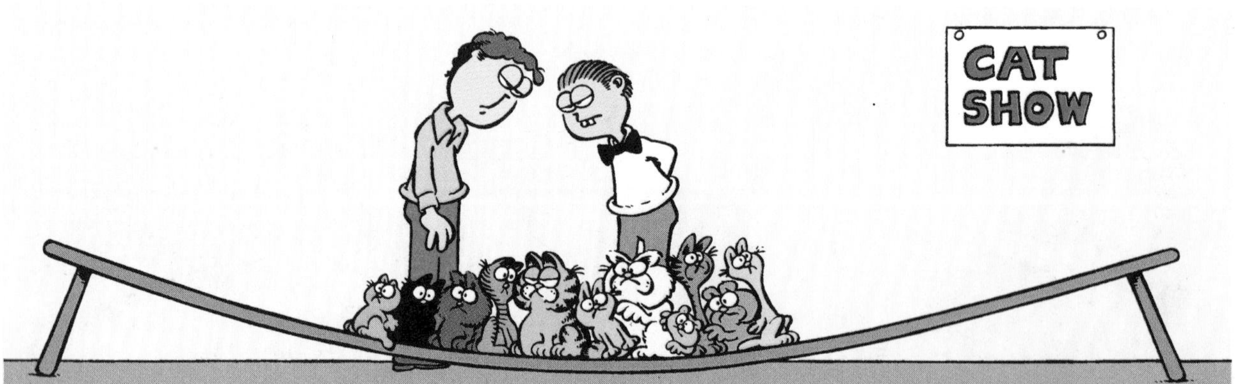
CAT SHOW

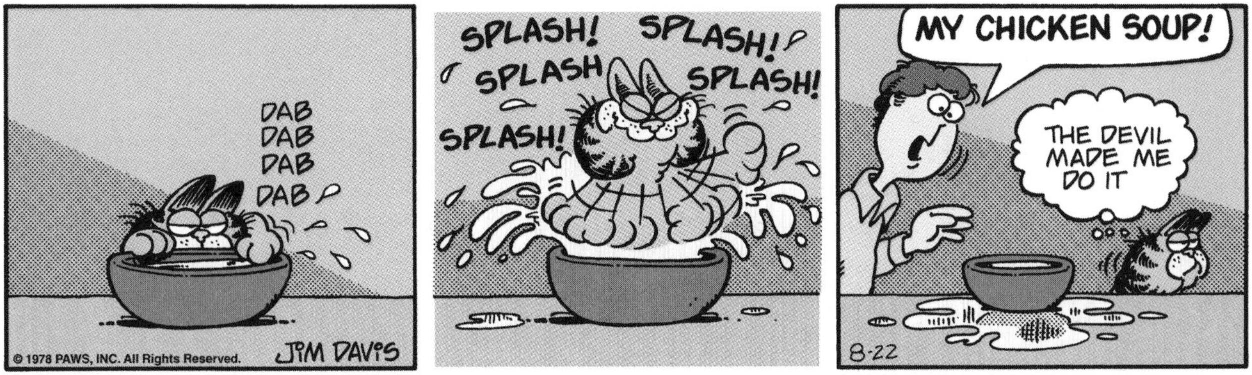
DAB
DAB
DAB
DAB
© 1978 PAWS, INC. All Rights Reserved.
JIM DAVIS
SPLASH! SPLASH!
SPLASH
SPLASH!
SPLASH!
MY CHICKEN SOUP!
THE DEVIL MADE ME DO IT
8-22

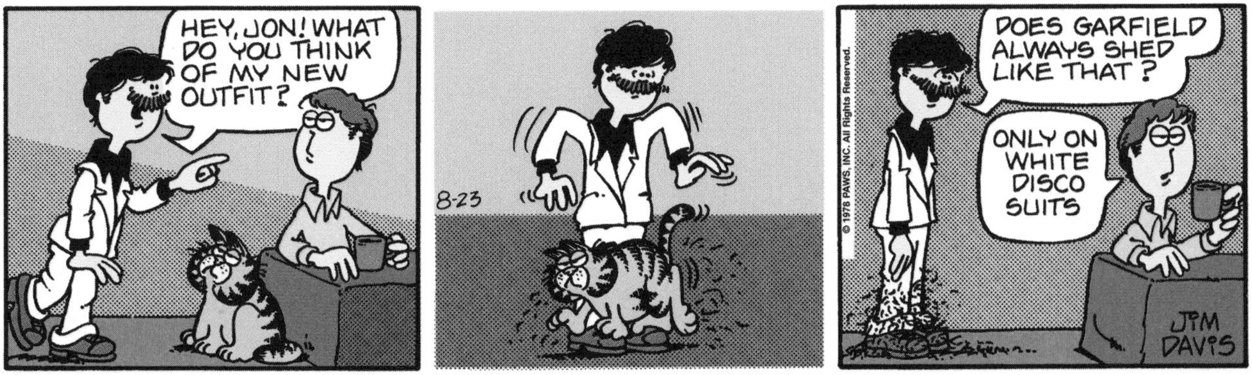
HEY, JON! WHAT DO YOU THINK OF MY NEW OUTFIT?
8-23
© 1978 PAWS, INC. All Rights Reserved.
DOES GARFIELD ALWAYS SHED LIKE THAT?
ONLY ON WHITE DISCO SUITS
JIM DAVIS

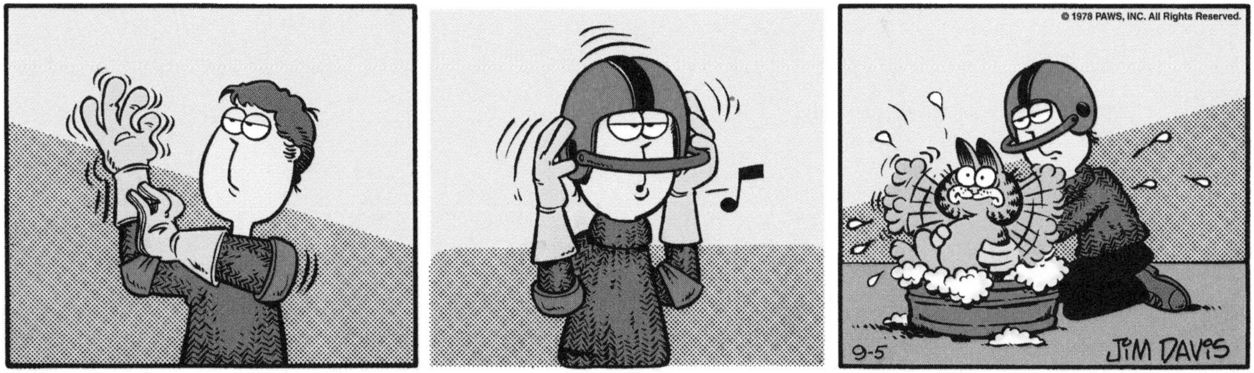
© 1978 PAWS, INC. All Rights Reserved.
9-5
JIM DAVIS

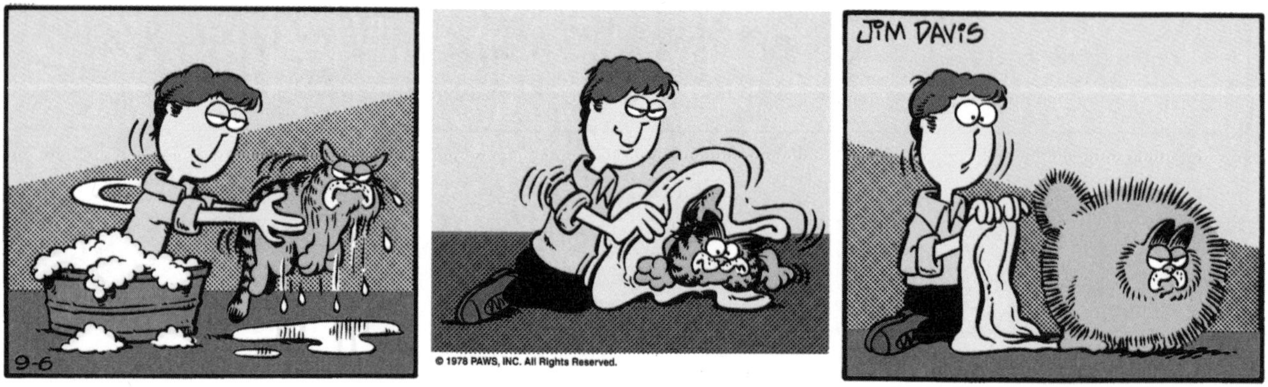
9-6
© 1978 PAWS, INC. All Rights Reserved.
JIM DAVIS

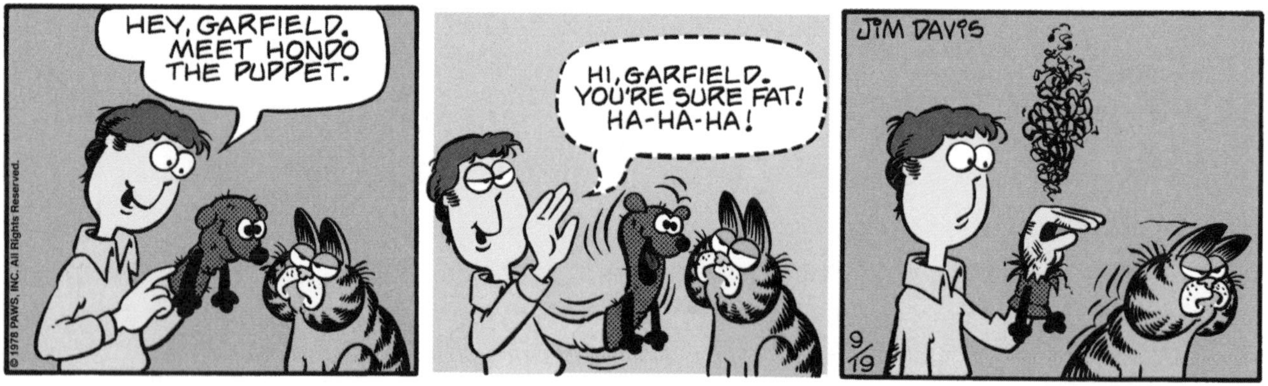
HEY, GARFIELD. MEET HONDO THE PUPPET.
© 1978 PAWS, INC. All Rights Reserved.
HI, GARFIELD. YOU'RE SURE FAT! HA-HA-HA!
JIM DAVIS
9/19

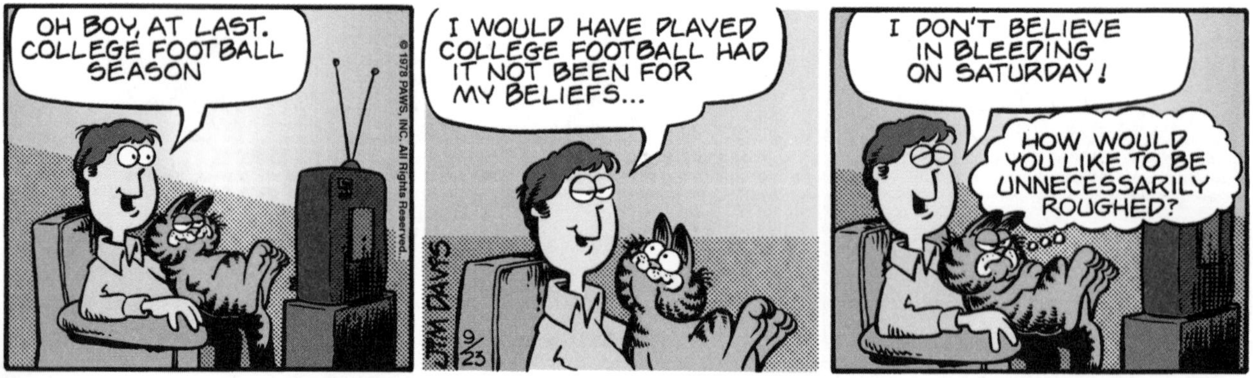
OH BOY, AT LAST. COLLEGE FOOTBALL SEASON
© 1978 PAWS, INC. All Rights Reserved.
I WOULD HAVE PLAYED COLLEGE FOOTBALL HAD IT NOT BEEN FOR MY BELIEFS...
JIM DAVIS
9/23
I DON'T BELIEVE IN BLEEDING ON SATURDAY!
HOW WOULD YOU LIKE TO BE UNNECESSARILY ROUGHED?

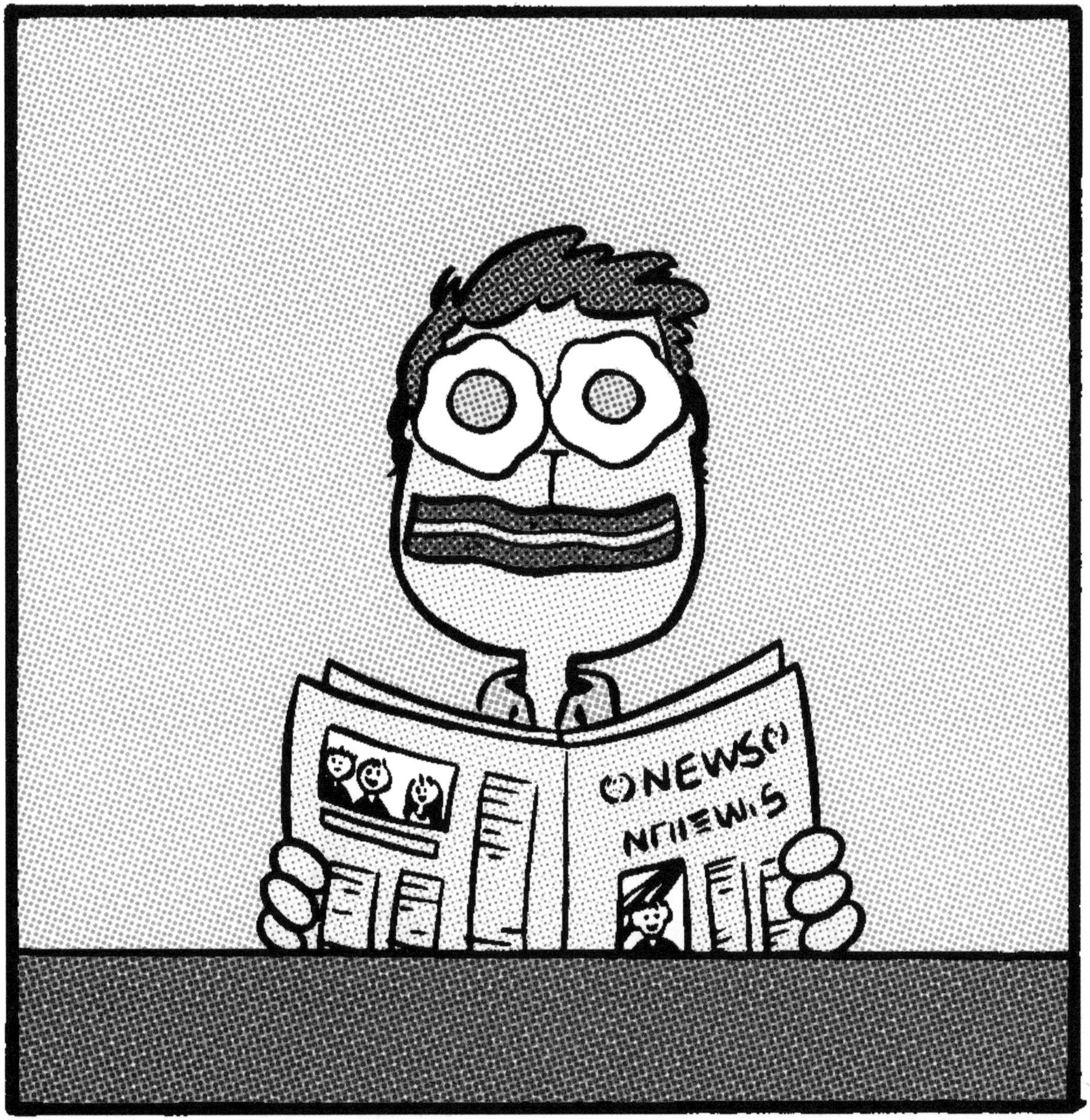
NEWS

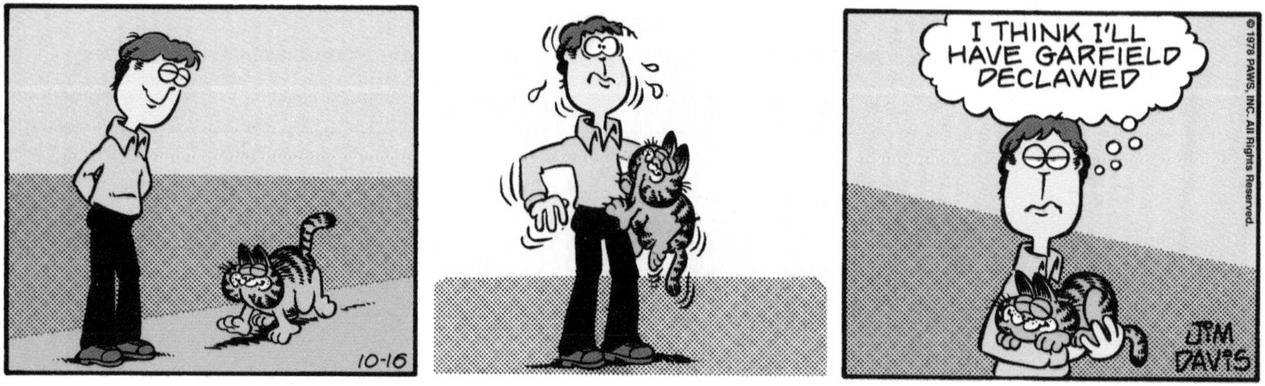
10-16
I THINK I'LL HAVE GARFIELD DECLAWED
© 1978 PAWS, INC. All Rights Reserved.
JIM DAVIS

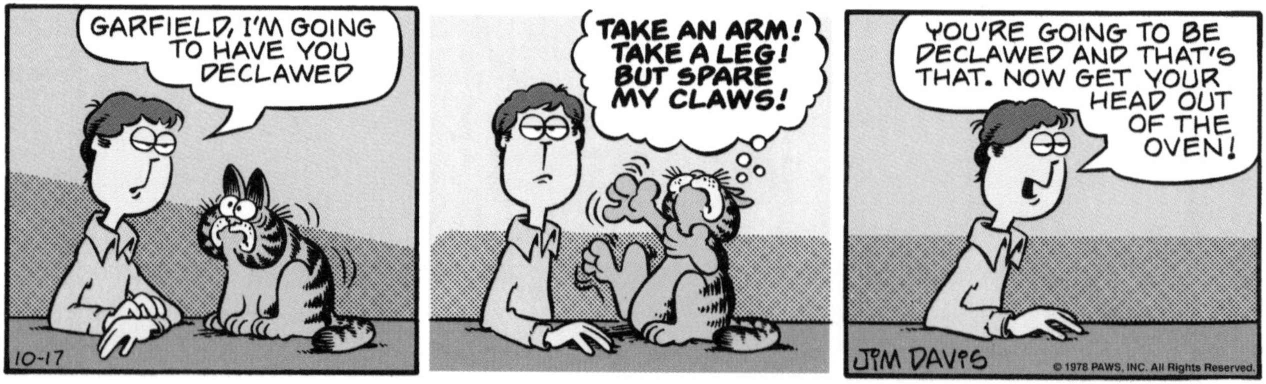
GARFIELD, I'M GOING TO HAVE YOU DECLAWED
10-17
TAKE AN ARM! TAKE A LEG! BUT SPARE MY CLAWS!
YOU'RE GOING TO BE DECLAWED AND THAT'S THAT. NOW GET YOUR HEAD OUT OF THE OVEN!
JIM DAVIS
© 1978 PAWS, INC. All Rights Reserved.

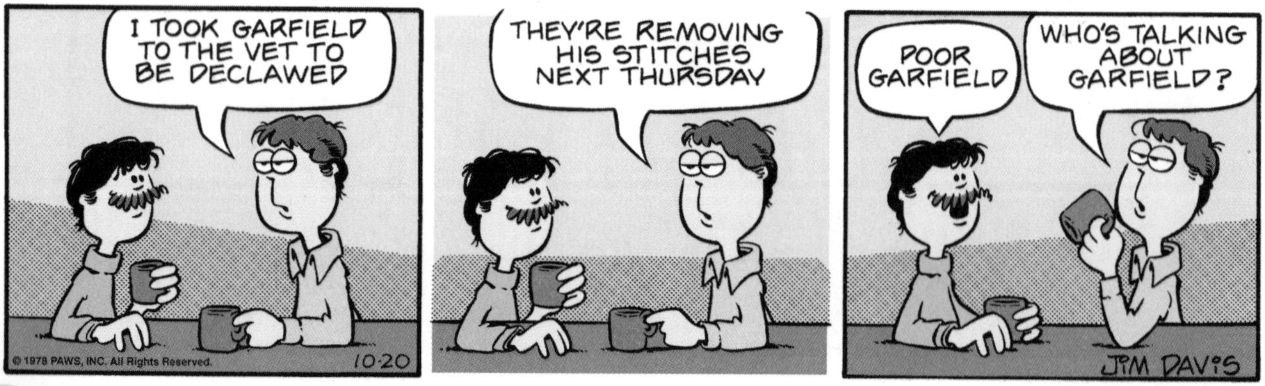
I TOOK GARFIELD TO THE VET TO BE DECLAWED
© 1978 PAWS, INC. All Rights Reserved.
10-20
THEY'RE REMOVING HIS STITCHES NEXT THURSDAY
POOR GARFIELD
WHO'S TALKING ABOUT GARFIELD?
JIM DAVIS

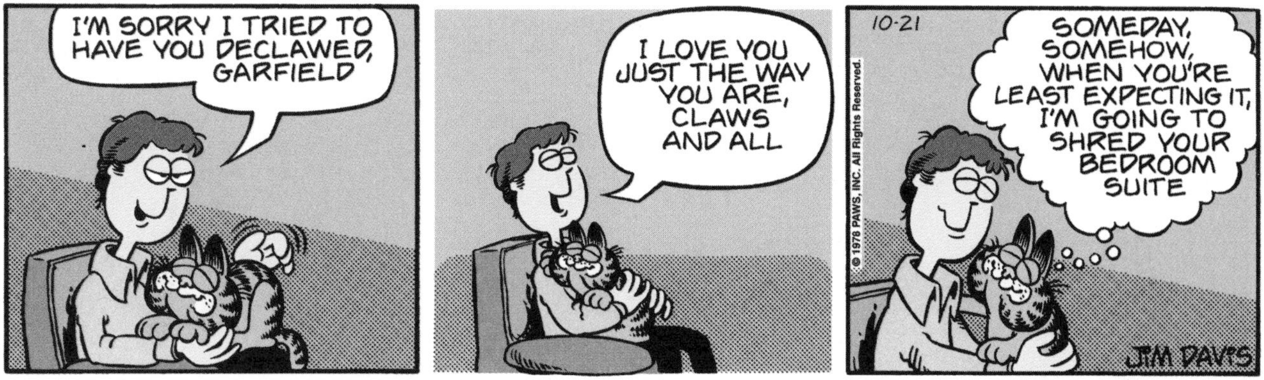
I'M SORRY I TRIED TO HAVE YOU DECLAWED, GARFIELD
I LOVE YOU JUST THE WAY YOU ARE, CLAWS AND ALL
10-21
© 1978 PAWS, INC. All Rights Reserved.
SOMEDAY, SOMEHOW, WHEN YOU'RE LEAST EXPECTING IT, I'M GOING TO SHRED YOUR BEDROOM SUITE
JIM DAVIS

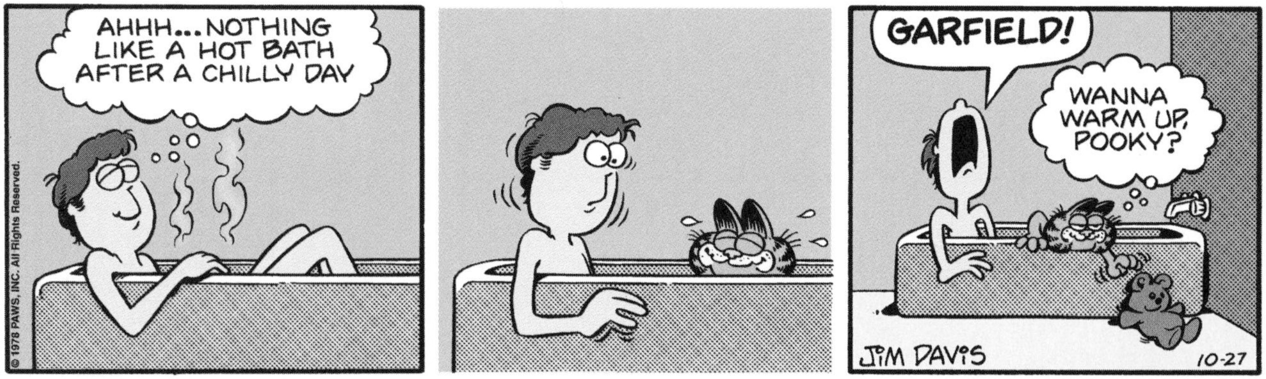
© 1978 PAWS, INC. All Rights Reserved.
AHHH...NOTHING LIKE A HOT BATH AFTER A CHILLY DAY
GARFIELD!
WANNA WARM UP, POOKY?
JIM DAVIS
10-27

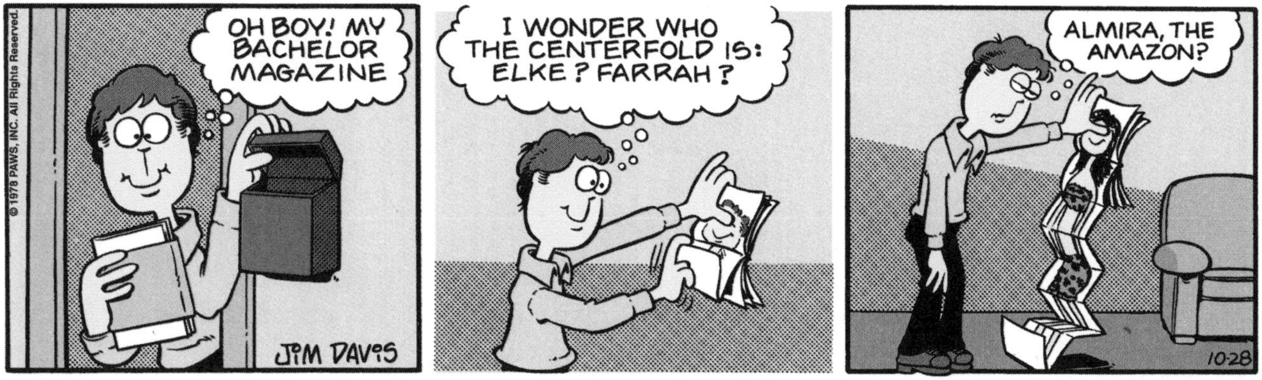
© 1978 PAWS, INC. All Rights Reserved.
OH BOY! MY BACHELOR MAGAZINE
JIM DAVIS
I WONDER WHO THE CENTERFOLD IS: ELKE? FARRAH?
ALMIRA, THE AMAZON?
10-28

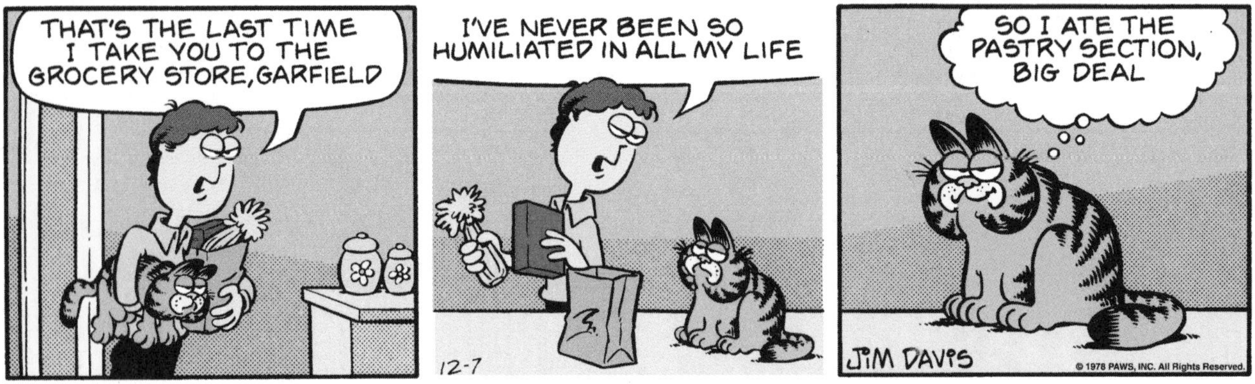
THAT'S THE LAST TIME I TAKE YOU TO THE GROCERY STORE, GARFIELD
I'VE NEVER BEEN SO HUMILIATED IN ALL MY LIFE
12-7
SO I ATE THE PASTRY SECTION, BIG DEAL
JIM DAVIS
© 1978 PAWS, INC. All Rights Reserved.

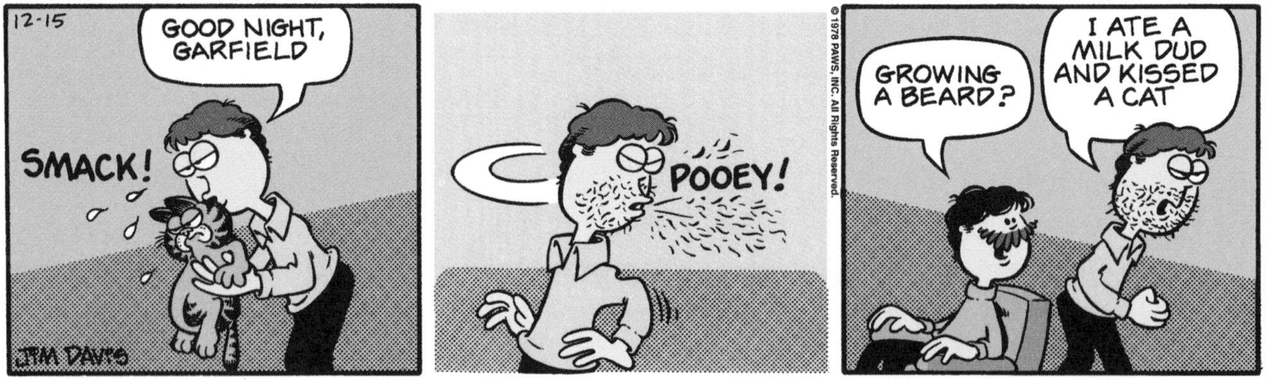
12-15
GOOD NIGHT, GARFIELD
SMACK!
JIM DAVIS
POOEY!
© 1978 PAWS, INC. All Rights Reserved.
GROWING A BEARD?
I ATE A MILK DUD AND KISSED A CAT

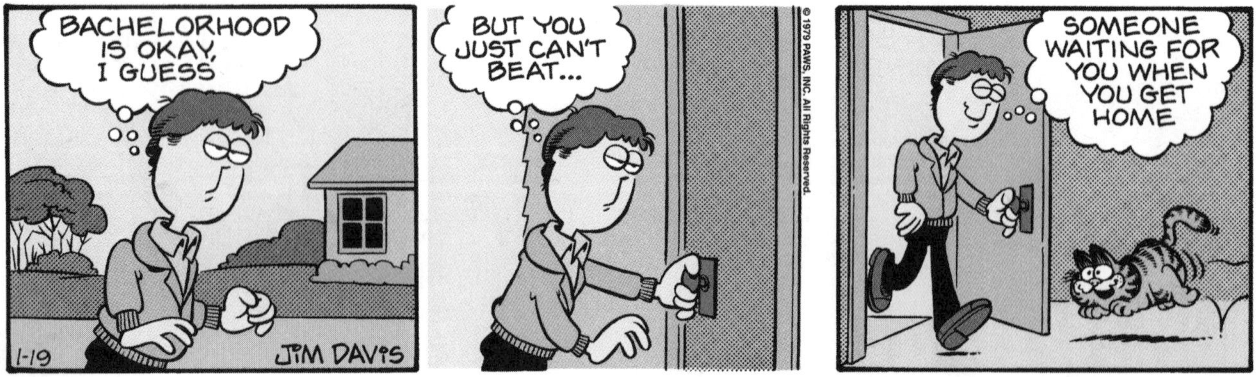
BACHELORHOOD IS OKAY, I GUESS
1-19
JIM DAVIS
BUT YOU JUST CAN'T BEAT...
© 1979 PAWS, INC. All Rights Reserved.
SOMEONE WAITING FOR YOU WHEN YOU GET HOME

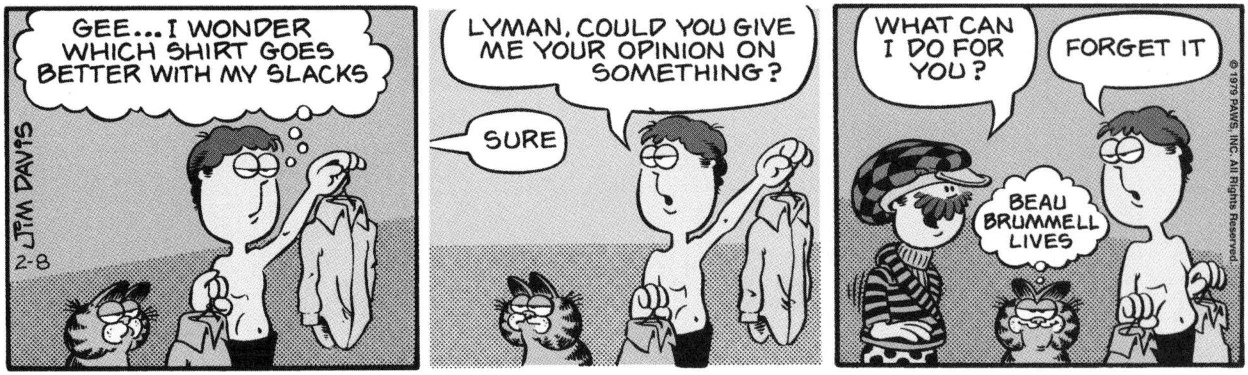
GEE...I WONDER WHICH SHIRT GOES BETTER WITH MY SLACKS
JIM DAVIS
2-8
LYMAN, COULD YOU GIVE ME YOUR OPINION ON SOMETHING?
SURE
WHAT CAN I DO FOR YOU?
FORGET IT
BEAU BRUMMELL LIVES
© 1979 PAWS, INC. All Rights Reserved.

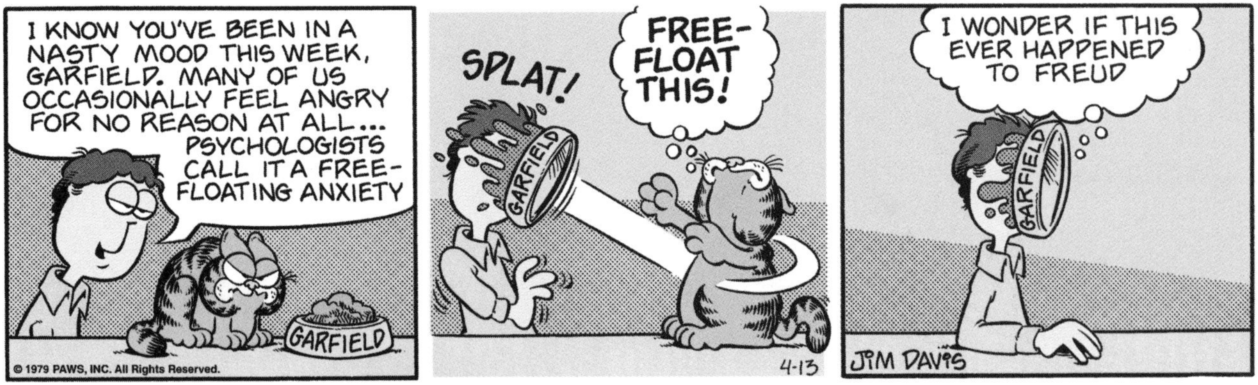
I KNOW YOU'VE BEEN IN A NASTY MOOD THIS WEEK, GARFIELD. MANY OF US OCCASIONALLY FEEL ANGRY FOR NO REASON AT ALL... PSYCHOLOGISTS CALL IT A FREE-FLOATING ANXIETY
GARFIELD
© 1979 PAWS, INC. All Rights Reserved.
SPLAT!
FREE-FLOAT THIS!
GARFIELD
4-13
I WONDER IF THIS EVER HAPPENED TO FREUD
GARFIELD
JIM DAVIS

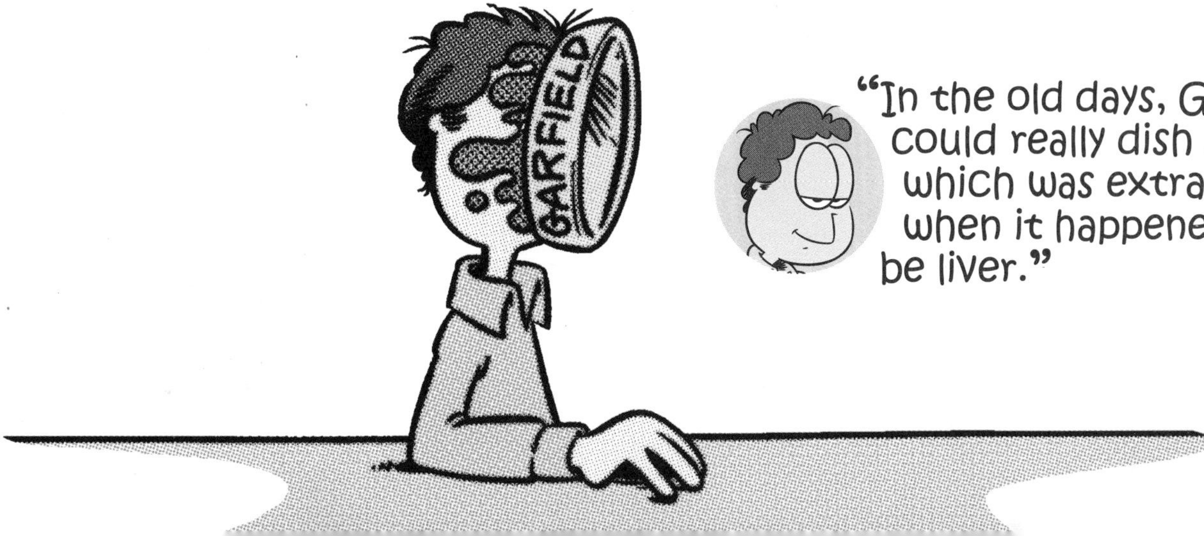
GARFIELD

"In the old days, Garfield could really dish it out... which was extra gross when it happened to be liver."

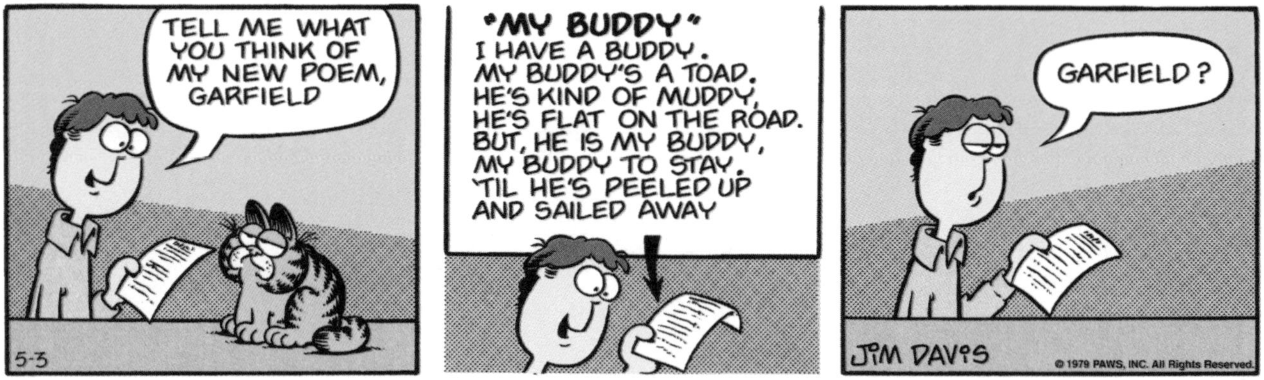
TELL ME WHAT YOU THINK OF MY NEW POEM, GARFIELD
"MY BUDDY"
I HAVE A BUDDY.
MY BUDDY'S A TOAD.
HE'S KIND OF MUDDY,
HE'S FLAT ON THE ROAD.
BUT, HE IS MY BUDDY,
MY BUDDY TO STAY.
'TIL HE'S PEELED UP
AND SAILED AWAY
GARFIELD?
5-3
JIM DAVIS
© 1979 PAWS, INC. All Rights Reserved.

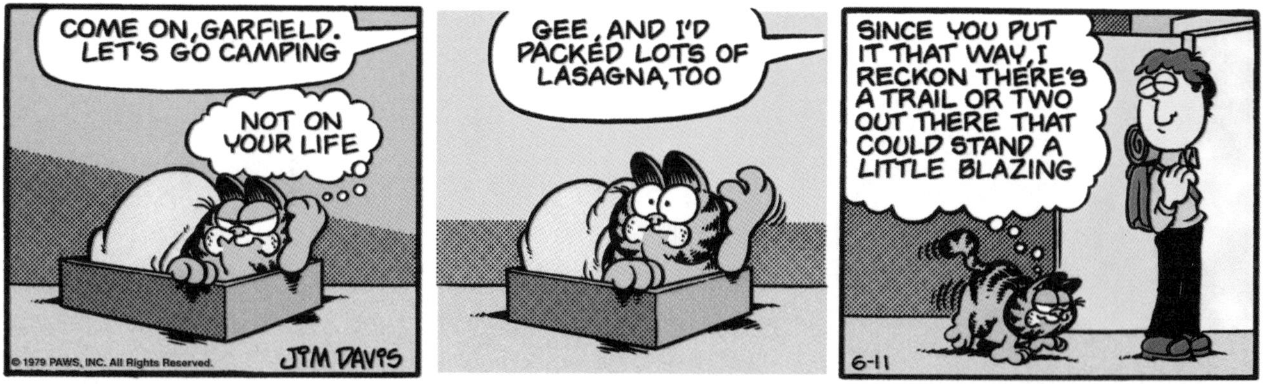
COME ON, GARFIELD. LET'S GO CAMPING
NOT ON YOUR LIFE
© 1979 PAWS, INC. All Rights Reserved.
JIM DAVIS
GEE, AND I'D PACKED LOTS OF LASAGNA, TOO
SINCE YOU PUT IT THAT WAY, I RECKON THERE'S A TRAIL OR TWO OUT THERE THAT COULD STAND A LITTLE BLAZING
6-11

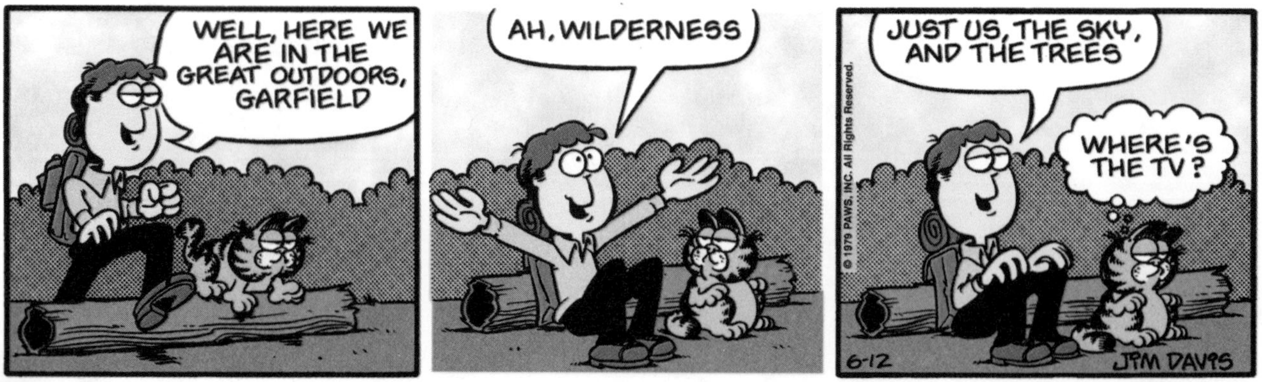
WELL, HERE WE ARE IN THE GREAT OUTDOORS, GARFIELD
AH, WILDERNESS
JUST US, THE SKY, AND THE TREES
WHERE'S THE TV?
© 1979 PAWS, INC. All Rights Reserved.
6-12
JIM DAVIS

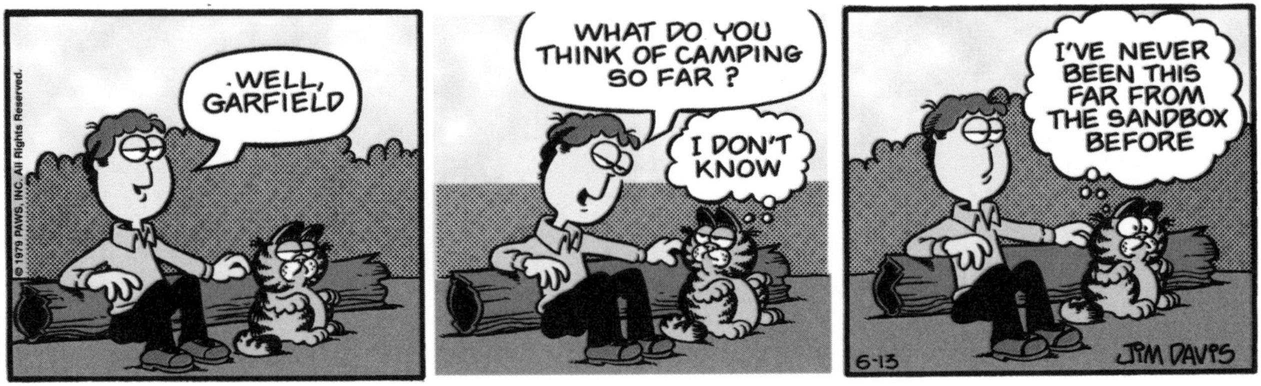
© 1979 PAWS, INC. All Rights Reserved.
WELL, GARFIELD
WHAT DO YOU THINK OF CAMPING SO FAR ?
I DON'T KNOW
I'VE NEVER BEEN THIS FAR FROM THE SANDBOX BEFORE
6-13
JIM DAVIS

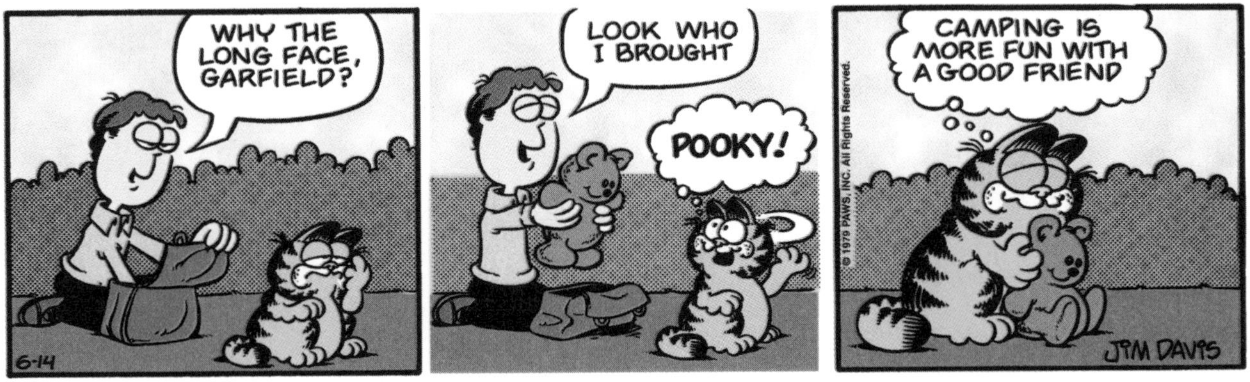
WHY THE LONG FACE, GARFIELD?
6-14
LOOK WHO I BROUGHT
POOKY!
© 1979 PAWS, INC. All Rights Reserved.
CAMPING IS MORE FUN WITH A GOOD FRIEND
JIM DAVIS

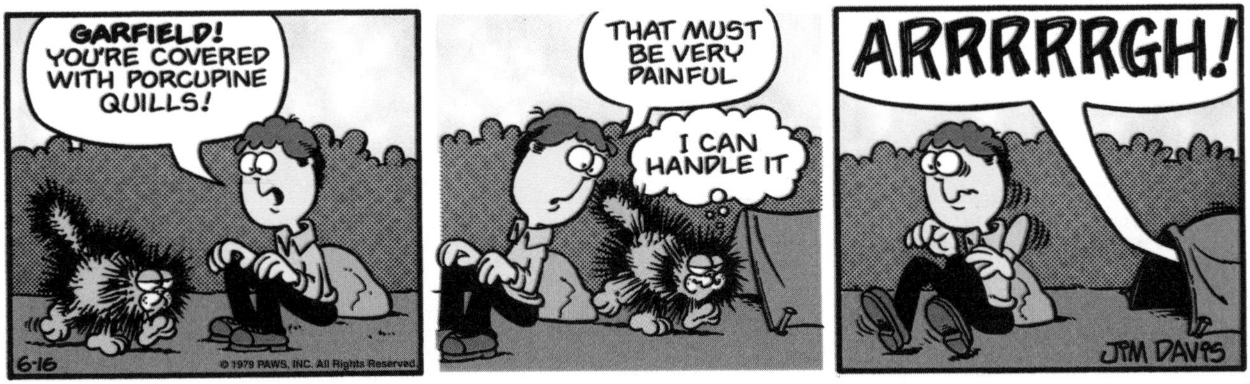
GARFIELD! YOU'RE COVERED WITH PORCUPINE QUILLS!
6-16
© 1979 PAWS, INC. All Rights Reserved.
THAT MUST BE VERY PAINFUL
I CAN HANDLE IT
ARRRRRGH!
JIM DAVIS

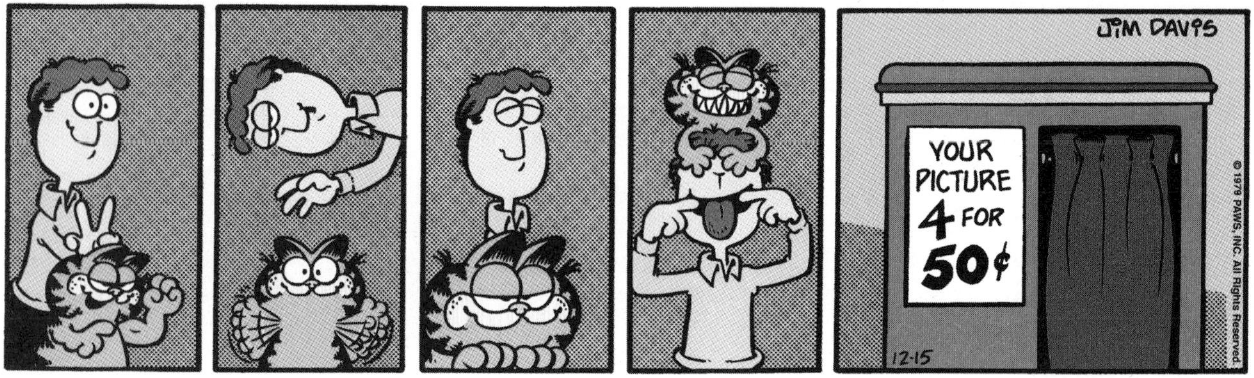
JIM DAVIS
YOUR PICTURE 4 FOR 50¢
12-15
© 1979 PAWS, INC. All Rights Reserved.

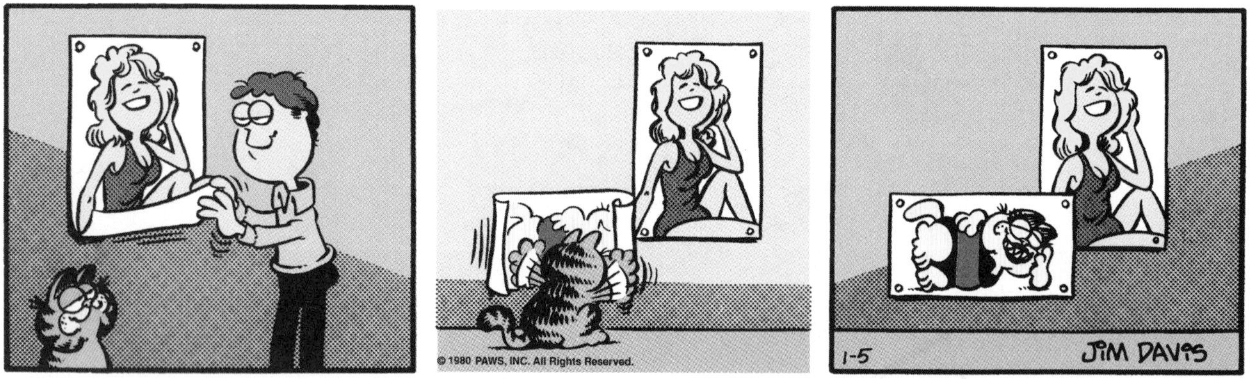
© 1980 PAWS, INC. All Rights Reserved.
1-5
JIM DAVIS

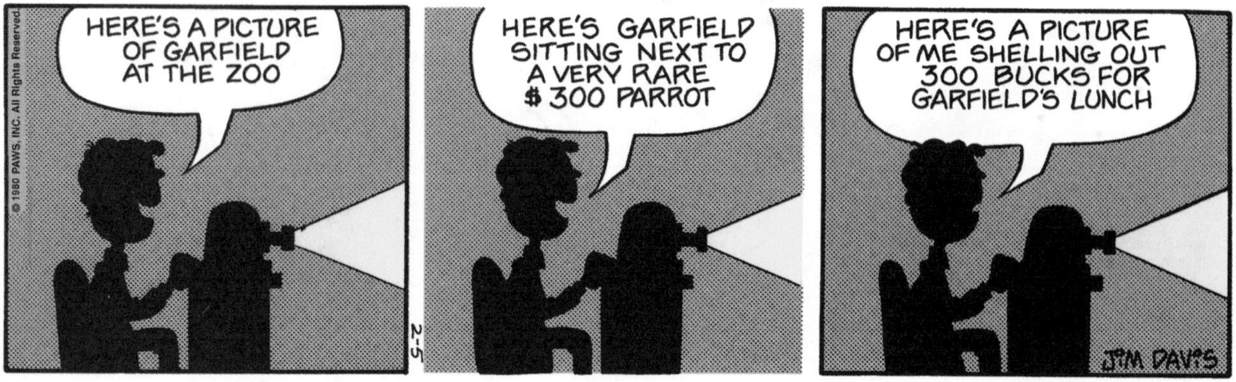
© 1980 PAWS, INC. All Rights Reserved.
HERE'S A PICTURE OF GARFIELD AT THE ZOO
2-5
HERE'S GARFIELD SITTING NEXT TO A VERY RARE $ 300 PARROT
HERE'S A PICTURE OF ME SHELLING OUT 300 BUCKS FOR GARFIELD'S LUNCH
JIM DAVIS

I KNOW YOU CATS ARE INQUISITIVE BY NATURE, GARFIELD
© 1980 PAWS, INC. All Rights Reserved.
AND I KNOW THIS IS YOUR HOME AS WELL AS MINE . . .
BUT STAY OUT OF MY UNDERWEAR DRAWER!!
3-19
JIM DAVIS

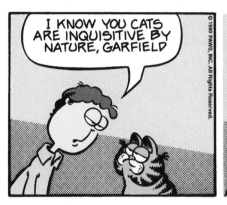

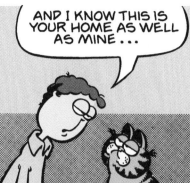

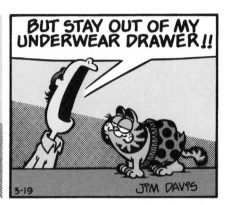

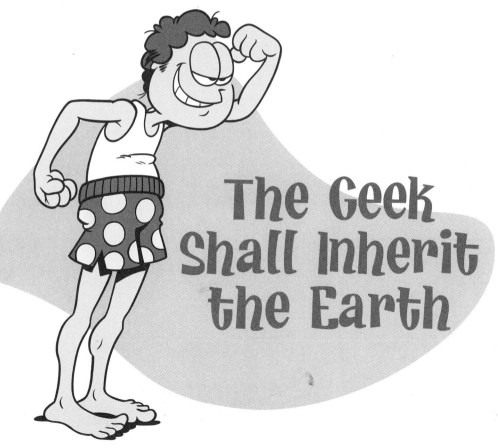

The Geek Shall Inherit the Earth

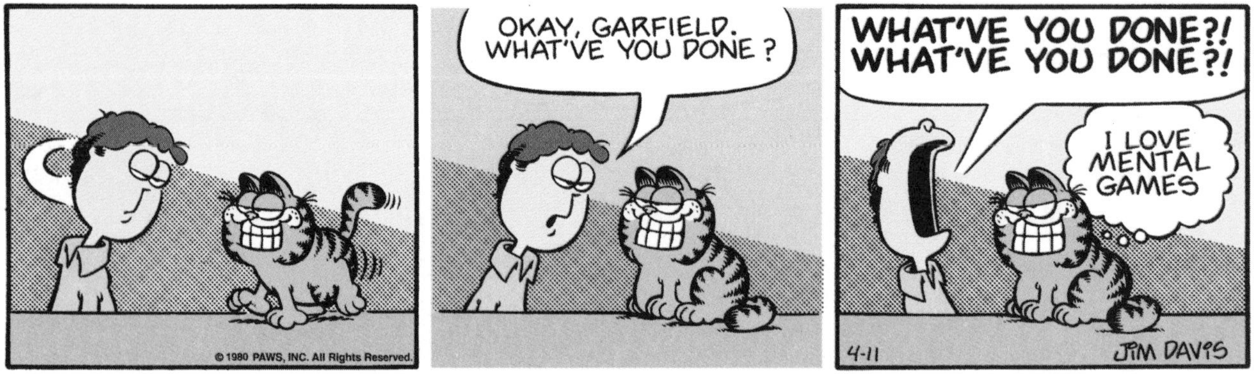
© 1980 PAWS, INC. All Rights Reserved.
OKAY, GARFIELD. WHAT'VE YOU DONE?
WHAT'VE YOU DONE?! WHAT'VE YOU DONE?!
I LOVE MENTAL GAMES
4-11
JIM DAVIS

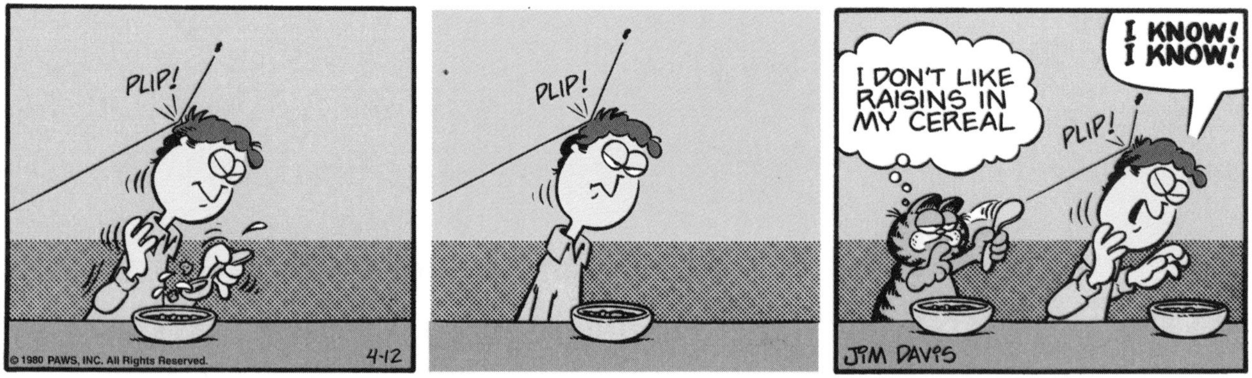
PLIP!
© 1980 PAWS, INC. All Rights Reserved.
4-12
PLIP!
I DON'T LIKE RAISINS IN MY CEREAL
I KNOW! I KNOW!
PLIP!
JIM DAVIS

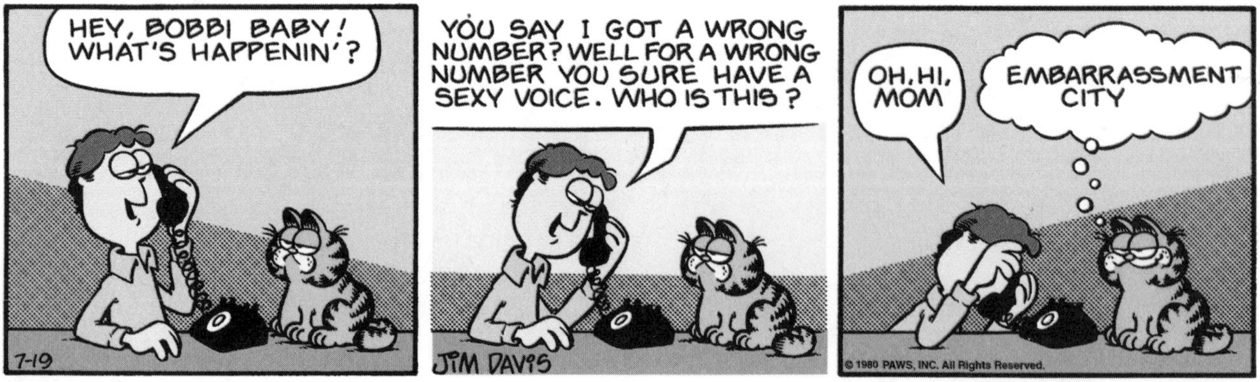
HEY, BOBBI BABY! WHAT'S HAPPENIN'?
7-19
YOU SAY I GOT A WRONG NUMBER? WELL FOR A WRONG NUMBER YOU SURE HAVE A SEXY VOICE. WHO IS THIS?
JIM DAVIS
OH, HI, MOM
EMBARRASSMENT CITY
© 1980 PAWS, INC. All Rights Reserved.

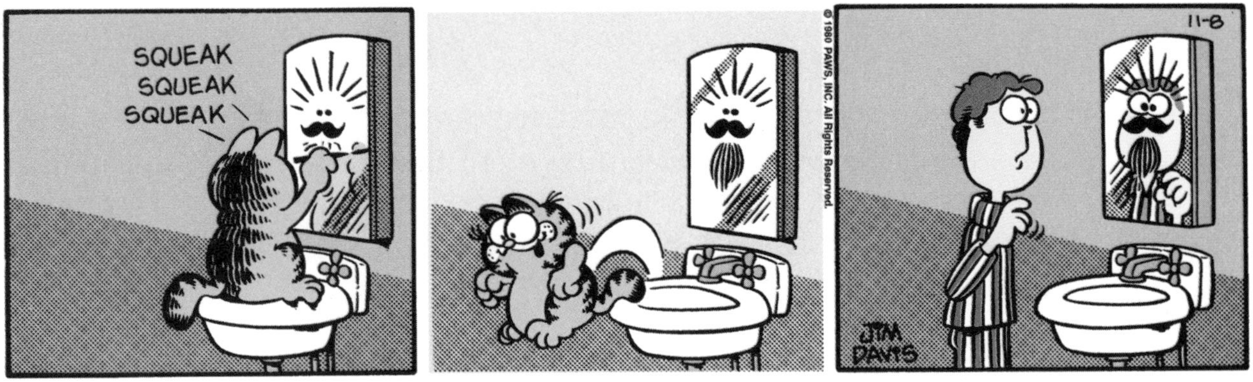
SQUEAK
SQUEAK
SQUEAK
SQUEAK
© 1980 PAWS, INC. All Rights Reserved.
11-8
JIM DAVIS

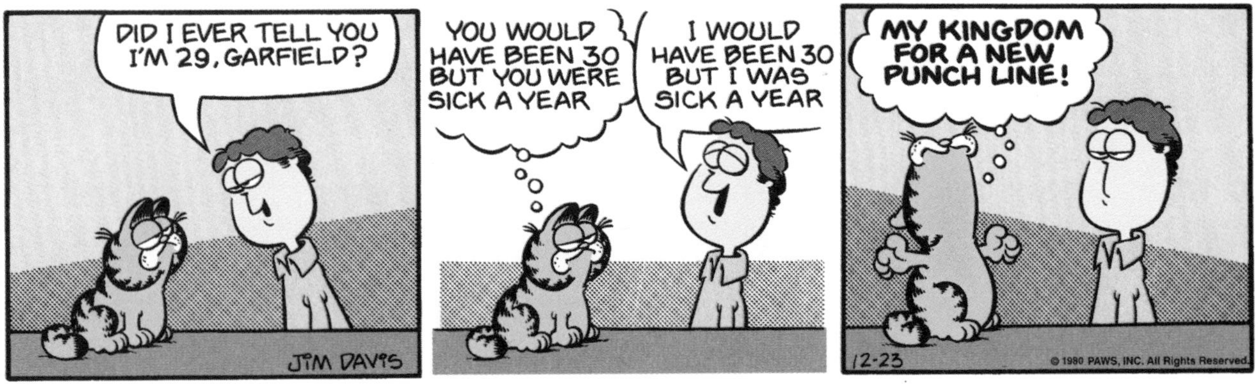
DID I EVER TELL YOU I'M 29, GARFIELD?
JIM DAVIS
YOU WOULD HAVE BEEN 30 BUT YOU WERE SICK A YEAR
I WOULD HAVE BEEN 30 BUT I WAS SICK A YEAR
MY KINGDOM FOR A NEW PUNCH LINE!
12-23
© 1980 PAWS, INC. All Rights Reserved.

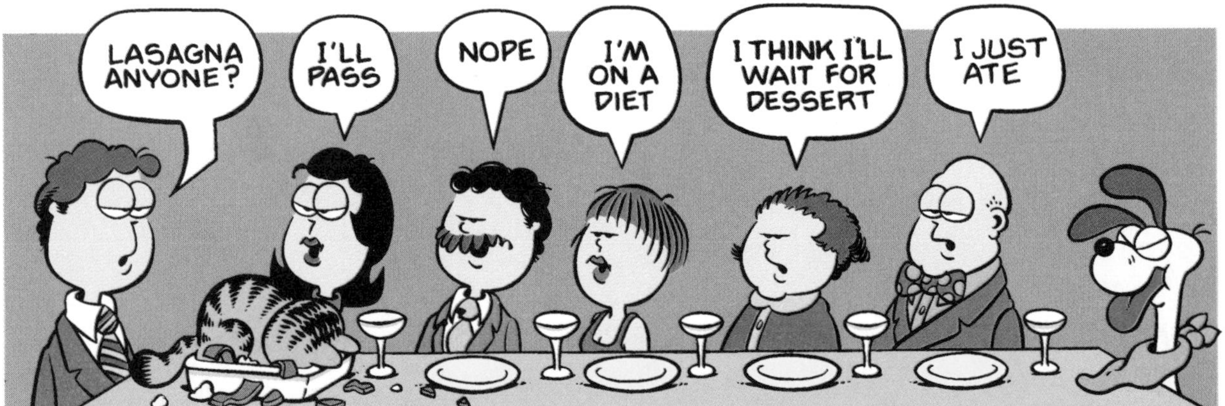
LASAGNA ANYONE?
I'LL PASS
NOPE
I'M ON A DIET
I THINK I'LL WAIT FOR DESSERT
I JUST ATE

DOWN ON THE FARM

The Garfield comic strip is firmly rooted in Jim Davis's family life. Jim grew up on a small farm near Fairmount, Indiana, with his dad, Jim, his mom, Betty, and his brother. Jim used those family members as characters, modeling Jon Arbuckle's farm folks after his own. (Incidentally, the cantankerous cat was named after Jim's curmudgeonly grandfather, James A. Garfield Davis.)

However, it took more than a year and a half before Jon's parents actually appeared in the strip on February 13, 1980, when Jon went back home (with a reluctant Garfield in tow) to visit. Since that time, Jon has made several trips to the farm—and his countrified clan has even ventured into the big city. The clash of cultures has resulted in some knee-slappin' hi-larity (e.g., Dad's tractor double-parked in the city street).

Jon's dad is a down-to-earth guy—literally. He's a hardworking farmer who enjoys the simple pleasures of the country, where a man can walk his pig in peace.

Jon's mom is a loving, hardworking farm wife who's very proud of her husband and sons. She's also a wonderful cook who believes strongly in both quality and quantity. As she sees it, the two most important food groups are potatoes and pies.

Jon's only sibling, Doc Boy, lives on the Arbuckle farm with his parents. Like his city-slicker brother, Doc Boy leads a pretty boring life, although he does occasionally get a date with the Hog Queen (and sometimes with the hog). Fun fact: Doc Boy was named after Jim's brother, Dave "Doc" Davis. Doc isn't nearly as goofy as his cartoon namesake; he's goofier!

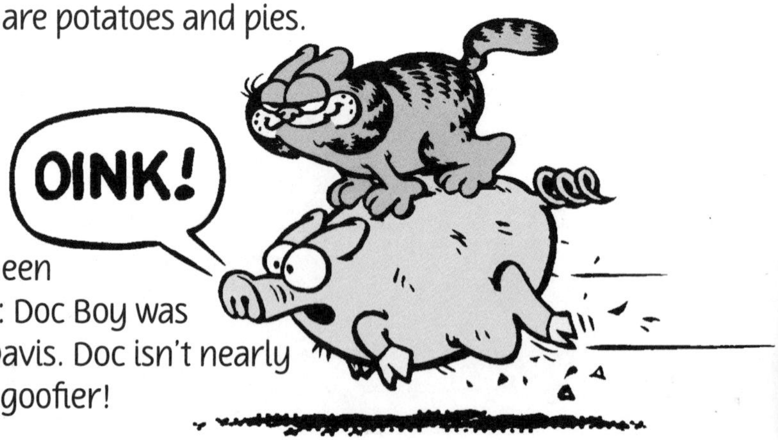
OINK!

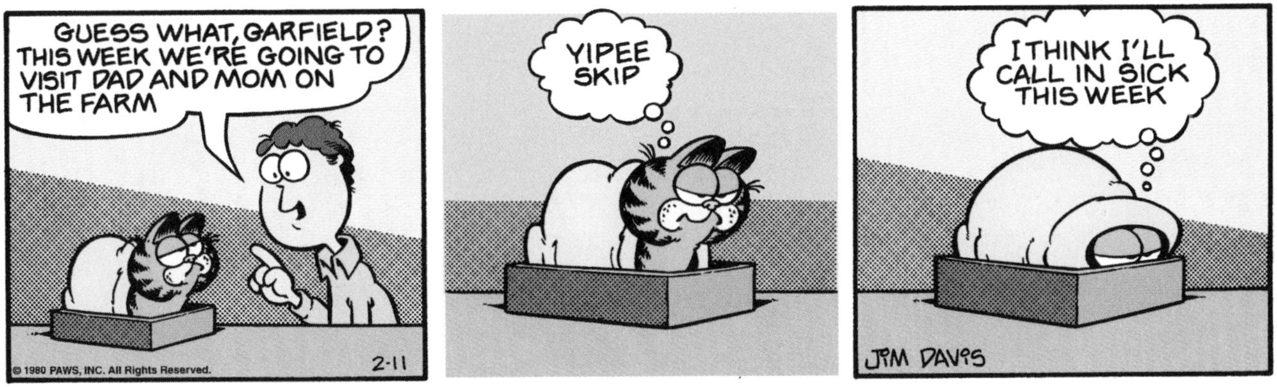
GUESS WHAT, GARFIELD? THIS WEEK WE'RE GOING TO VISIT DAD AND MOM ON THE FARM
YIPEE SKIP
I THINK I'LL CALL IN SICK THIS WEEK
© 1980 PAWS, INC. All Rights Reserved.
2-11
JIM DAVIS

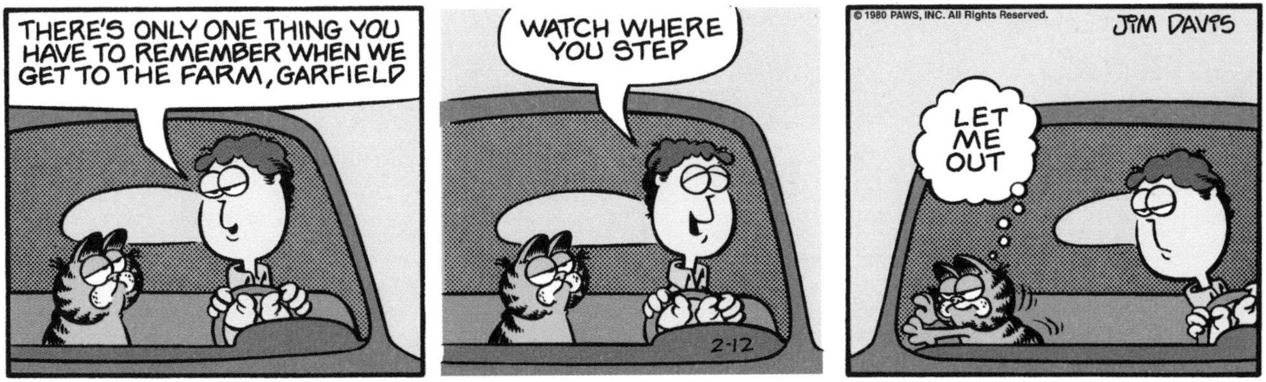
THERE'S ONLY ONE THING YOU HAVE TO REMEMBER WHEN WE GET TO THE FARM, GARFIELD
WATCH WHERE YOU STEP
LET ME OUT
2-12
© 1980 PAWS, INC. All Rights Reserved.
JIM DAVIS

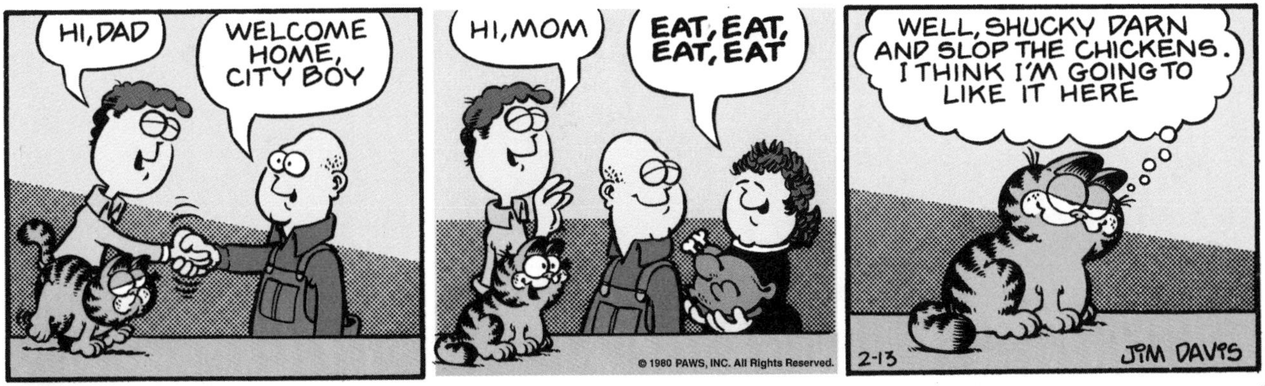
HI, DAD
WELCOME HOME, CITY BOY
HI, MOM
EAT, EAT, EAT, EAT
WELL, SHUCKY DARN AND SLOP THE CHICKENS. I THINK I'M GOING TO LIKE IT HERE
© 1980 PAWS, INC. All Rights Reserved.
2-13
JIM DAVIS

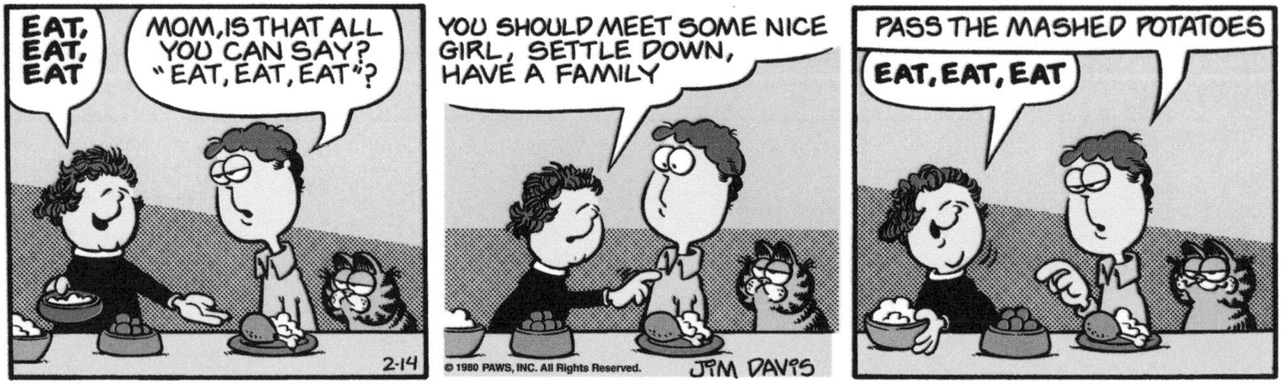
EAT, EAT, EAT
MOM, IS THAT ALL YOU CAN SAY? "EAT, EAT, EAT"?
YOU SHOULD MEET SOME NICE GIRL, SETTLE DOWN, HAVE A FAMILY
PASS THE MASHED POTATOES
EAT, EAT, EAT
2-14
© 1980 PAWS, INC. All Rights Reserved.
JIM DAVIS

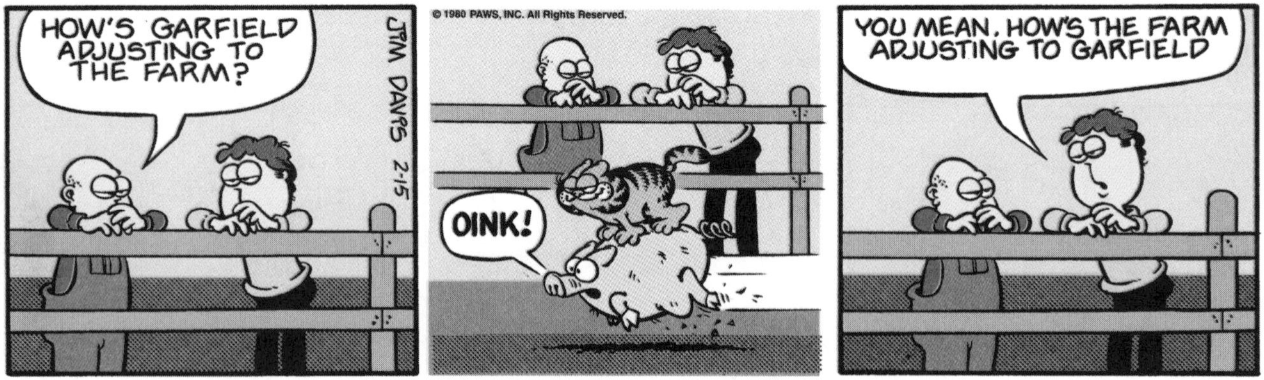
HOW'S GARFIELD ADJUSTING TO THE FARM?
JIM DAVIS 2-15
© 1980 PAWS, INC. All Rights Reserved.
OINK!
YOU MEAN, HOW'S THE FARM ADJUSTING TO GARFIELD

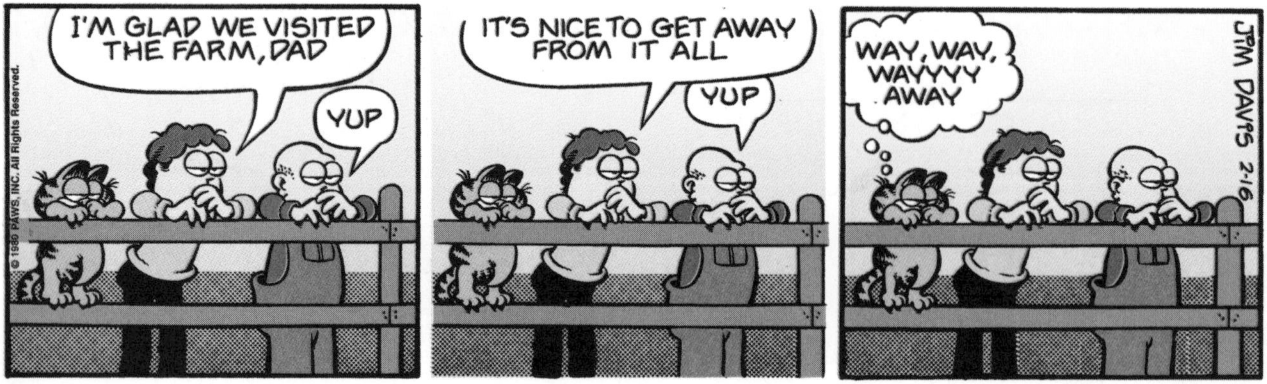
I'M GLAD WE VISITED THE FARM, DAD
YUP
© 1980 PAWS, INC. All Rights Reserved.
IT'S NICE TO GET AWAY FROM IT ALL
YUP
WAY, WAY, WAYYYY AWAY
JIM DAVIS 2-16

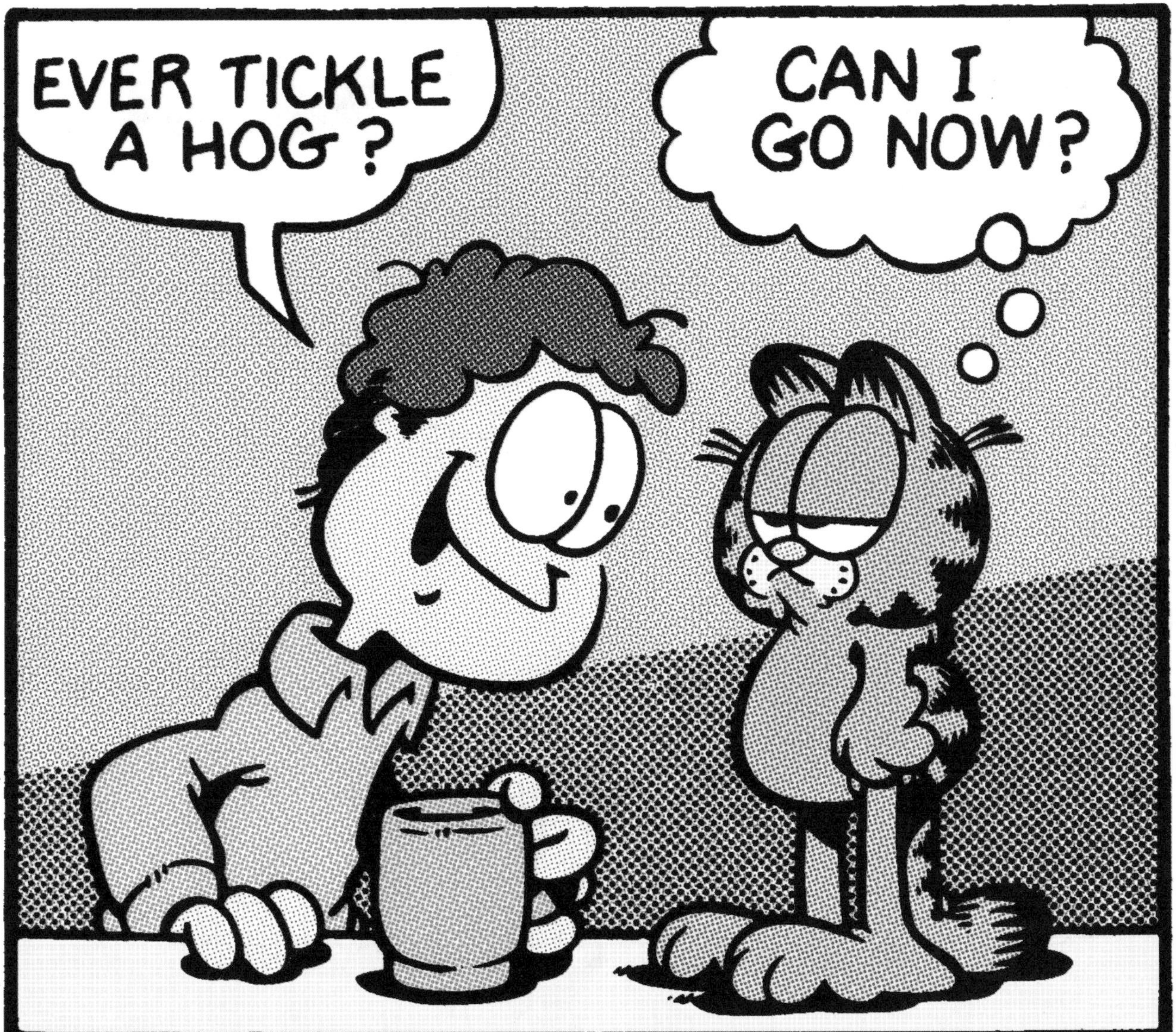
EVER TICKLE A HOG?
CAN I GO NOW?

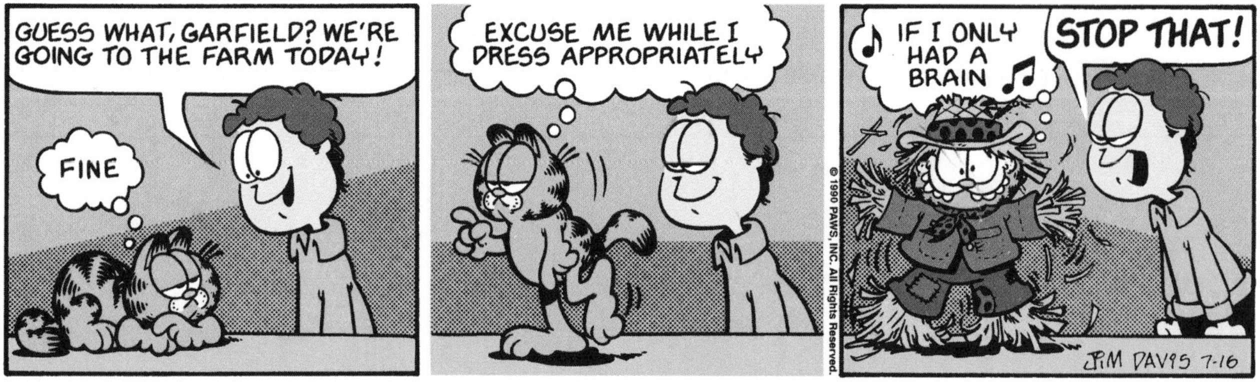
GUESS WHAT, GARFIELD? WE'RE GOING TO THE FARM TODAY!
FINE
EXCUSE ME WHILE I DRESS APPROPRIATELY
IF I ONLY HAD A BRAIN
STOP THAT!
© 1990 PAWS, INC. All Rights Reserved.
JIM DAVIS 7-16

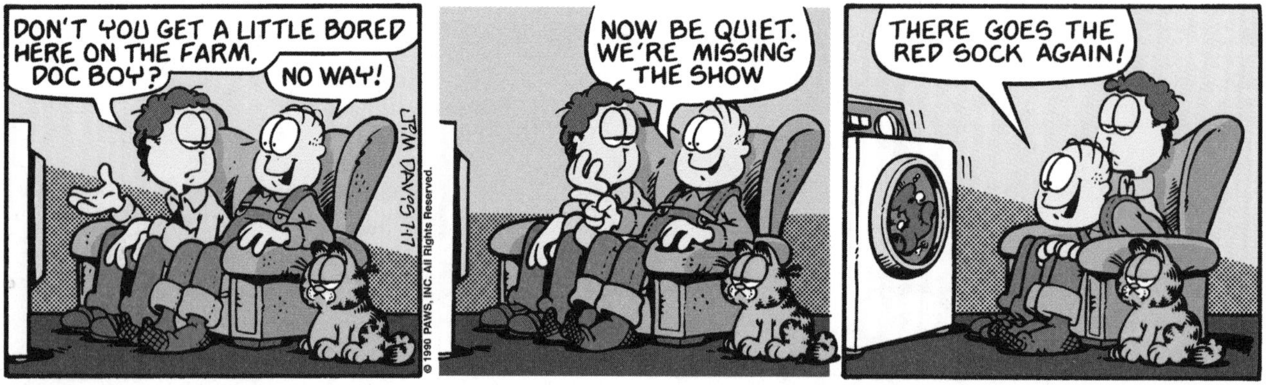
DON'T YOU GET A LITTLE BORED HERE ON THE FARM, DOC BOY?
NO WAY!
JIM DAVIS 7-17
© 1990 PAWS, INC. All Rights Reserved.
NOW BE QUIET. WE'RE MISSING THE SHOW
THERE GOES THE RED SOCK AGAIN!

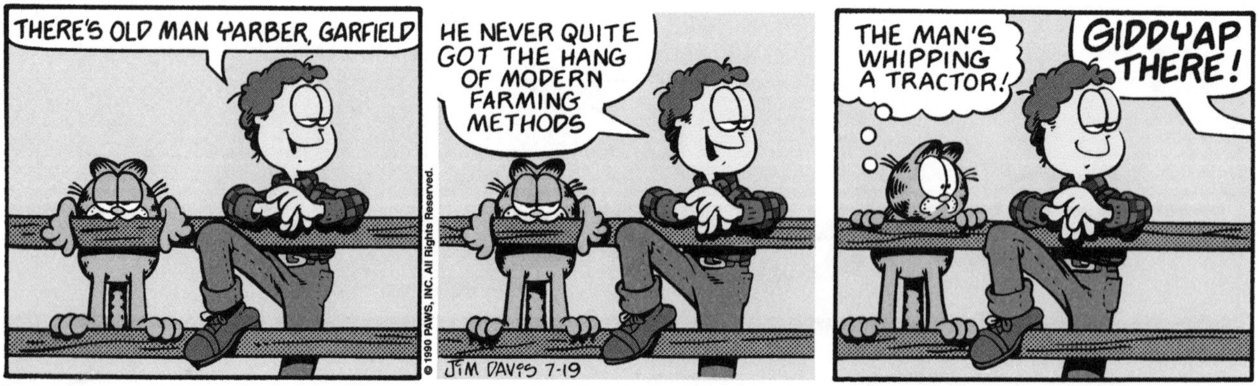
THERE'S OLD MAN YARBER, GARFIELD
© 1990 PAWS, INC. All Rights Reserved.
HE NEVER QUITE GOT THE HANG OF MODERN FARMING METHODS
JIM DAVIS 7-19
THE MAN'S WHIPPING A TRACTOR!
GIDDYAP THERE!

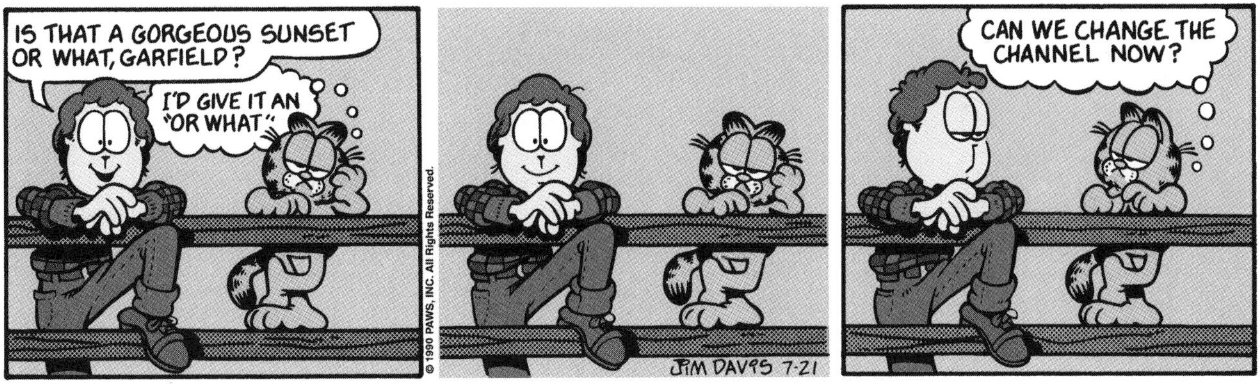
IS THAT A GORGEOUS SUNSET OR WHAT, GARFIELD?
I'D GIVE IT AN "OR WHAT"
© 1990 PAWS, INC. All Rights Reserved.
JIM DAVIS 7-21
CAN WE CHANGE THE CHANNEL NOW?

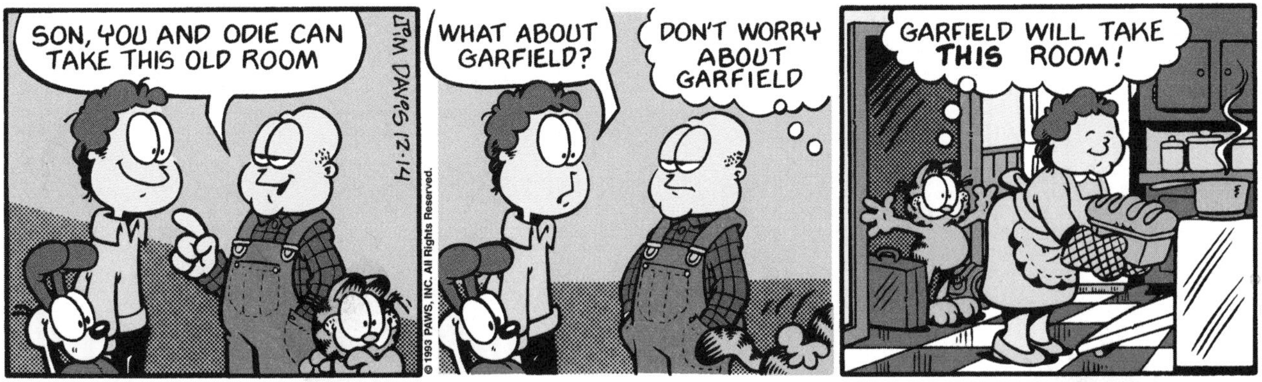
SON, YOU AND ODIE CAN TAKE THIS OLD ROOM
JIM DAVIS 12-14
© 1993 PAWS, INC. All Rights Reserved.
WHAT ABOUT GARFIELD?
DON'T WORRY ABOUT GARFIELD
GARFIELD WILL TAKE **THIS** ROOM!

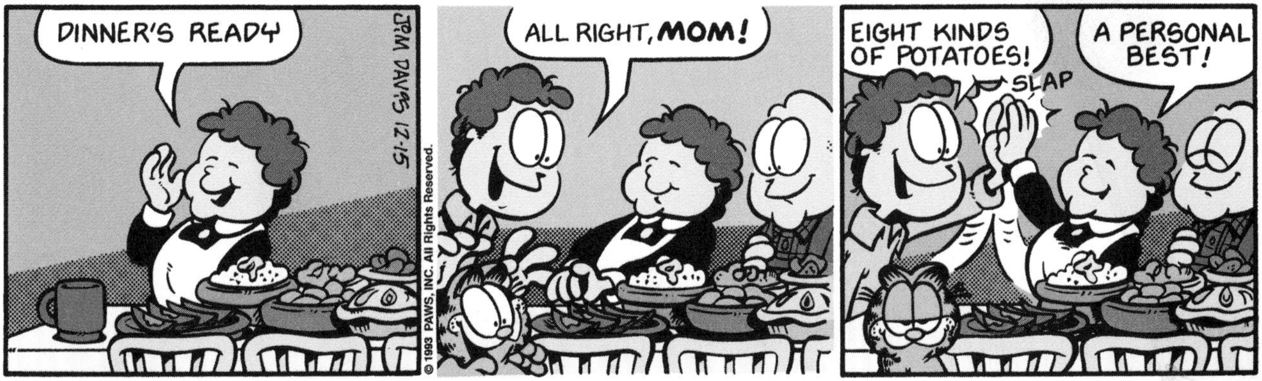
DINNER'S READY
JIM DAVIS 12-15
© 1993 PAWS, INC. All Rights Reserved.
ALL RIGHT, **MOM!**
EIGHT KINDS OF POTATOES!
SLAP
A PERSONAL BEST!

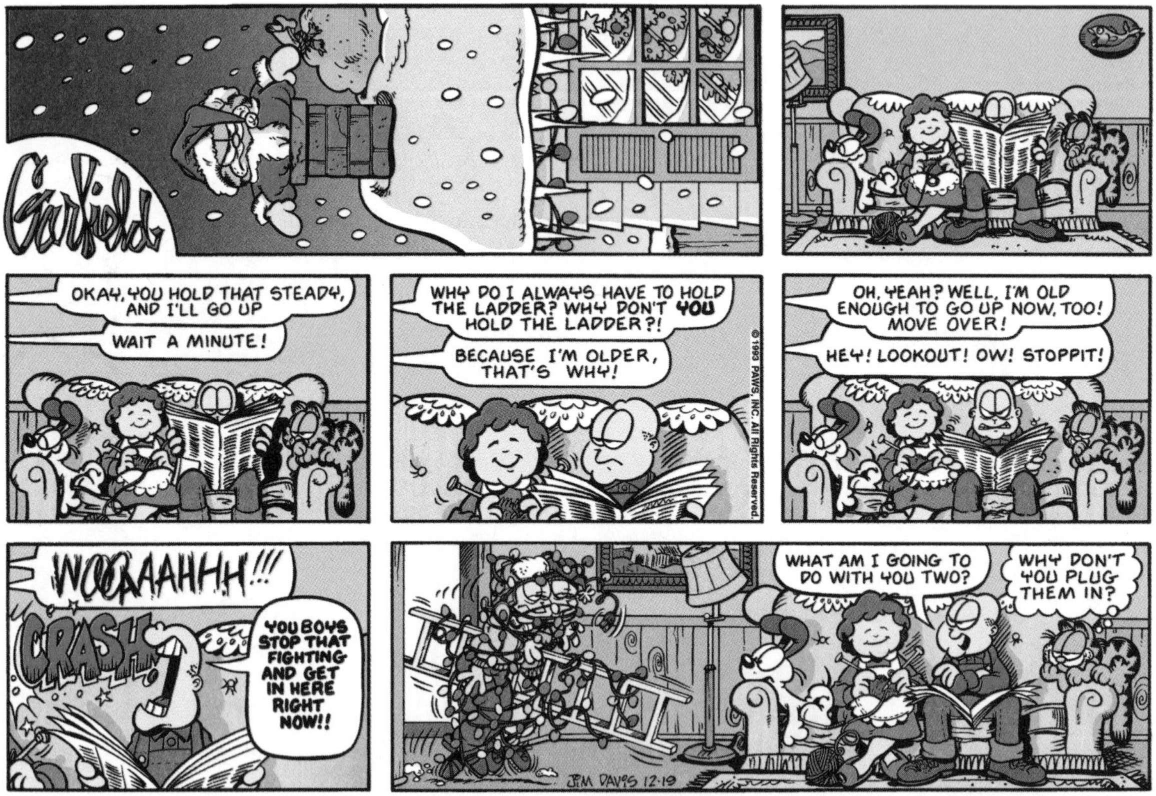
Garfield
OKAY, YOU HOLD THAT STEADY, AND I'LL GO UP
WAIT A MINUTE!
WHY DO I ALWAYS HAVE TO HOLD THE LADDER? WHY DON'T **YOU** HOLD THE LADDER?!
BECAUSE I'M OLDER, THAT'S WHY!
© 1993 PAWS, INC. All Rights Reserved.
OH, YEAH? WELL, I'M OLD ENOUGH TO GO UP NOW, TOO! MOVE OVER!
HEY! LOOKOUT! OW! STOPPIT!
WOOAAAHHH!!!
CRASH
YOU BOYS STOP THAT FIGHTING AND GET IN HERE RIGHT NOW!!
WHAT AM I GOING TO DO WITH YOU TWO?
WHY DON'T YOU PLUG THEM IN?
JIM DAVIS 12-19

TOP TEN MOST LIKELY MEANINGS FOR THE NAME "ARBUCKLE"

10. "wiener-chested"
9. "rash giver"
8. "pudding-brained"
7. "man of socks"
6. "dances with cows"
5. "he who giggles in battle"
4. "uh-oh, here he comes"
3. "royal bore"
2. "village dweeb"
1. "cat-whipped"

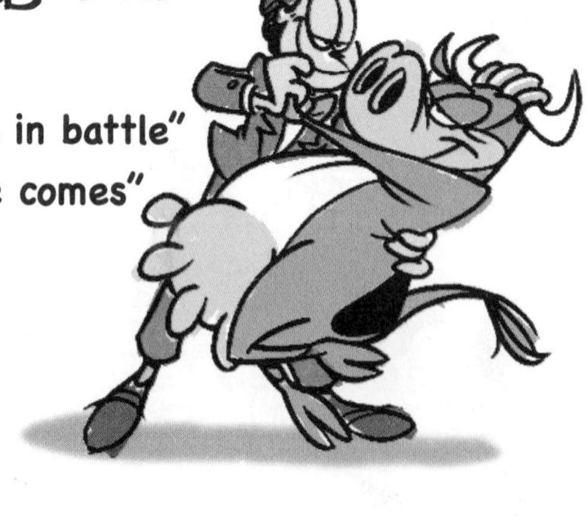

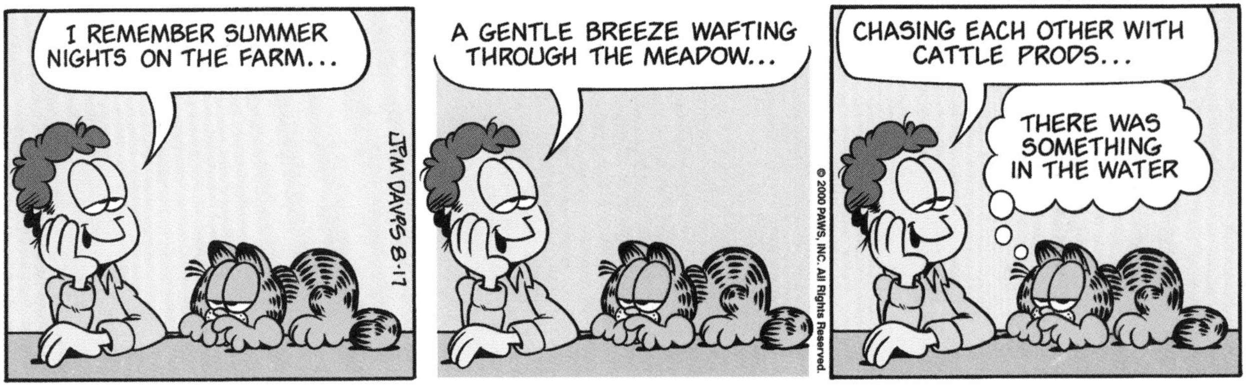
I REMEMBER SUMMER NIGHTS ON THE FARM...
JIM DAVIS 8-17
A GENTLE BREEZE WAFTING THROUGH THE MEADOW...
© 2000 PAWS, INC. All Rights Reserved.
CHASING EACH OTHER WITH CATTLE PRODS...
THERE WAS SOMETHING IN THE WATER

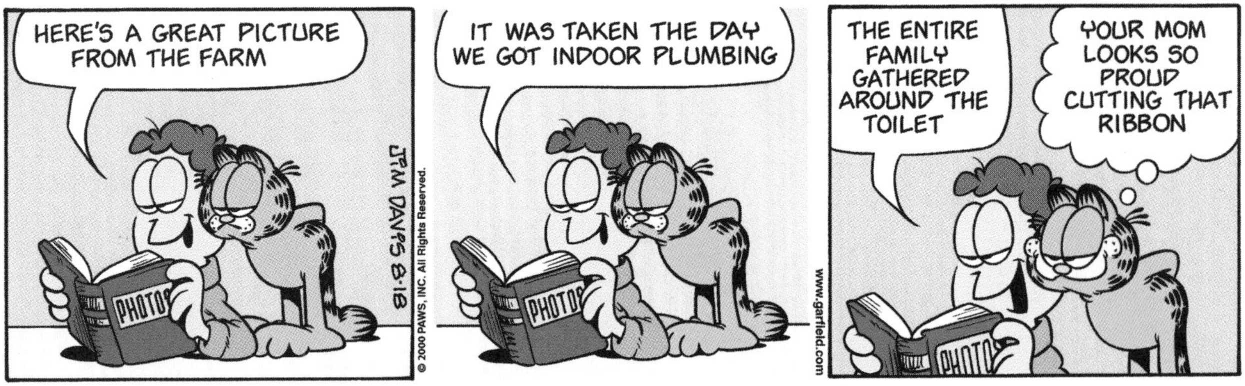
HERE'S A GREAT PICTURE FROM THE FARM
PHOTOS
JIM DAVIS 8-18
© 2000 PAWS, INC. All Rights Reserved.
IT WAS TAKEN THE DAY WE GOT INDOOR PLUMBING
PHOTOS
www.garfield.com
THE ENTIRE FAMILY GATHERED AROUND THE TOILET
YOUR MOM LOOKS SO PROUD CUTTING THAT RIBBON

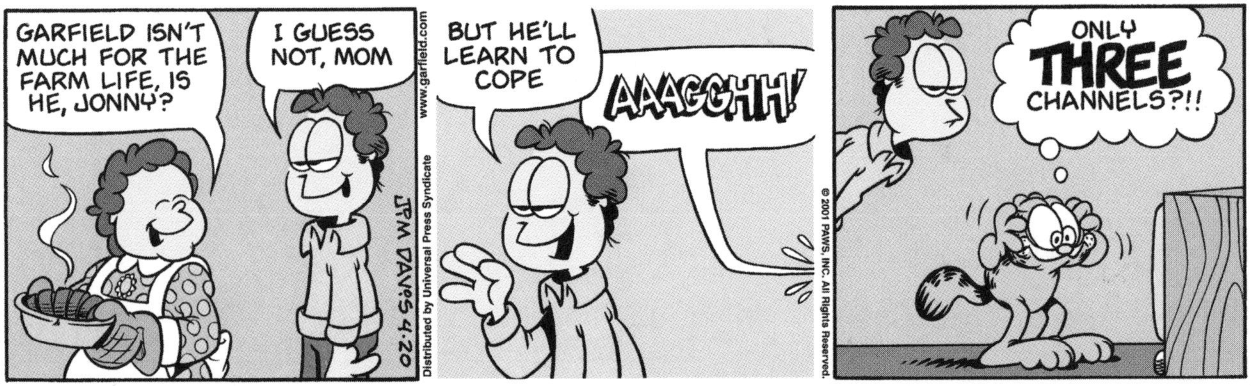
GARFIELD ISN'T MUCH FOR THE FARM LIFE, IS HE, JONNY?
I GUESS NOT, MOM
JIM DAVIS 4-20
www.garfield.com
Distributed by Universal Press Syndicate
BUT HE'LL LEARN TO COPE
AAAGGHH!
© 2001 PAWS, INC. All Rights Reserved.
ONLY THREE CHANNELS?!!

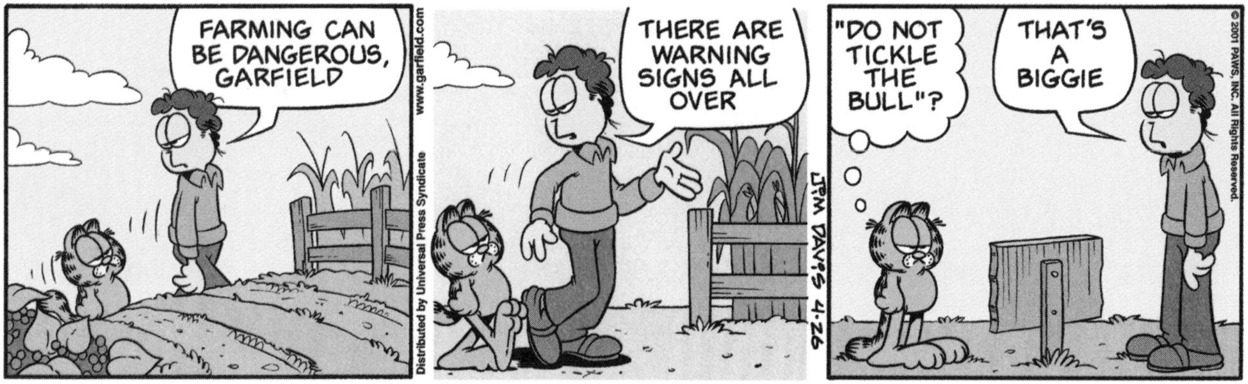
FARMING CAN BE DANGEROUS, GARFIELD
www.garfield.com
Distributed by Universal Press Syndicate
THERE ARE WARNING SIGNS ALL OVER
JIM DAVIS 4-26
"DO NOT TICKLE THE BULL"?
THAT'S A BIGGIE
© 2001 PAWS, INC. All Rights Reserved.

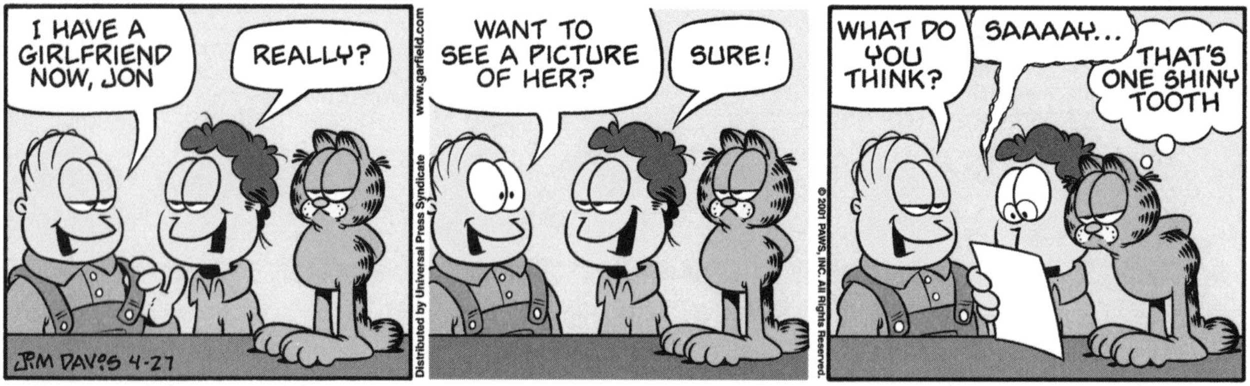
I HAVE A GIRLFRIEND NOW, JON
REALLY?
JIM DAVIS 4-27
www.garfield.com
Distributed by Universal Press Syndicate
WANT TO SEE A PICTURE OF HER?
SURE!
© 2001 PAWS, INC. All Rights Reserved.
WHAT DO YOU THINK?
SAAAAY...
THAT'S ONE SHINY TOOTH

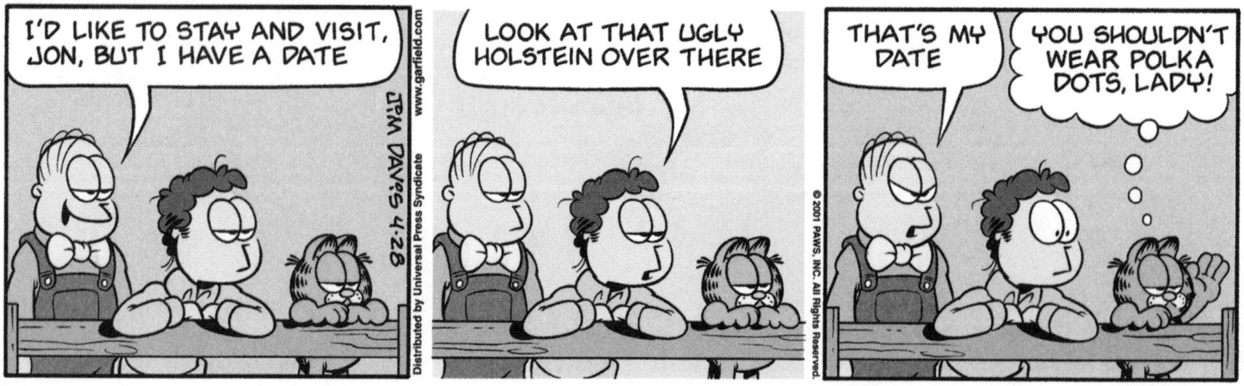
I'D LIKE TO STAY AND VISIT, JON, BUT I HAVE A DATE
JIM DAVIS 4-28
www.garfield.com
Distributed by Universal Press Syndicate
LOOK AT THAT UGLY HOLSTEIN OVER THERE
© 2001 PAWS, INC. All Rights Reserved.
THAT'S MY DATE
YOU SHOULDN'T WEAR POLKA DOTS, LADY!

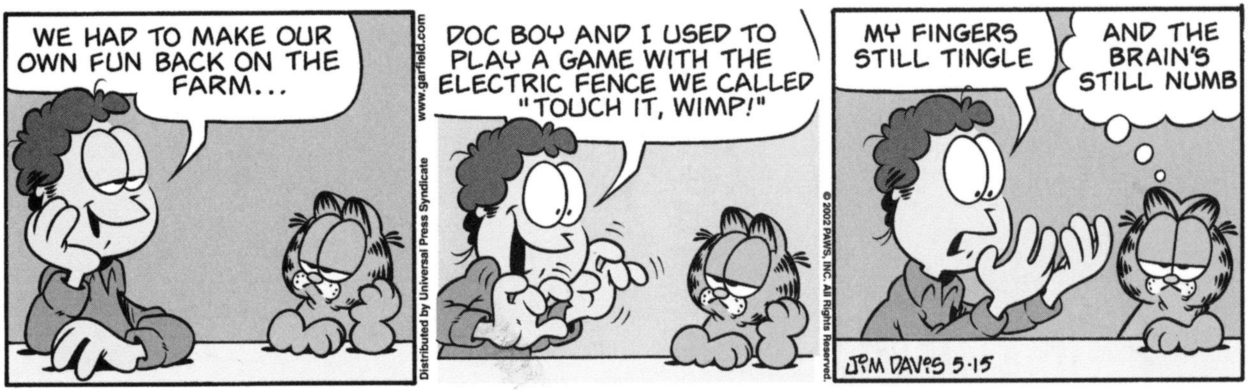
WE HAD TO MAKE OUR OWN FUN BACK ON THE FARM...
DOC BOY AND I USED TO PLAY A GAME WITH THE ELECTRIC FENCE WE CALLED "TOUCH IT, WIMP!"
MY FINGERS STILL TINGLE
AND THE BRAIN'S STILL NUMB
JIM DAVIS 5-15
www.garfield.com
Distributed by Universal Press Syndicate
© 2002 PAWS, INC. All Rights Reserved.

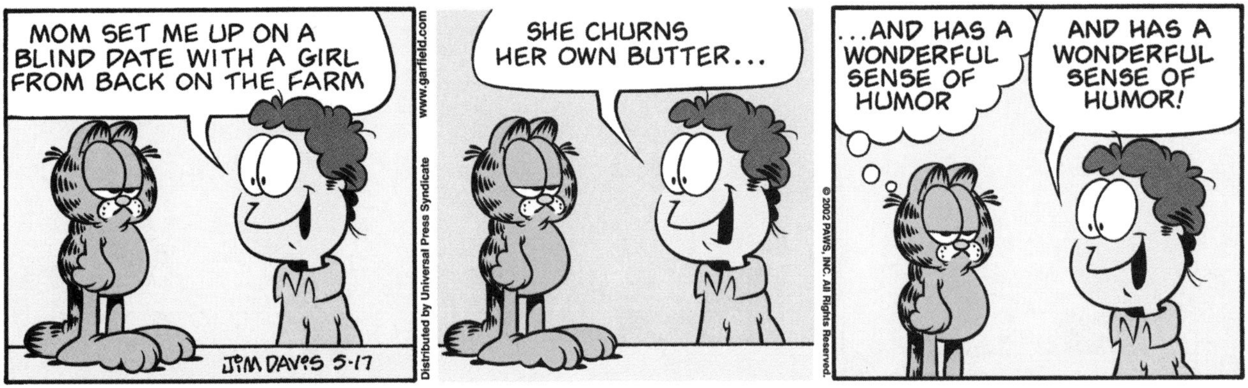
MOM SET ME UP ON A BLIND DATE WITH A GIRL FROM BACK ON THE FARM
SHE CHURNS HER OWN BUTTER...
...AND HAS A WONDERFUL SENSE OF HUMOR
AND HAS A WONDERFUL SENSE OF HUMOR!
JIM DAVIS 5-17
www.garfield.com
Distributed by Universal Press Syndicate
© 2002 PAWS, INC. All Rights Reserved.

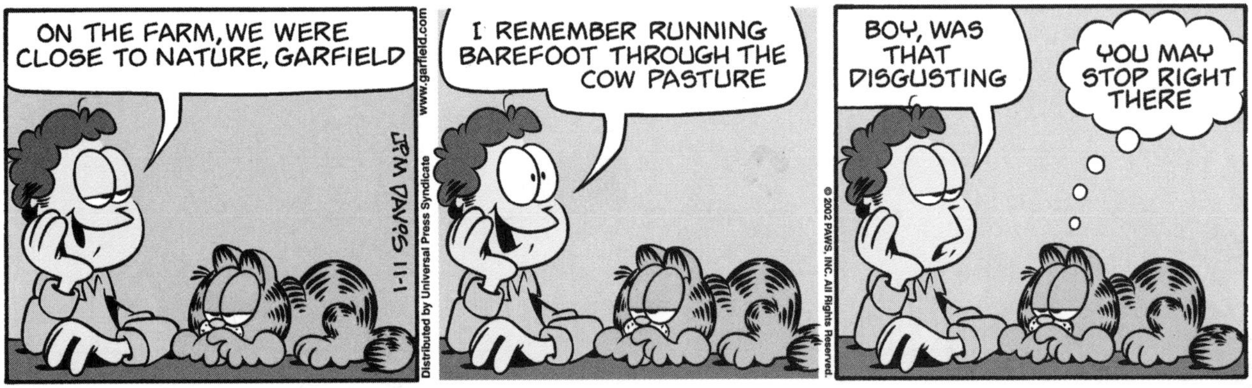
ON THE FARM, WE WERE CLOSE TO NATURE, GARFIELD
I REMEMBER RUNNING BAREFOOT THROUGH THE COW PASTURE
BOY, WAS THAT DISGUSTING
YOU MAY STOP RIGHT THERE
JIM DAVIS 11-1
www.garfield.com
Distributed by Universal Press Syndicate
© 2002 PAWS, INC. All Rights Reserved.

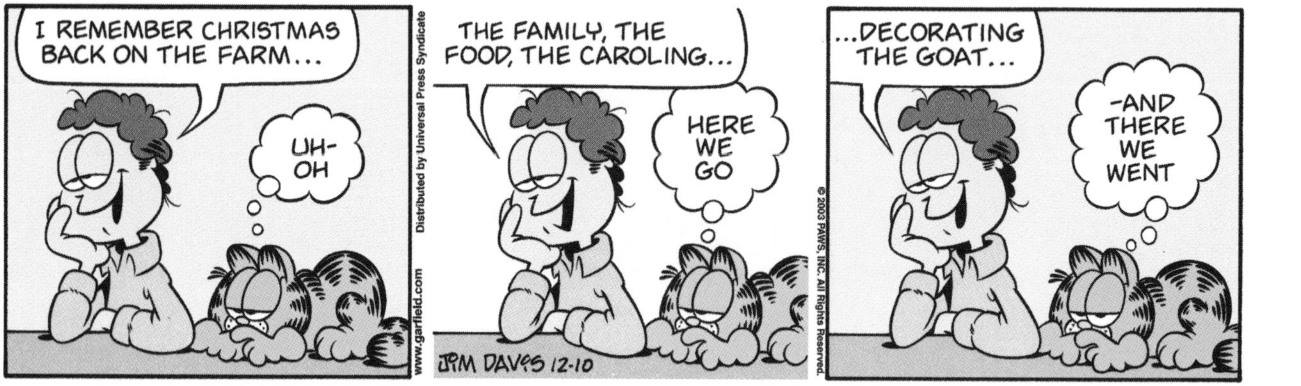
I REMEMBER CHRISTMAS BACK ON THE FARM...
UH-OH
THE FAMILY, THE FOOD, THE CAROLING...
HERE WE GO
...DECORATING THE GOAT...
-AND THERE WE WENT
JIM DAVIS 12-10
www.garfield.com
Distributed by Universal Press Syndicate
© 2003 PAWS, INC. All Rights Reserved.

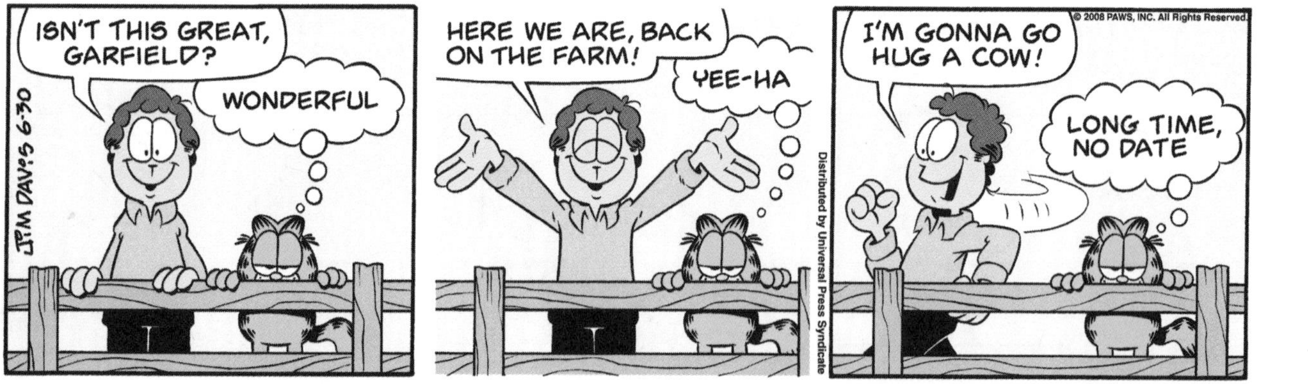
ISN'T THIS GREAT, GARFIELD?
WONDERFUL
HERE WE ARE, BACK ON THE FARM!
YEE-HA
I'M GONNA GO HUG A COW!
LONG TIME, NO DATE
JIM DAVIS 6-30
Distributed by Universal Press Syndicate
© 2008 PAWS, INC. All Rights Reserved.

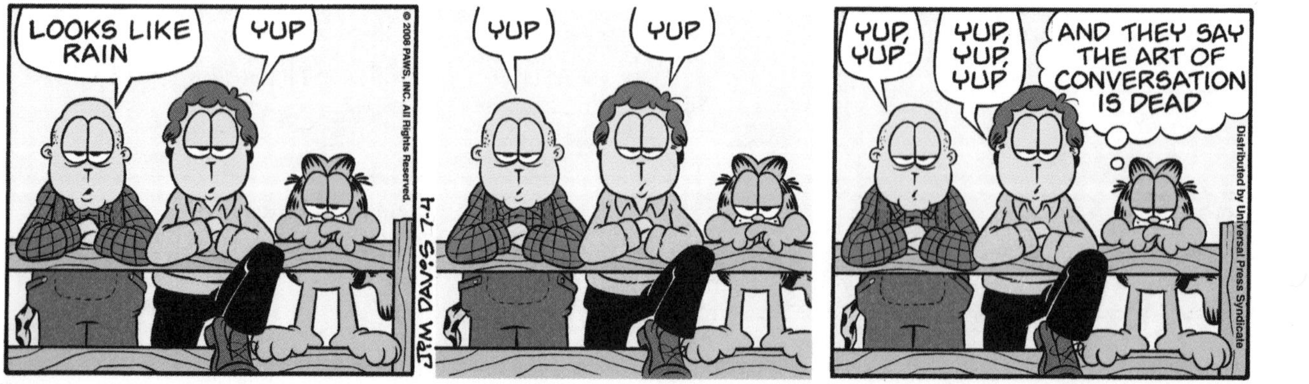
LOOKS LIKE RAIN
YUP
YUP
YUP
YUP, YUP
YUP, YUP, YUP
AND THEY SAY THE ART OF CONVERSATION IS DEAD
JIM DAVIS 7-4
© 2008 PAWS, INC. All Rights Reserved.
Distributed by Universal Press Syndicate

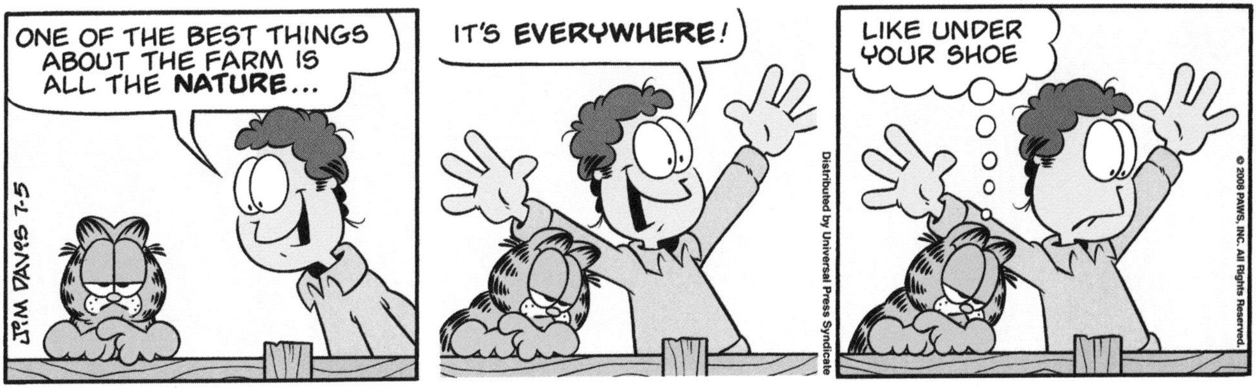
ONE OF THE BEST THINGS ABOUT THE FARM IS ALL THE NATURE...
JIM DAVIS 7-5
IT'S EVERYWHERE!
Distributed by Universal Press Syndicate
LIKE UNDER YOUR SHOE
© 2008 PAWS, INC. All Rights Reserved.

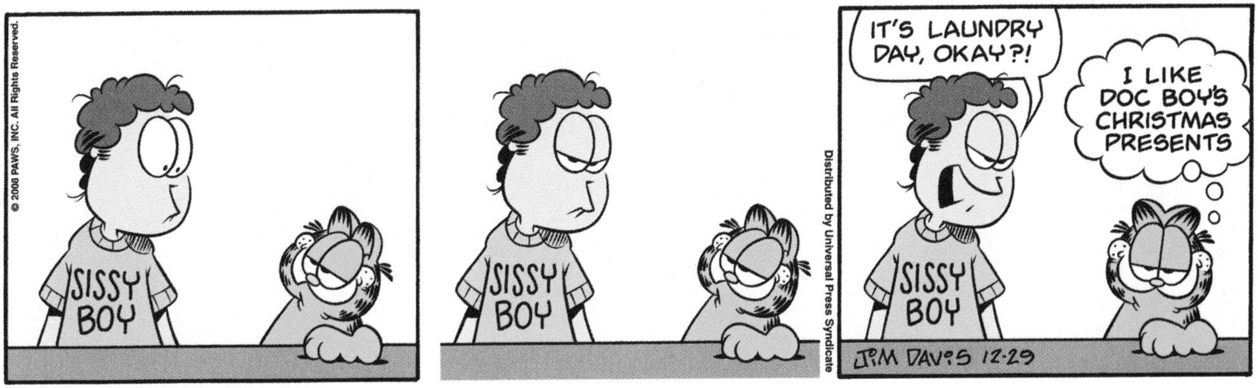
© 2008 PAWS, INC. All Rights Reserved.
SISSY BOY
SISSY BOY
Distributed by Universal Press Syndicate
IT'S LAUNDRY DAY, OKAY?!
I LIKE DOC BOY'S CHRISTMAS PRESENTS
SISSY BOY
JIM DAVIS 12-29

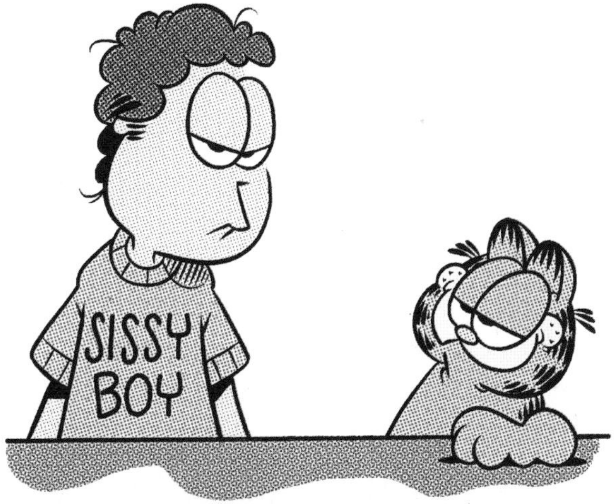
SISSY BOY

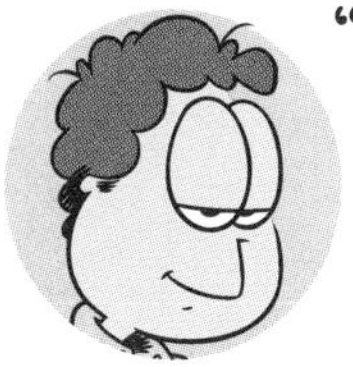

"I got even with Doc Boy. I had Garfield fertilize his overalls."

JON'S FAMILY ALBUM

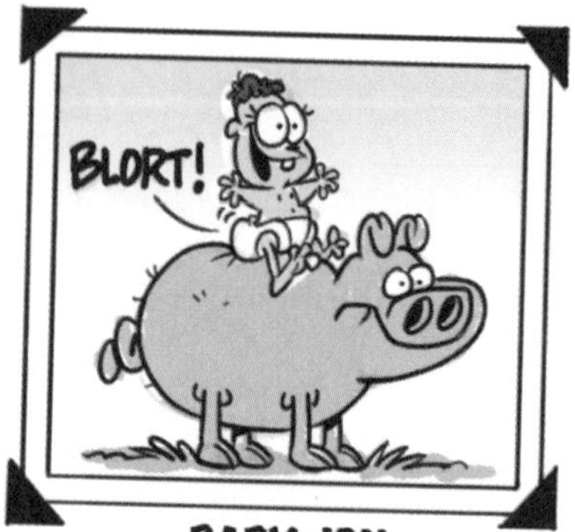
BLORT!

BABY JON

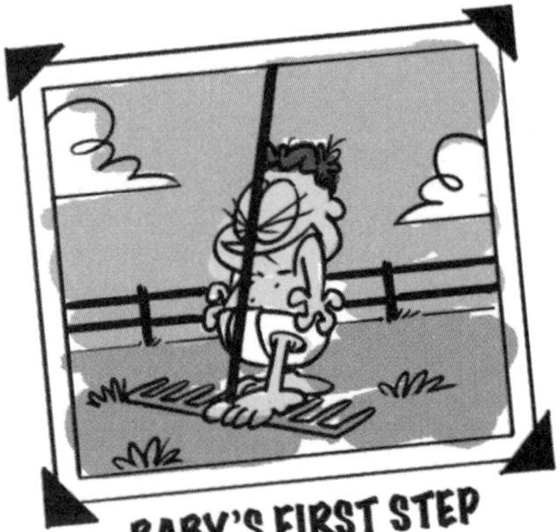

BABY'S FIRST STEP

"Clucky," my first pet chicken.

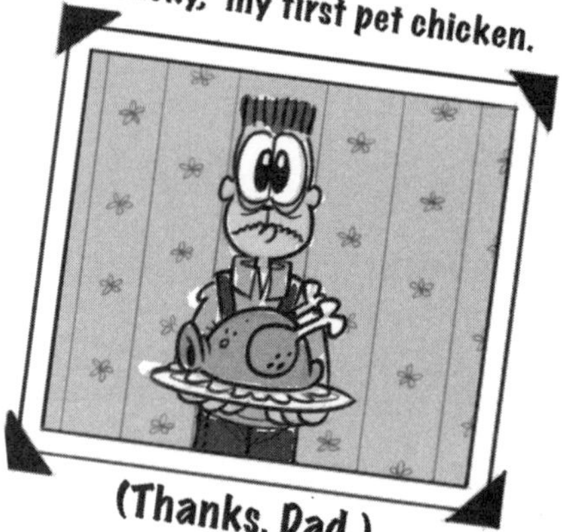

(Thanks, Dad.)

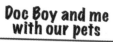

Doc Boy and me with our pets

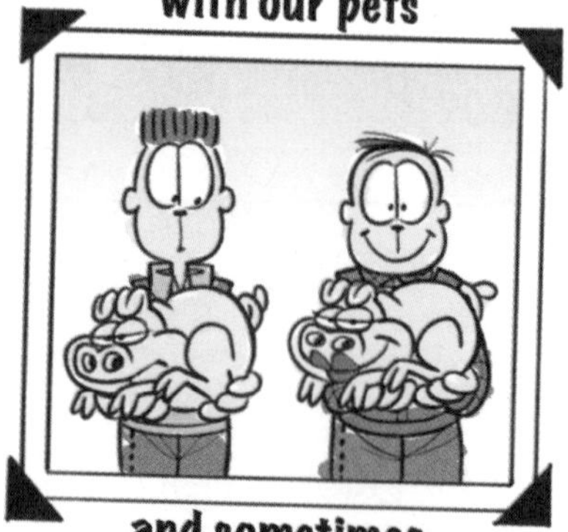

and sometimes dates.

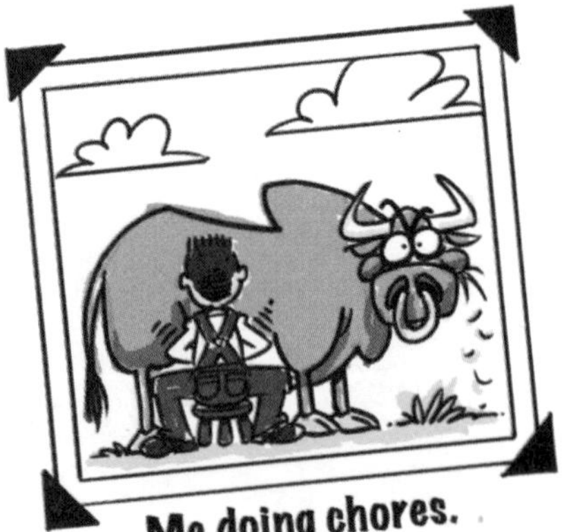

Me doing chores.

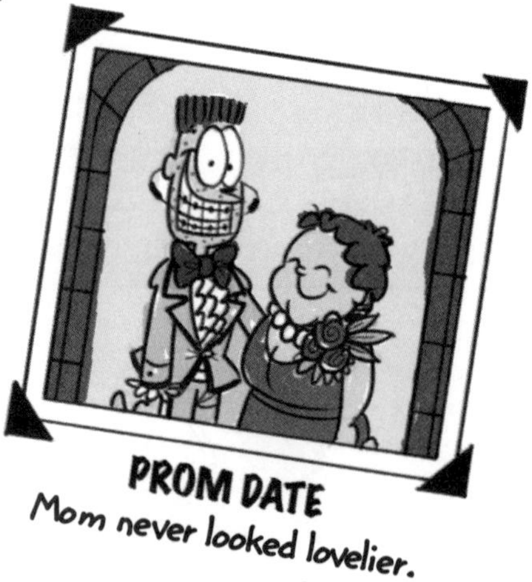

PROM DATE

Mom never looked lovelier.

Norbert

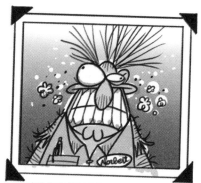

GREAT-UNCLE NORBERT
the color-blind electrician

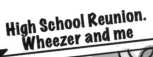

High School Reunion.
Wheezer and me

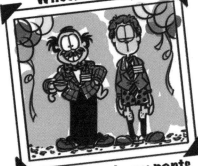

after he stole my pants.

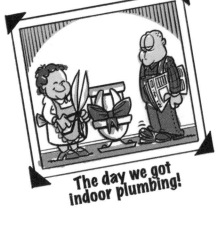

The day we got
indoor plumbing!

High School Reunion

GING
GING
STAMP
STAMP
STAMP
STAMP

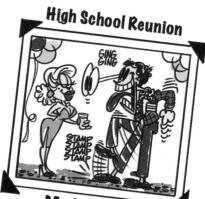

Mr. Suave sees
an old flame.

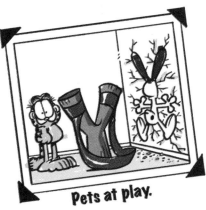

Pets at play.

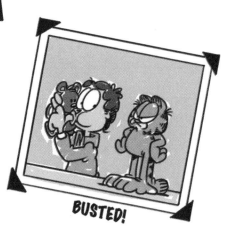

BUSTED!

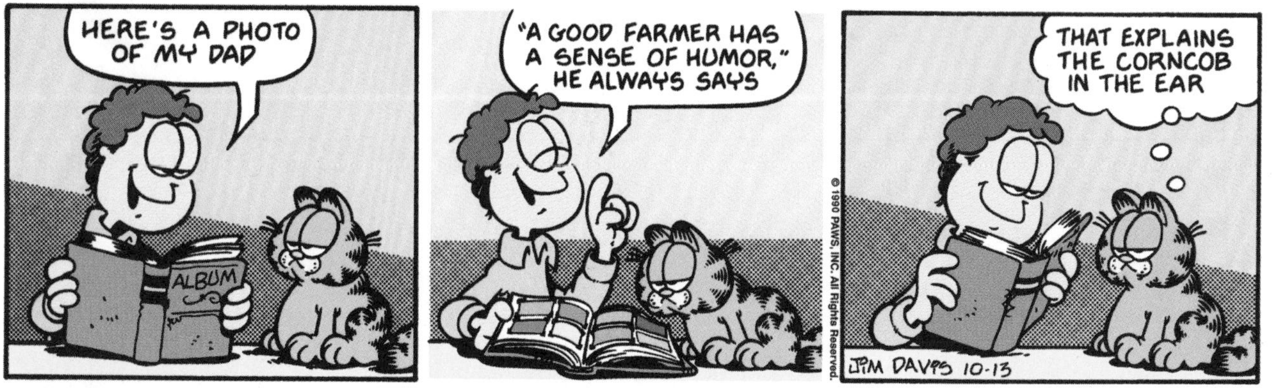
HERE'S A PHOTO OF MY DAD
"A GOOD FARMER HAS A SENSE OF HUMOR," HE ALWAYS SAYS
THAT EXPLAINS THE CORNCOB IN THE EAR
ALBUM
© 1990 PAWS, INC. All Rights Reserved.
JIM DAVIS 10-13

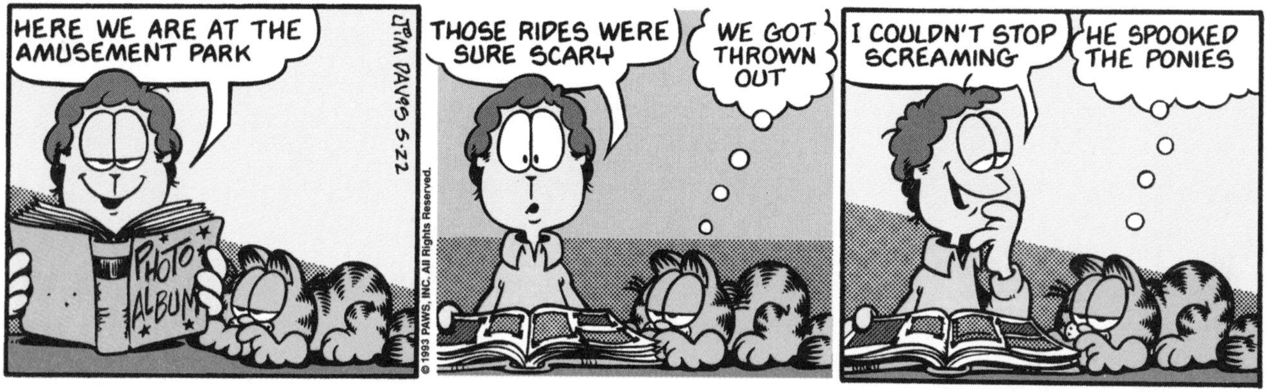
HERE WE ARE AT THE AMUSEMENT PARK
PHOTO ALBUM
JIM DAVIS 5-22
© 1993 PAWS, INC. All Rights Reserved.
THOSE RIDES WERE SURE SCARY
WE GOT THROWN OUT
I COULDN'T STOP SCREAMING
HE SPOOKED THE PONIES

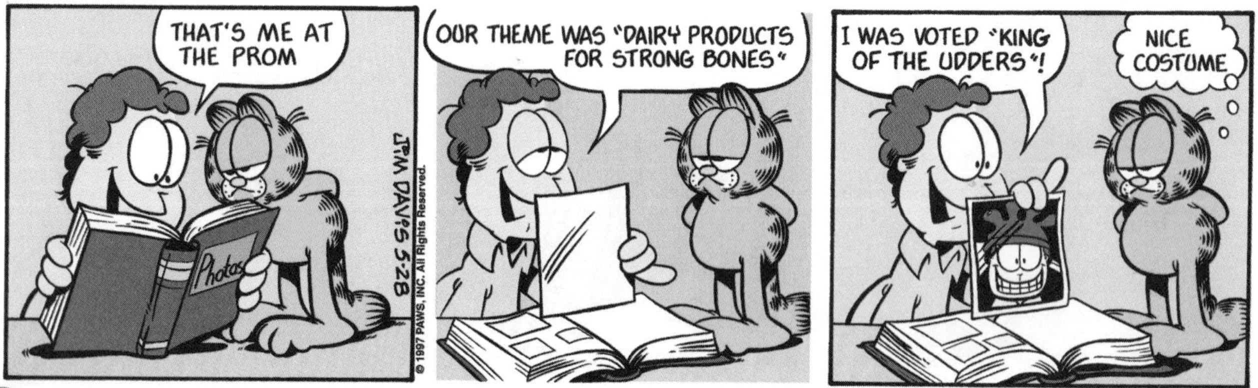
THAT'S ME AT THE PROM
Photos
JIM DAVIS 5-28
© 1997 PAWS, INC. All Rights Reserved.
OUR THEME WAS "DAIRY PRODUCTS FOR STRONG BONES"
I WAS VOTED "KING OF THE UDDERS"!
NICE COSTUME

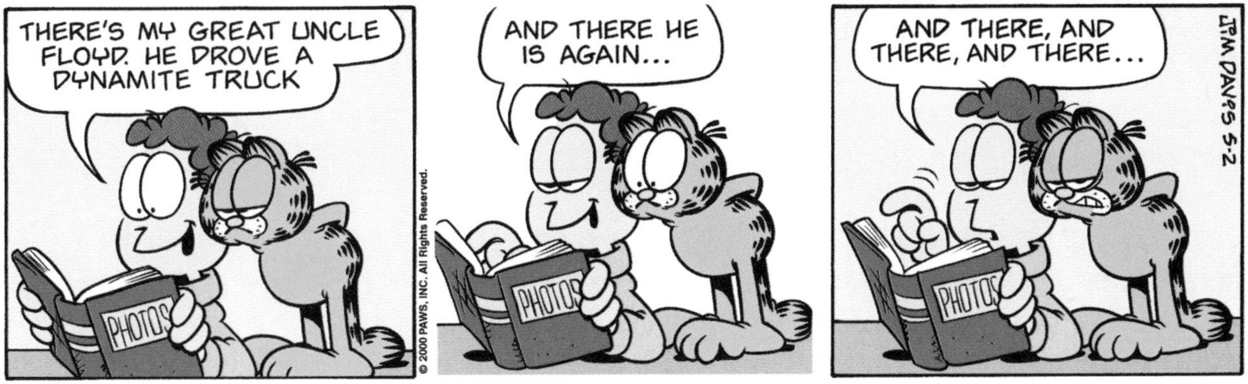
THERE'S MY GREAT UNCLE FLOYD. HE DROVE A DYNAMITE TRUCK
PHOTOS
© 2000 PAWS, INC. All Rights Reserved.
AND THERE HE IS AGAIN...
AND THERE, AND THERE, AND THERE...
JIM DAVIS 5-2

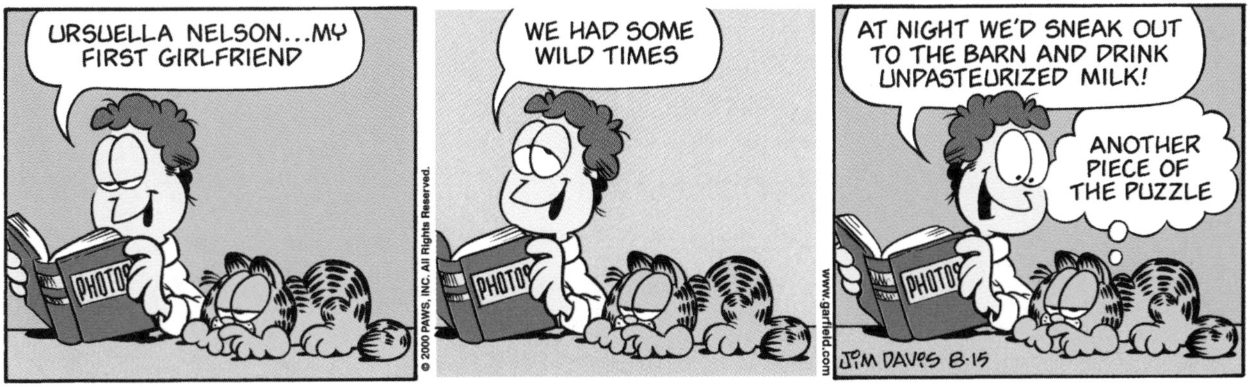
URSUELLA NELSON...MY FIRST GIRLFRIEND
© 2000 PAWS, INC. All Rights Reserved.
WE HAD SOME WILD TIMES
www.garfield.com
AT NIGHT WE'D SNEAK OUT TO THE BARN AND DRINK UNPASTEURIZED MILK!
ANOTHER PIECE OF THE PUZZLE
JIM DAVIS 8-15

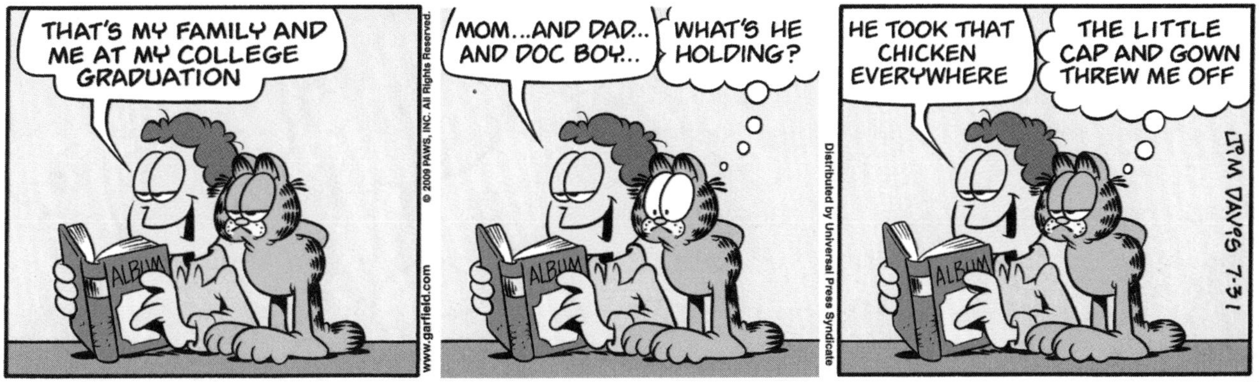
THAT'S MY FAMILY AND ME AT MY COLLEGE GRADUATION
ALBUM
© 2009 PAWS, INC. All Rights Reserved.
www.garfield.com
MOM...AND DAD... AND DOC BOY...
WHAT'S HE HOLDING?
Distributed by Universal Press Syndicate
HE TOOK THAT CHICKEN EVERYWHERE
THE LITTLE CAP AND GOWN THREW ME OFF
JIM DAVIS 7-31

PLAYFUL PETS

One thing's for certain: Life with Garfield and Odie is never boring. Frustrating? Maddening? Exasperating? Sure. But never boring.

Garfield and Mrs. Feeny, Jon's neighbor, are constantly battling: Garfield swipes her dentures for his sock puppet; Mrs. Feeny puts up an electrified fence; Garfield feeds her dog laxative-laced bran muffins; Mrs. Feeny adds a moat around her house; Garfield digs a tiger trap in her flower bed; Mrs. Feeny gets a restraining order. Typical suburban shenanigans.

When Garfield isn't harassing the neighbors, or kicking Odie off the table (or tying his ears to the ceiling fan), he's pestering Jon for food. Keeping the fat cat fed is a full-time job with endless overtime. No matter how many pizzas Jon orders, pans of lasagna he bakes, or gigantic-sized "Kitty Bags" he brings home, he just can't seem to fill up the flabby tabby's bottomless stomach. If it weren't for Garfield's marathon cat naps, Jon would never get a break.

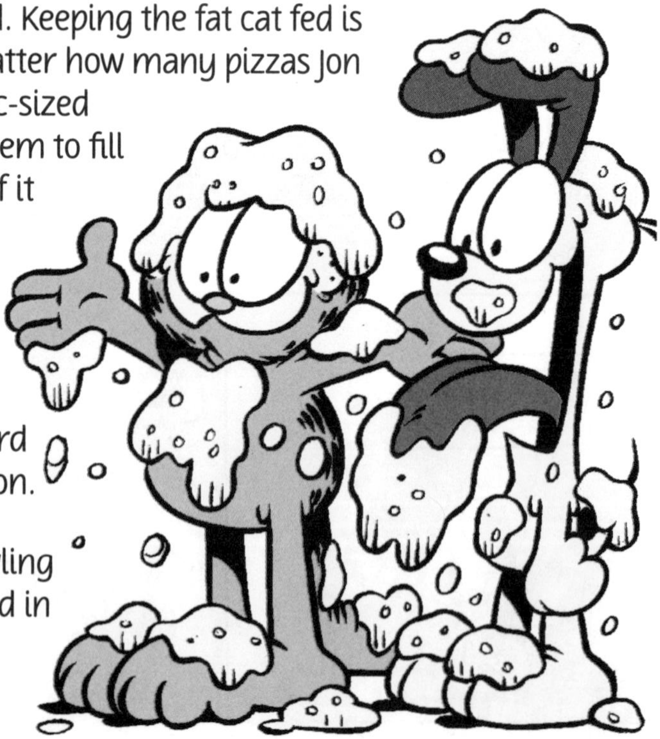

And Odie can be a handful, too, especially when he's drinking all the water from the wading pool or digging a hole in the backyard big enough to bury a Tyrannosaurus skeleton.

Shedding, shredding, digging, drooling, howling and yowling...that's life with pets. As Jon said in one strip, "I'm so happy to own a cat I could throw up."

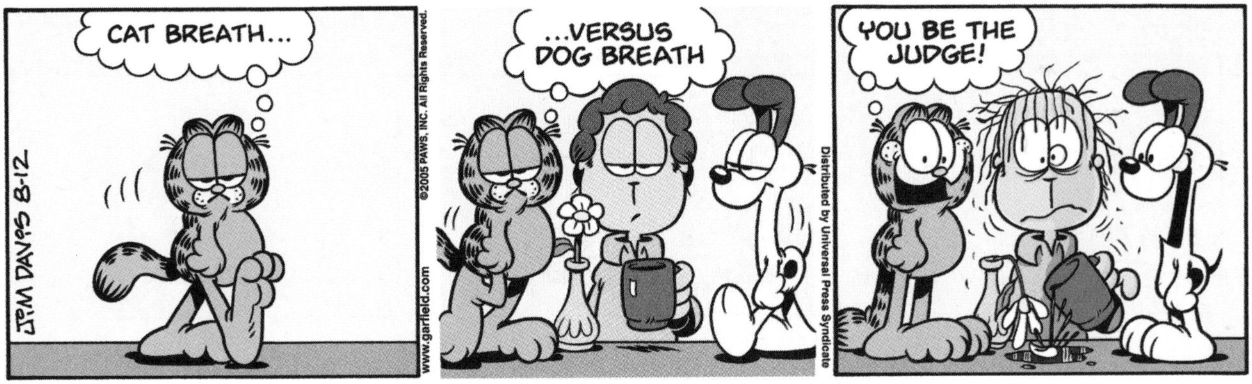
JPM DAVPS 8-12
CAT BREATH...
...VERSUS DOG BREATH
YOU BE THE JUDGE!
©2005 PAWS, INC. All Rights Reserved.
www.garfield.com
Distributed by Universal Press Syndicate

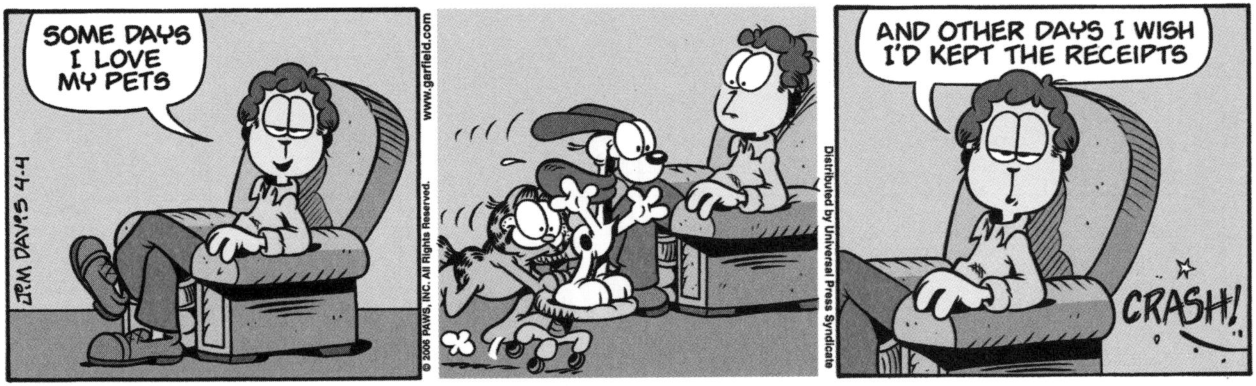
JPM DAVPS 4-4
SOME DAYS I LOVE MY PETS
AND OTHER DAYS I WISH I'D KEPT THE RECEIPTS
CRASH!
© 2006 PAWS, INC. All Rights Reserved.
www.garfield.com
Distributed by Universal Press Syndicate

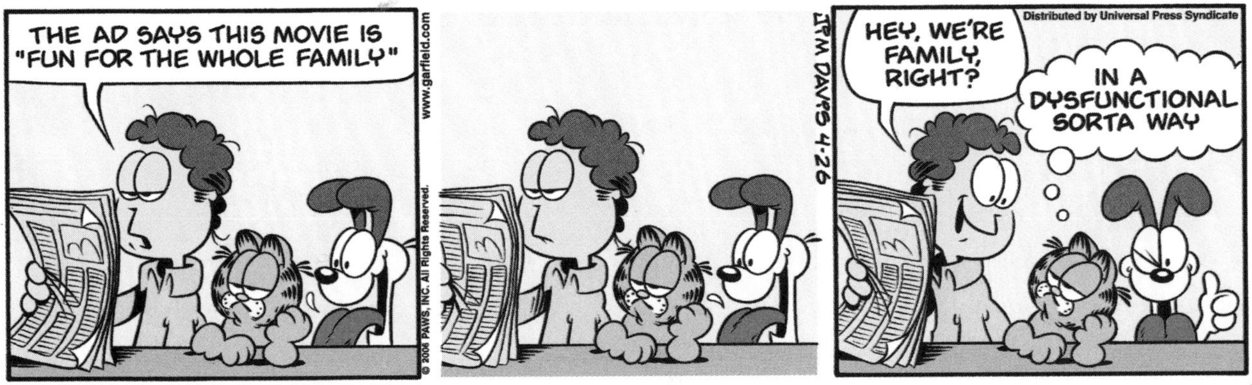
THE AD SAYS THIS MOVIE IS "FUN FOR THE WHOLE FAMILY"
HEY, WE'RE FAMILY, RIGHT?
IN A DYSFUNCTIONAL SORTA WAY
JPM DAVPS 4-26
© 2006 PAWS, INC. All Rights Reserved.
www.garfield.com
Distributed by Universal Press Syndicate

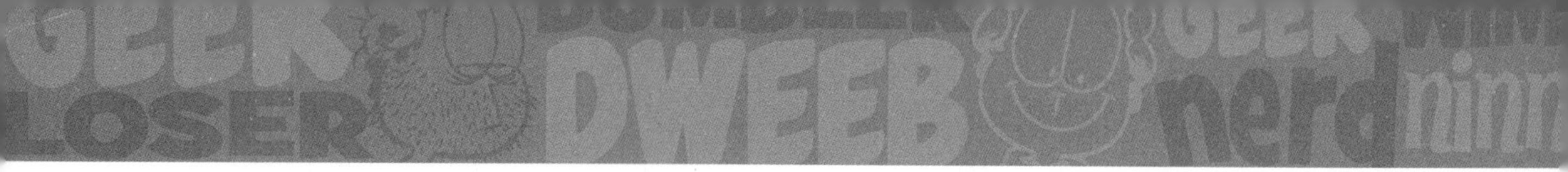
LOSER
DWEEB
nerd

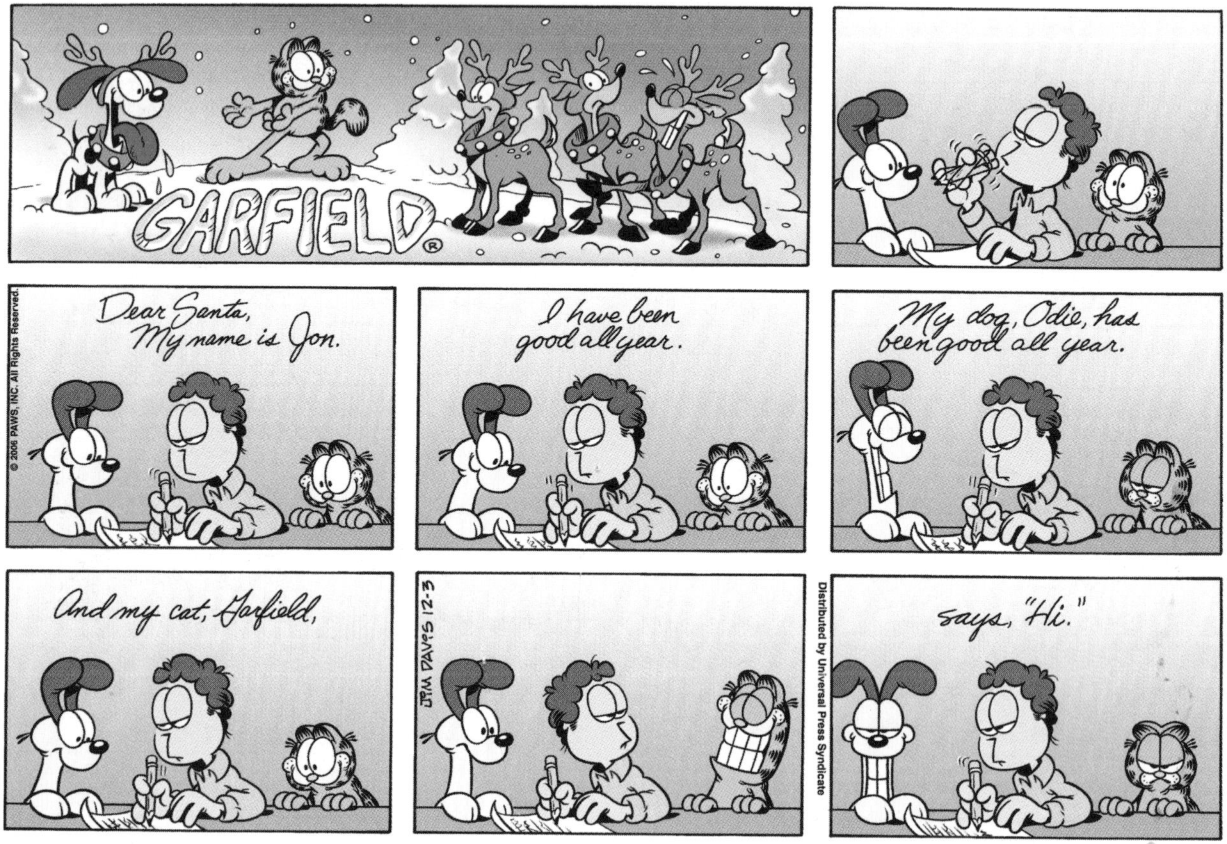
GARFIELD
© 2006 PAWS, INC. All Rights Reserved.
Dear Santa,
My name is Jon.
I have been good all year.
My dog, Odie, has been good all year.
And my cat, Garfield,
JPM DAVIS 12-3
Distributed by Universal Press Syndicate
says, "Hi."

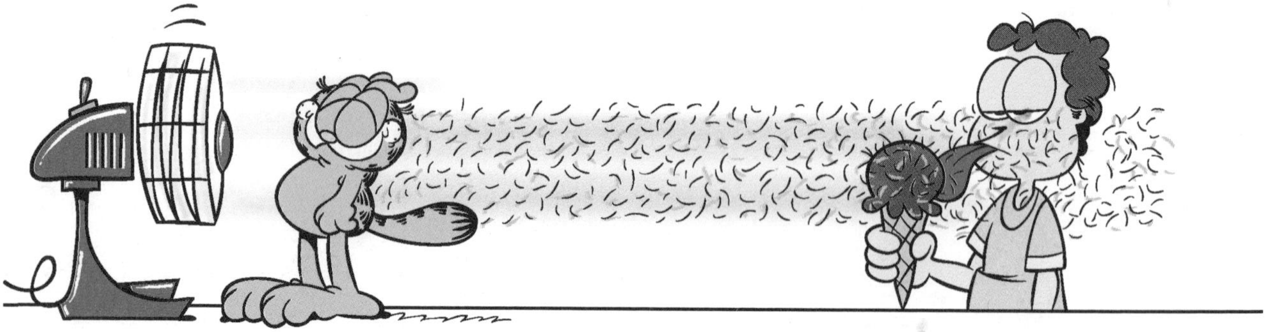

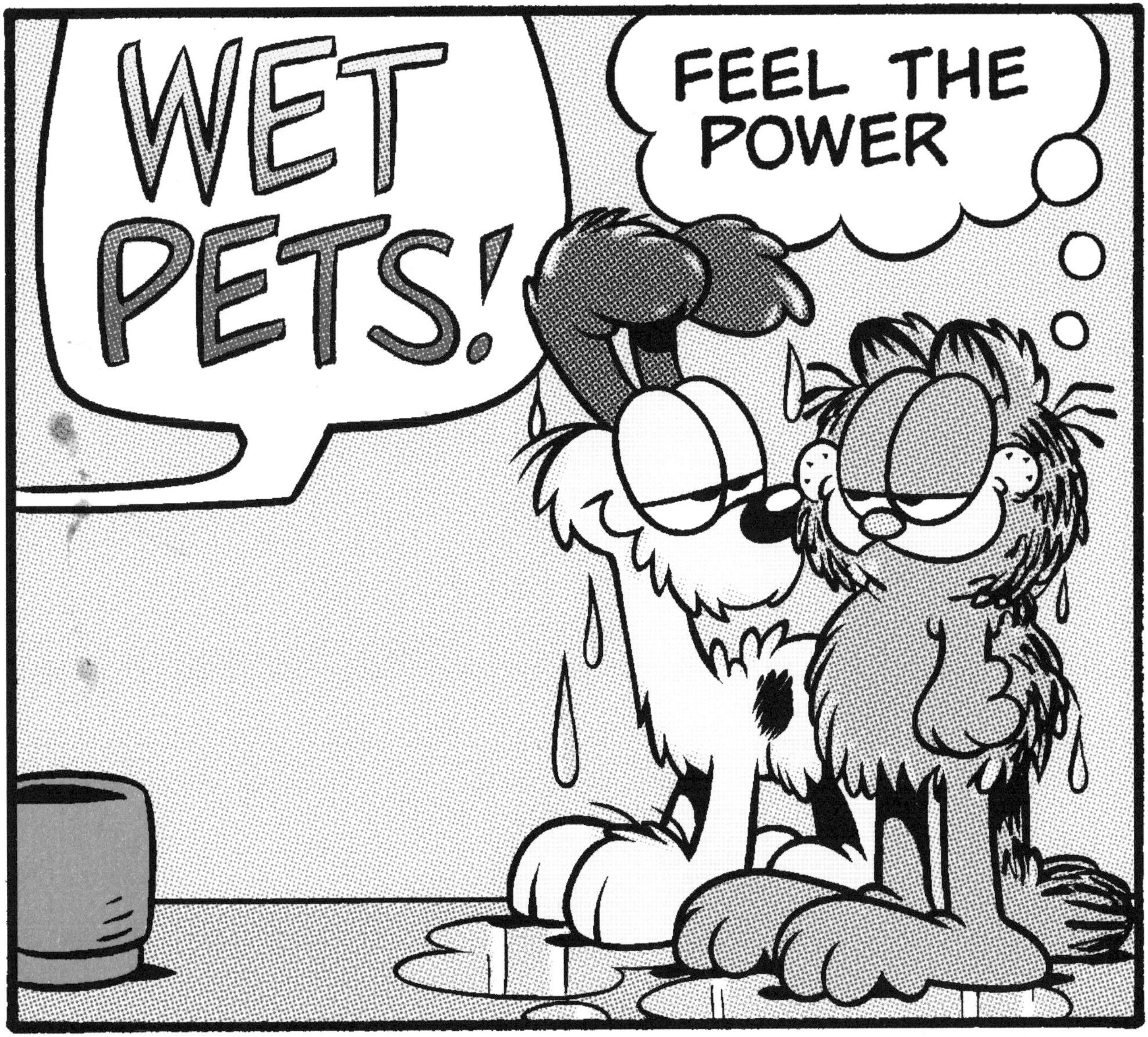
WET PETS!
FEEL THE POWER

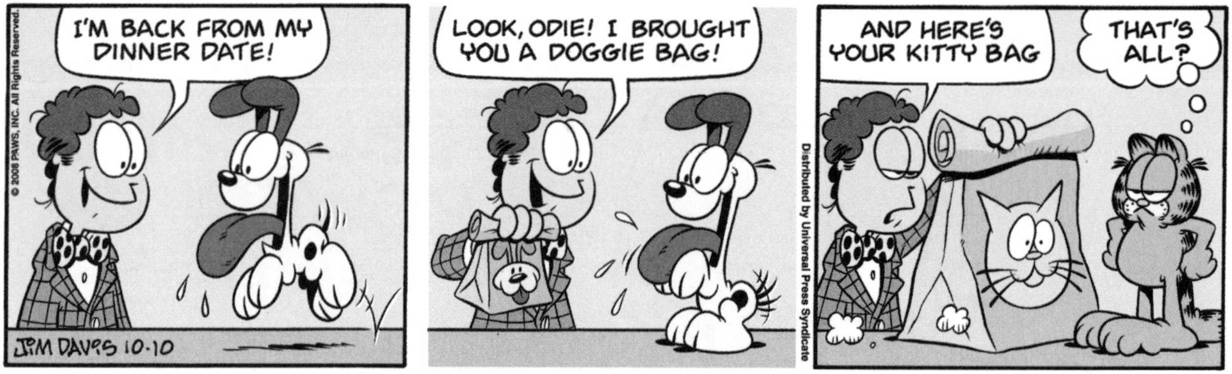
© 2008 PAWS, INC. All Rights Reserved.
I'M BACK FROM MY DINNER DATE!
JIM DAVIS 10-10
LOOK, ODIE! I BROUGHT YOU A DOGGIE BAG!
Distributed by Universal Press Syndicate
AND HERE'S YOUR KITTY BAG
THAT'S ALL?

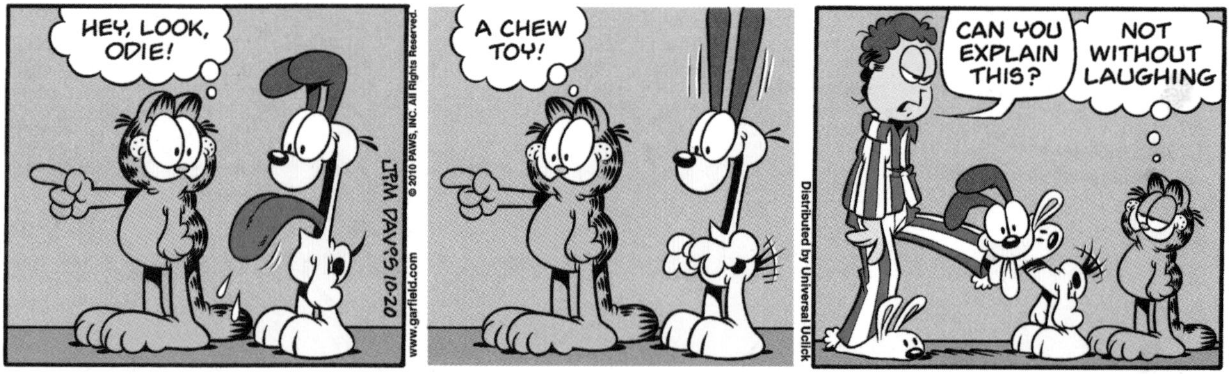
HEY, LOOK, ODIE!
JIM DAVIS 10-20
© 2010 PAWS, INC. All Rights Reserved.
www.garfield.com
A CHEW TOY!
Distributed by Universal Uclick
CAN YOU EXPLAIN THIS?
NOT WITHOUT LAUGHING

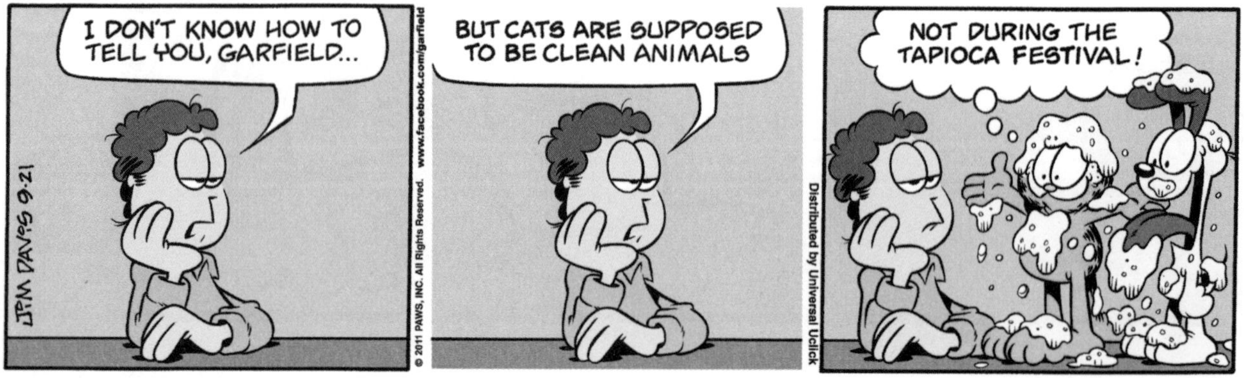
I DON'T KNOW HOW TO TELL YOU, GARFIELD...
JIM DAVIS 9-21
© 2011 PAWS, INC. All Rights Reserved. www.facebook.com/garfield
BUT CATS ARE SUPPOSED TO BE CLEAN ANIMALS
Distributed by Universal Uclick
NOT DURING THE TAPIOCA FESTIVAL!

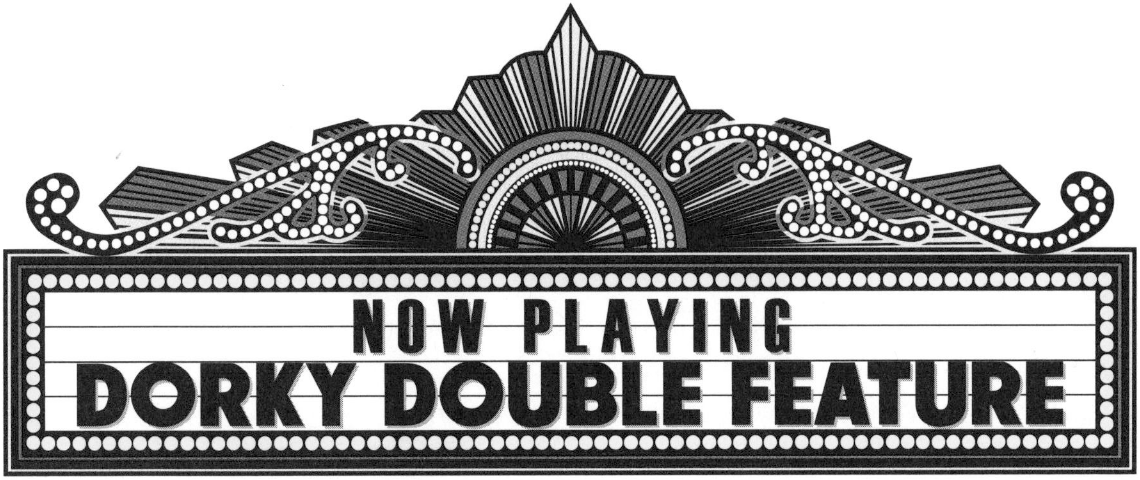
NOW PLAYING
DORKY DOUBLE FEATURE

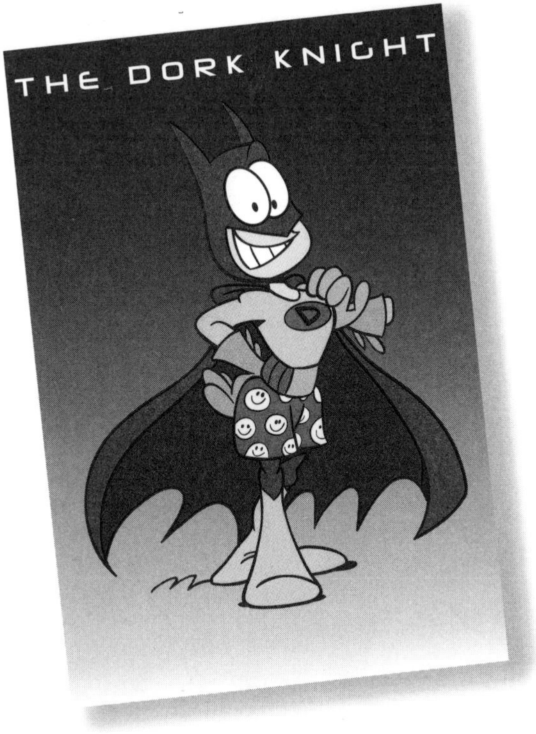
THE DORK KNIGHT

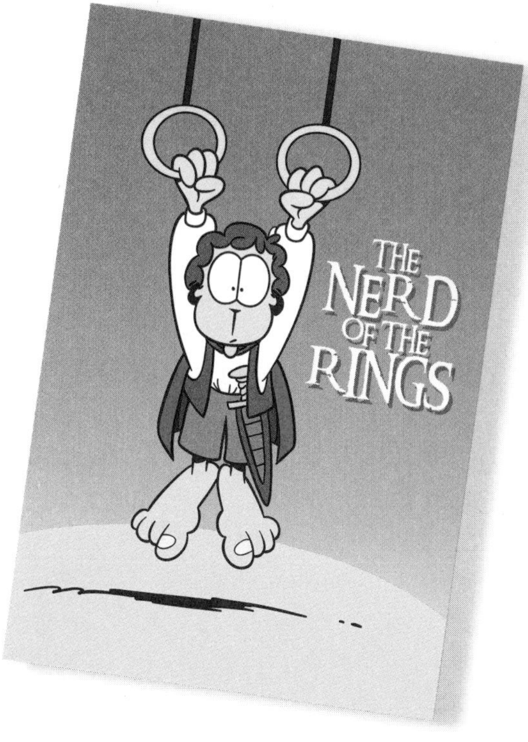
THE NERD OF THE RINGS

The dating scene is never easy, but it's especially hard for Jon. Once he tried a dating service that matched him with a lovely woman nicknamed "The Widow Maker." Newly paroled, she was eager to start dating again and only had to be sedated twice during her night on the town with Jon.

Blind dates haven't been any better. There was the girl who had a craving for raw meat; the girl with the "great personality" who won first place at the county fair pork rind–eating contest; and then the girl who sucker-punched Jon on the way to the front porch and ran away (some people will do anything to get out of a goodnight kiss, it seems).

Jon once said he was "as desperate as a monkey in a banana famine." Maybe that's why he's had so many close encounters of the weird kind with women (a mime, a female wrestler, and Zelda the Toad Woman. Jon must love girls in show business!).

Then there's Ellen. She's shot down the clueless Casanova more than fifty times. Ellen's insulted Jon; yelled at him; hung up on him (repeatedly); sent him a Christmas card that said, "Stop asking me out, you dork!"; used a voodoo doll; she even got a restraining order (or two). Luckily, Jon hooked up with Liz, or poor Ellen might have been forced to enter the Witness Relocation Program to escape his annoying advances.

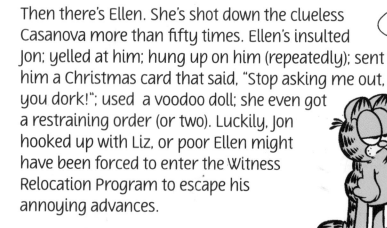

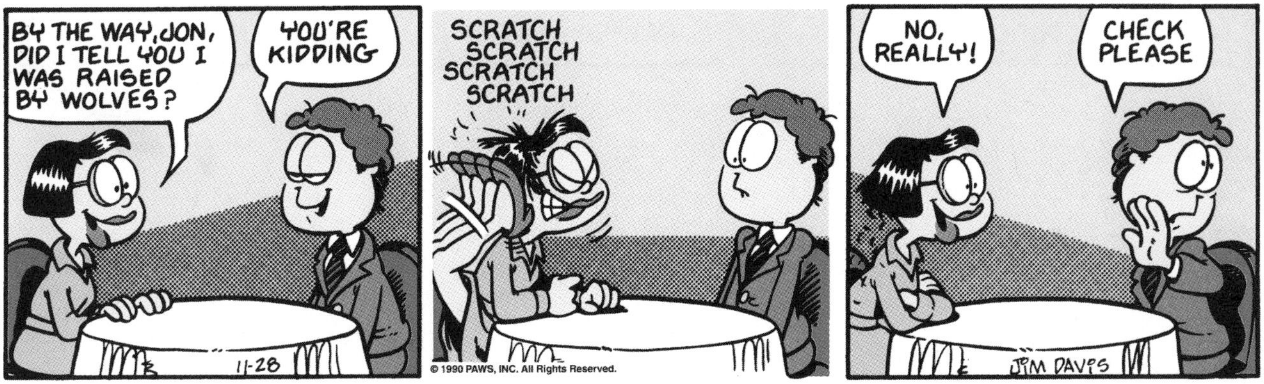
BY THE WAY, JON, DID I TELL YOU I WAS RAISED BY WOLVES?
YOU'RE KIDDING
11-28
SCRATCH SCRATCH SCRATCH SCRATCH
© 1990 PAWS, INC. All Rights Reserved.
NO, REALLY!
CHECK PLEASE
JIM DAVIS

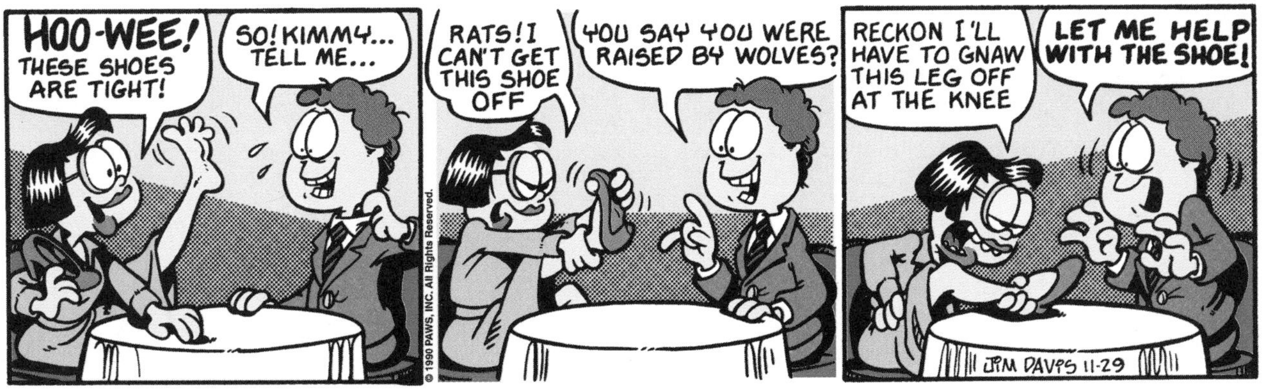
HOO-WEE! THESE SHOES ARE TIGHT!
SO! KIMMY... TELL ME...
© 1990 PAWS, INC. All Rights Reserved.
RATS! I CAN'T GET THIS SHOE OFF
YOU SAY YOU WERE RAISED BY WOLVES?
RECKON I'LL HAVE TO GNAW THIS LEG OFF AT THE KNEE
LET ME HELP WITH THE SHOE!
JIM DAVIS 11-29

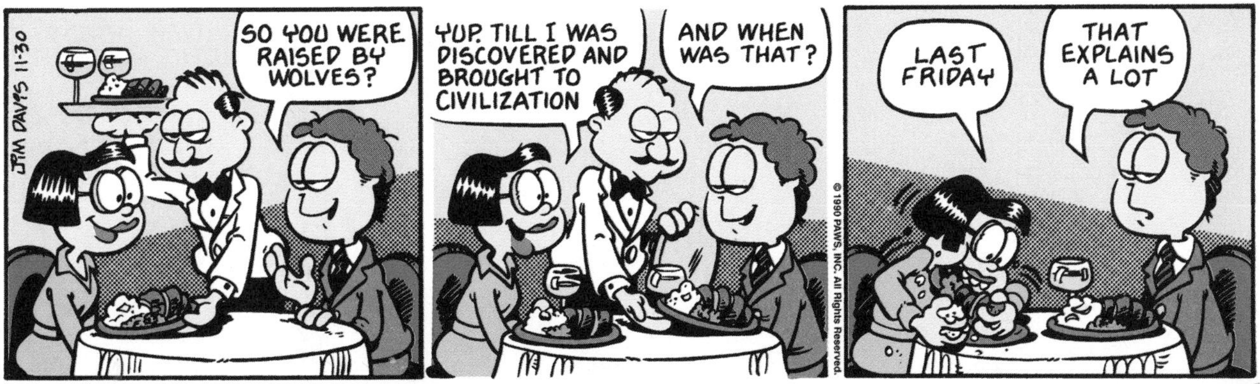
JIM DAVIS 11-30
SO YOU WERE RAISED BY WOLVES?
YUP. TILL I WAS DISCOVERED AND BROUGHT TO CIVILIZATION
AND WHEN WAS THAT?
© 1990 PAWS, INC. All Rights Reserved.
LAST FRIDAY
THAT EXPLAINS A LOT

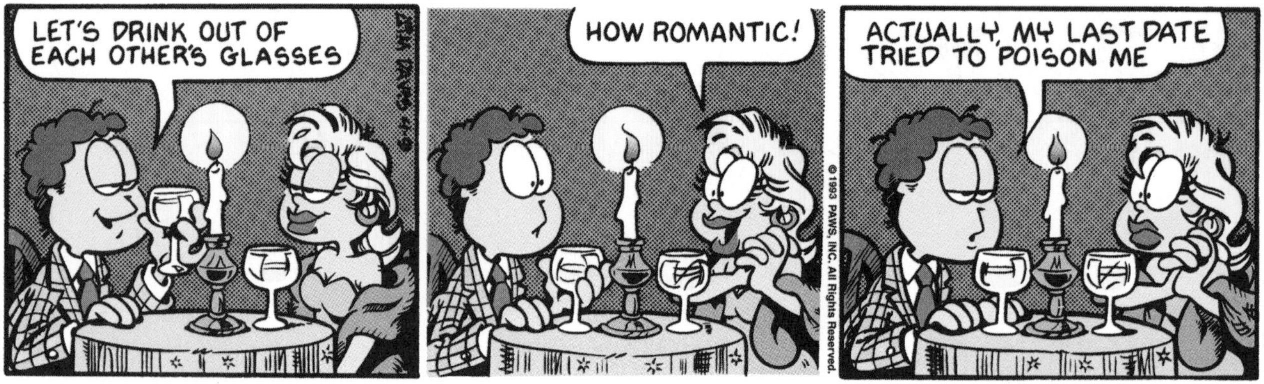
LET'S DRINK OUT OF EACH OTHER'S GLASSES
JIM DAVIS 4-9
HOW ROMANTIC!
ACTUALLY, MY LAST DATE TRIED TO POISON ME

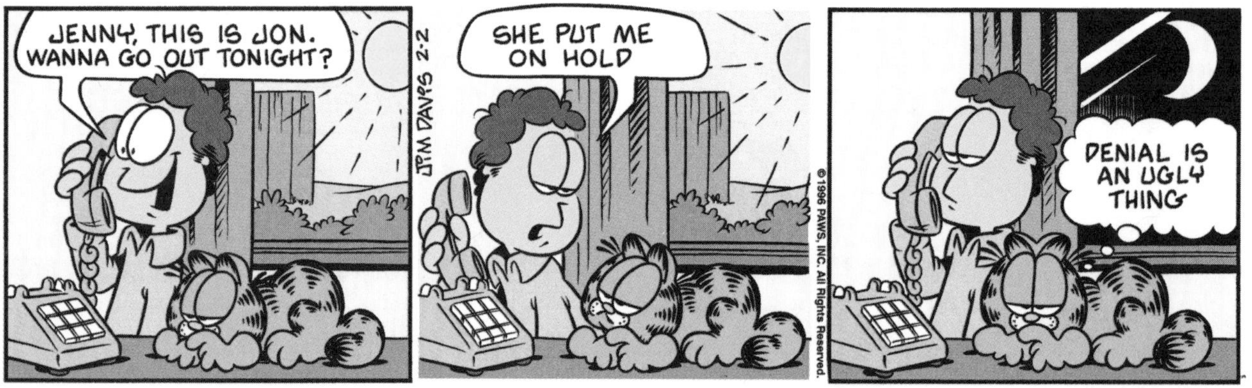
JENNY, THIS IS JON. WANNA GO OUT TONIGHT?
JIM DAVIS 2-2
SHE PUT ME ON HOLD
DENIAL IS AN UGLY THING

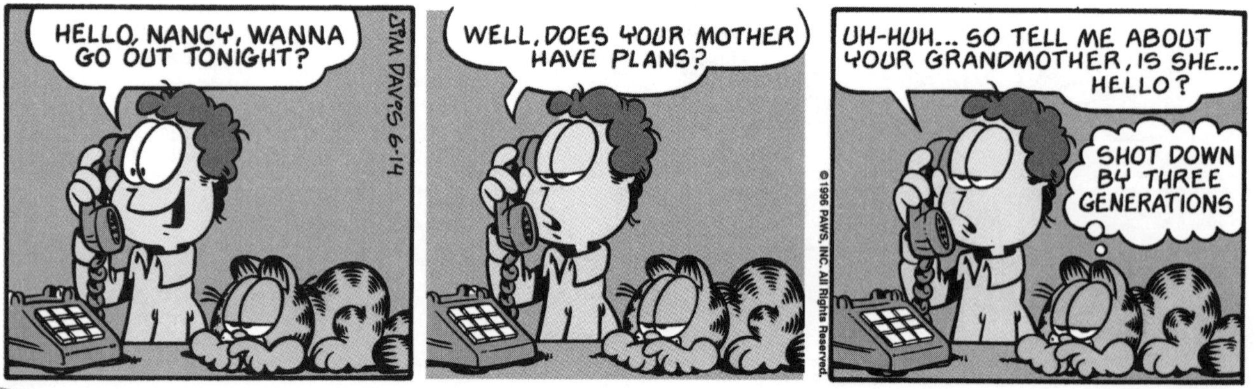
HELLO, NANCY, WANNA GO OUT TONIGHT?
JIM DAVIS 6-14
WELL, DOES YOUR MOTHER HAVE PLANS?
UH-HUH... SO TELL ME ABOUT YOUR GRANDMOTHER, IS SHE... HELLO?
SHOT DOWN BY THREE GENERATIONS

Top Ten Dating Dodges Women Use On Jon

10. "Sorry, I Don't Date Outside My Species."

9. "I'll Be Washing My hair All That Week. Each One. Individually."

8. "I'm Getting a Sex-change Operation."

7. "I Came Down With a Severe Case of Toe Jam."

6. "Darn, I have to Pick Up My Wombat From the Taxidermist that Night."

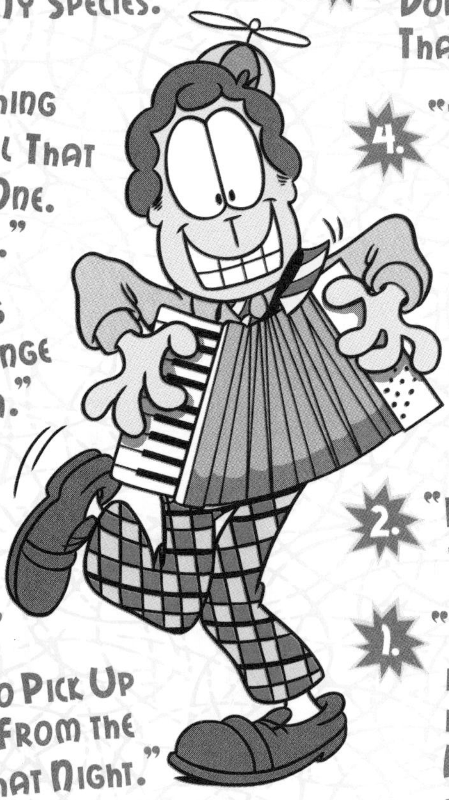

5. "No Can Do. I'm Donating My Kidney That Weekend."

4. "That's the Night I Wax My Grandmother's Mustache."

3. "I have to Stay home and Floss My Otter."

2. "I'm Allergic to Geeks."

1. "I'd Rather Swim in Piranha-infested Waters Dressed as a Meat Loaf."

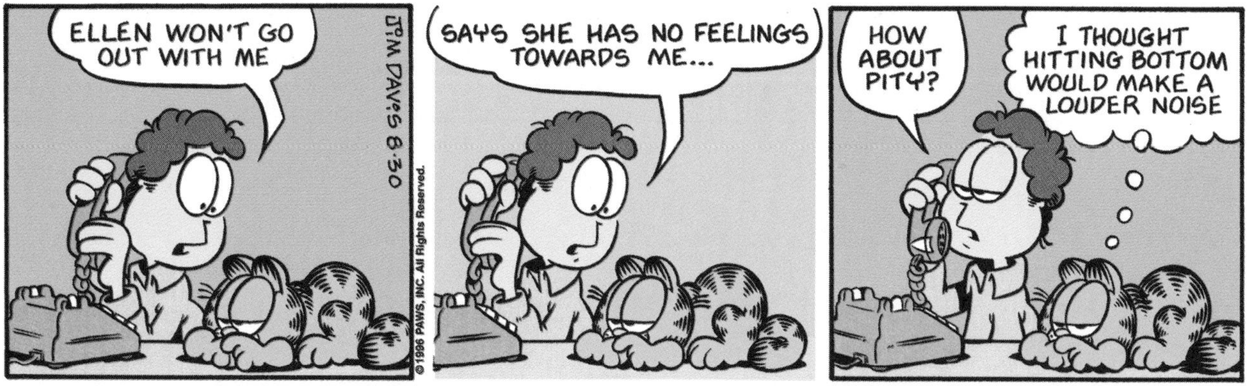
ELLEN WON'T GO OUT WITH ME
JPM DAVIS 8-30
© 1996 PAWS, INC. All Rights Reserved.
SAYS SHE HAS NO FEELINGS TOWARDS ME...
HOW ABOUT PITY?
I THOUGHT HITTING BOTTOM WOULD MAKE A LOUDER NOISE

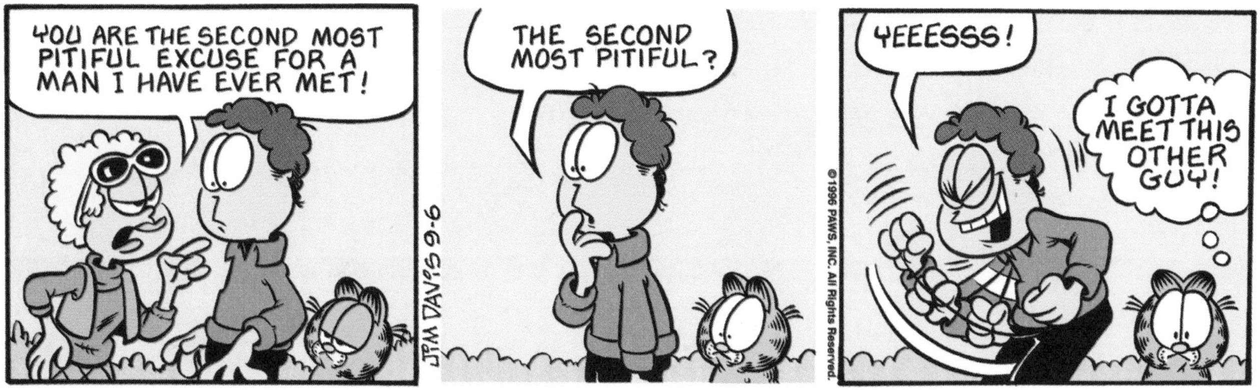
YOU ARE THE SECOND MOST PITIFUL EXCUSE FOR A MAN I HAVE EVER MET!
JPM DAVIS 9-6
THE SECOND MOST PITIFUL?
© 1996 PAWS, INC. All Rights Reserved.
YEEESSS!
I GOTTA MEET THIS OTHER GUY!

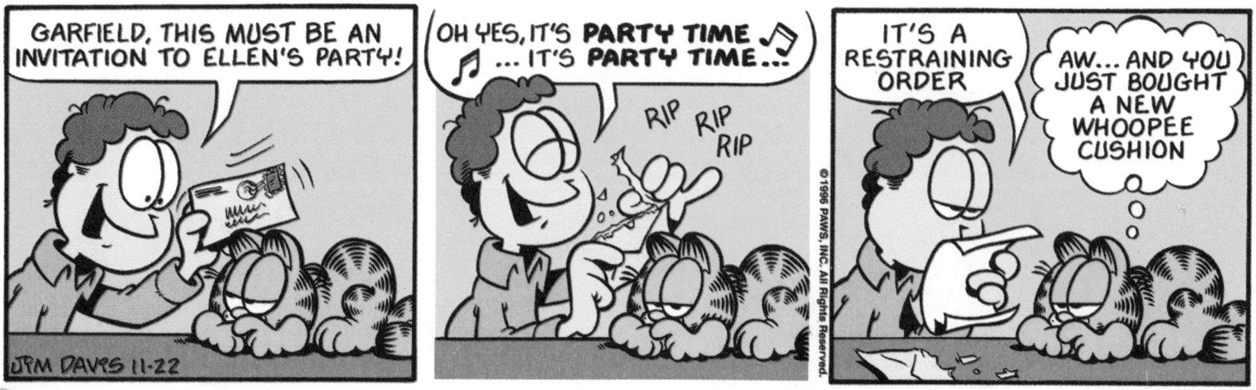
GARFIELD, THIS MUST BE AN INVITATION TO ELLEN'S PARTY!
JPM DAVIS 11-22
OH YES, IT'S **PARTY TIME** ... IT'S **PARTY TIME**...
RIP
RIP
RIP
© 1996 PAWS, INC. All Rights Reserved.
IT'S A RESTRAINING ORDER
AW... AND YOU JUST BOUGHT A NEW WHOOPEE CUSHION

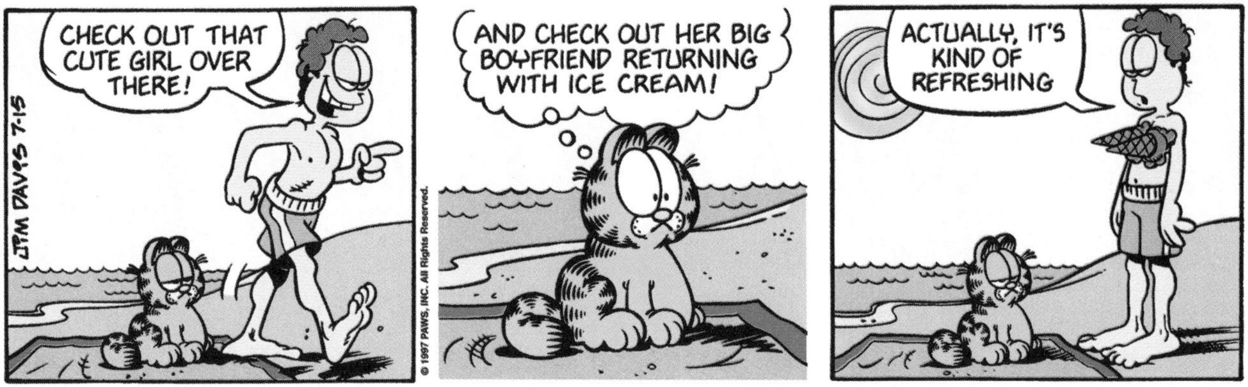
JIM DAVIS 7-15
CHECK OUT THAT CUTE GIRL OVER THERE!
AND CHECK OUT HER BIG BOYFRIEND RETURNING WITH ICE CREAM!
ACTUALLY, IT'S KIND OF REFRESHING
© 1997 PAWS, INC. All Rights Reserved.

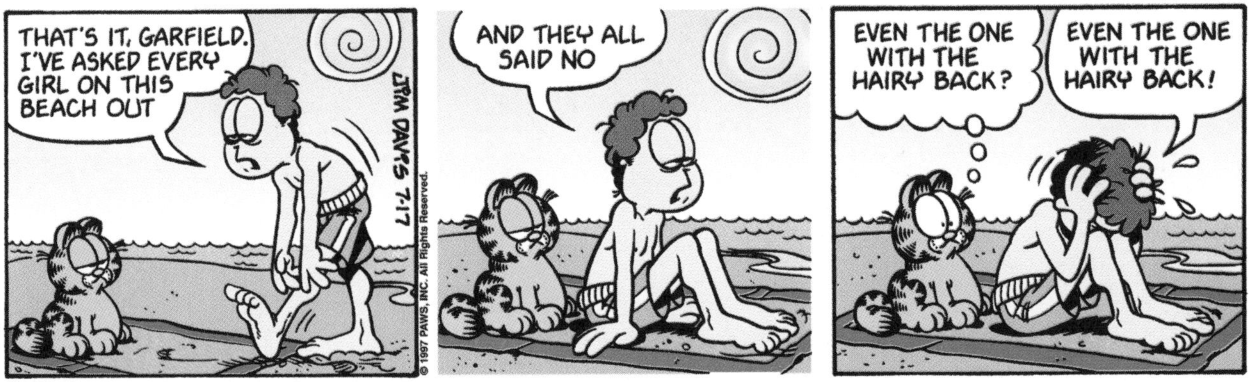
JIM DAVIS 7-17
THAT'S IT, GARFIELD. I'VE ASKED EVERY GIRL ON THIS BEACH OUT
AND THEY ALL SAID NO
EVEN THE ONE WITH THE HAIRY BACK?
EVEN THE ONE WITH THE HAIRY BACK!
© 1997 PAWS, INC. All Rights Reserved.

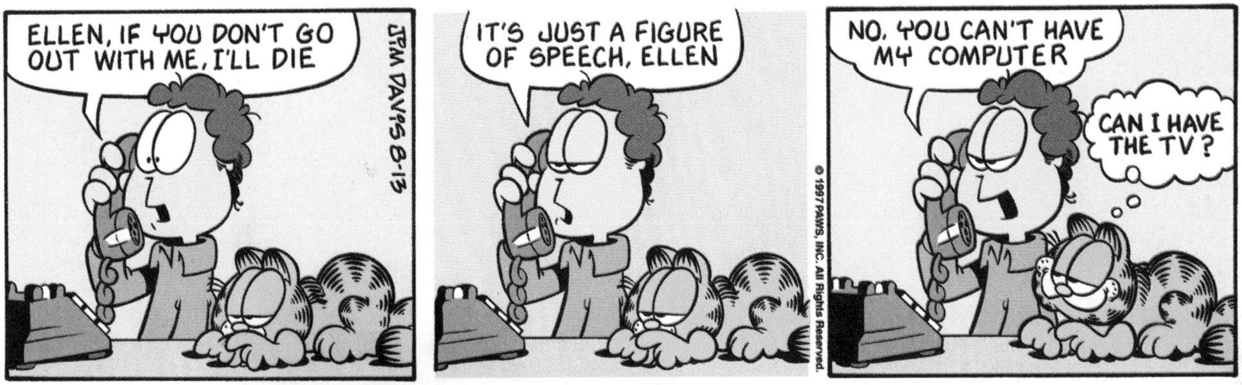
JIM DAVIS 8-13
ELLEN, IF YOU DON'T GO OUT WITH ME, I'LL DIE
IT'S JUST A FIGURE OF SPEECH, ELLEN
NO. YOU CAN'T HAVE MY COMPUTER
CAN I HAVE THE TV?
© 1997 PAWS, INC. All Rights Reserved.

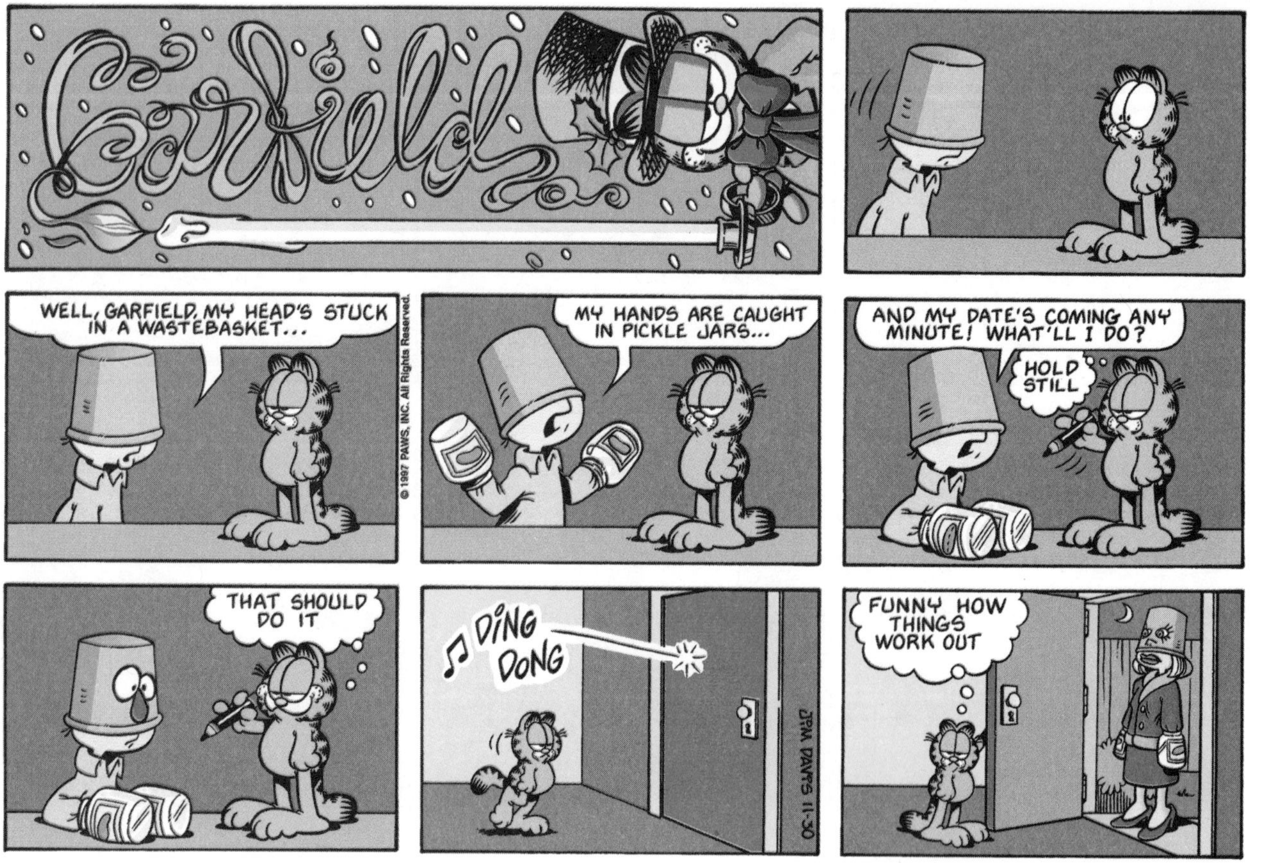
Garfield
WELL, GARFIELD, MY HEAD'S STUCK IN A WASTEBASKET...
© 1997 PAWS, INC. All Rights Reserved.
MY HANDS ARE CAUGHT IN PICKLE JARS...
AND MY DATE'S COMING ANY MINUTE! WHAT'LL I DO?
HOLD STILL
THAT SHOULD DO IT
DING DONG
JPM DAVIS 11-30
FUNNY HOW THINGS WORK OUT

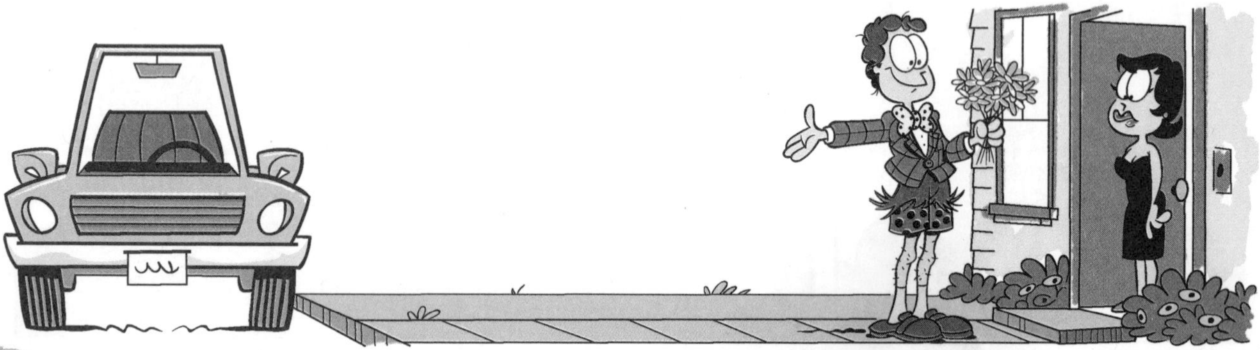

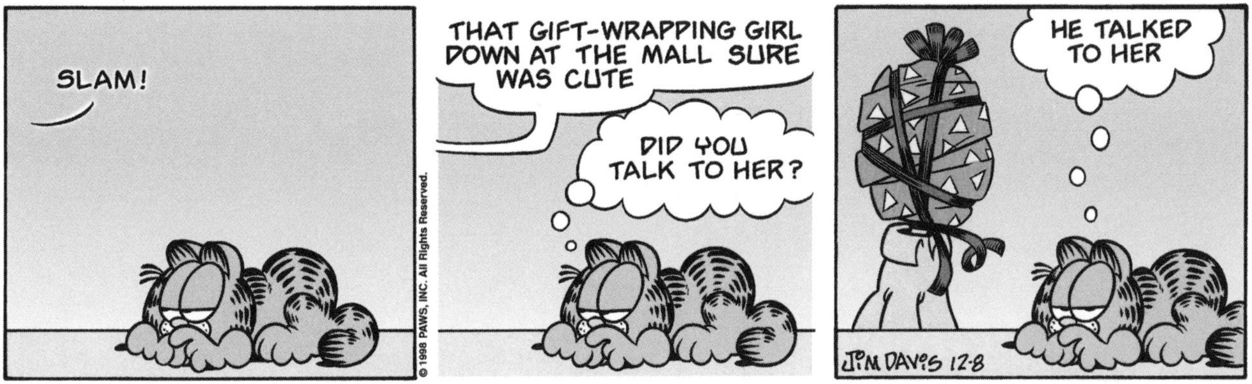
SLAM!
THAT GIFT-WRAPPING GIRL DOWN AT THE MALL SURE WAS CUTE
DID YOU TALK TO HER?
HE TALKED TO HER
JIM DAVIS 12-8

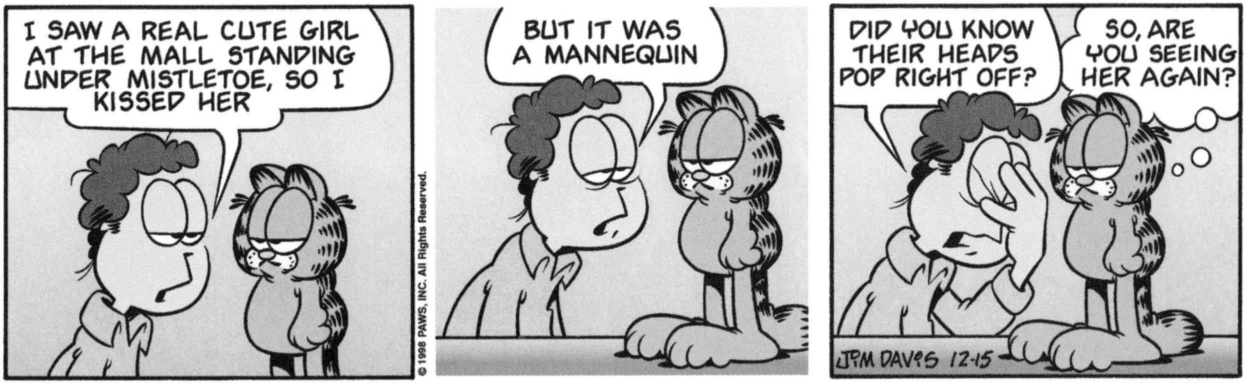
I SAW A REAL CUTE GIRL AT THE MALL STANDING UNDER MISTLETOE, SO I KISSED HER
BUT IT WAS A MANNEQUIN
DID YOU KNOW THEIR HEADS POP RIGHT OFF?
SO, ARE YOU SEEING HER AGAIN?
JIM DAVIS 12-15

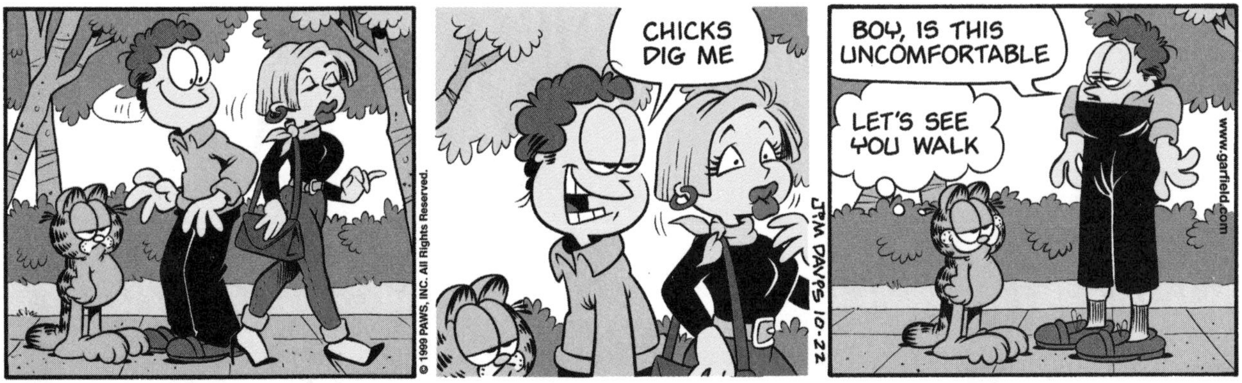
CHICKS DIG ME
JIM DAVIS 10-22
BOY, IS THIS UNCOMFORTABLE
LET'S SEE YOU WALK
www.garfield.com

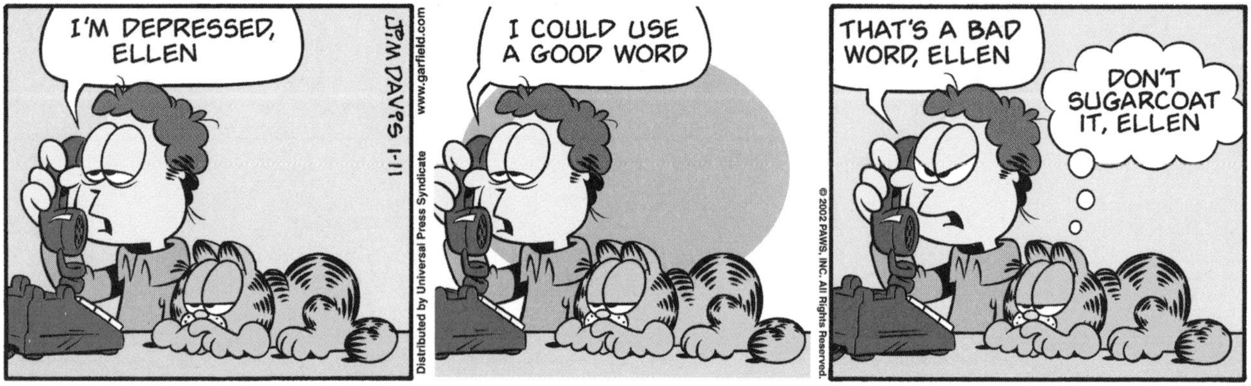
I'M DEPRESSED, ELLEN
JIM DAVIS 1-11
www.garfield.com
Distributed by Universal Press Syndicate
I COULD USE A GOOD WORD
© 2002 PAWS, INC. All Rights Reserved.
THAT'S A BAD WORD, ELLEN
DON'T SUGARCOAT IT, ELLEN

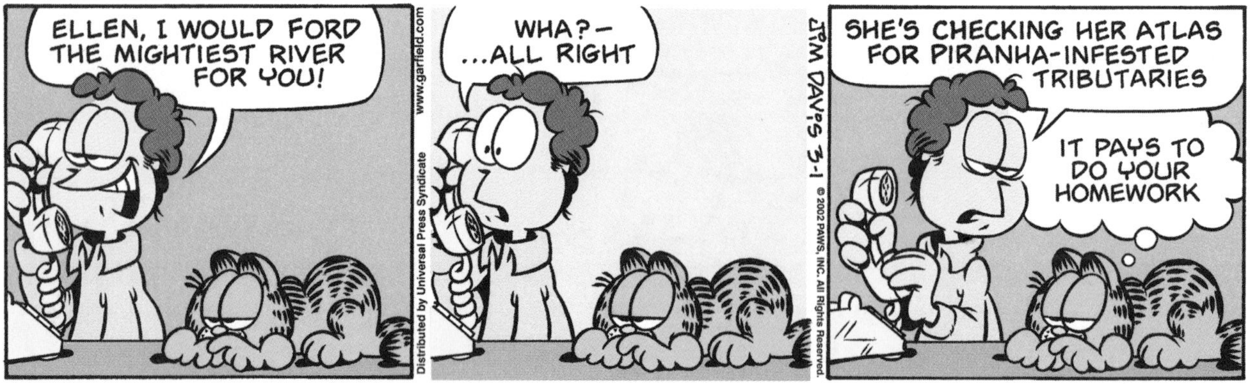
ELLEN, I WOULD FORD THE MIGHTIEST RIVER FOR YOU!
www.garfield.com
Distributed by Universal Press Syndicate
WHA?— ...ALL RIGHT
JIM DAVIS 3-1
© 2002 PAWS, INC. All Rights Reserved.
SHE'S CHECKING HER ATLAS FOR PIRANHA-INFESTED TRIBUTARIES
IT PAYS TO DO YOUR HOMEWORK

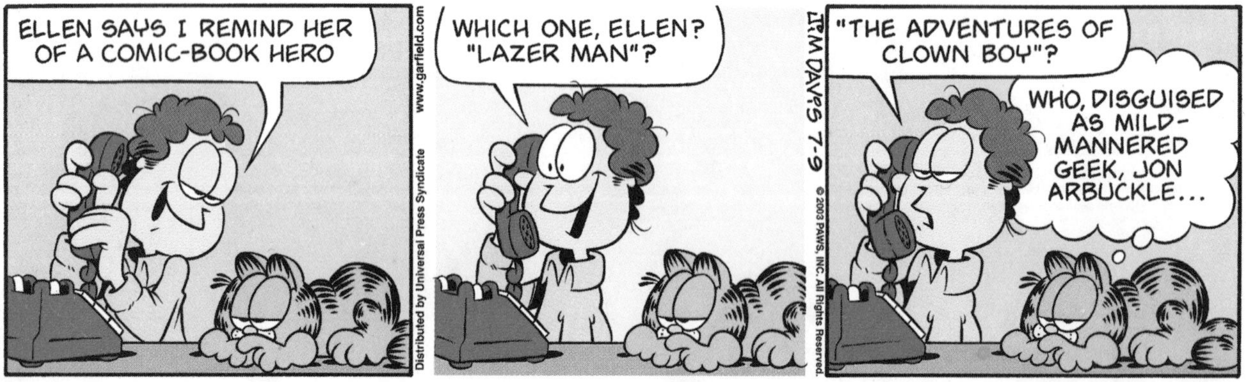
ELLEN SAYS I REMIND HER OF A COMIC-BOOK HERO
www.garfield.com
Distributed by Universal Press Syndicate
WHICH ONE, ELLEN? "LAZER MAN"?
JIM DAVIS 7-9
© 2003 PAWS, INC. All Rights Reserved.
"THE ADVENTURES OF CLOWN BOY"?
WHO, DISGUISED AS MILD-MANNERED GEEK, JON ARBUCKLE...

Jon's Scariest Dates

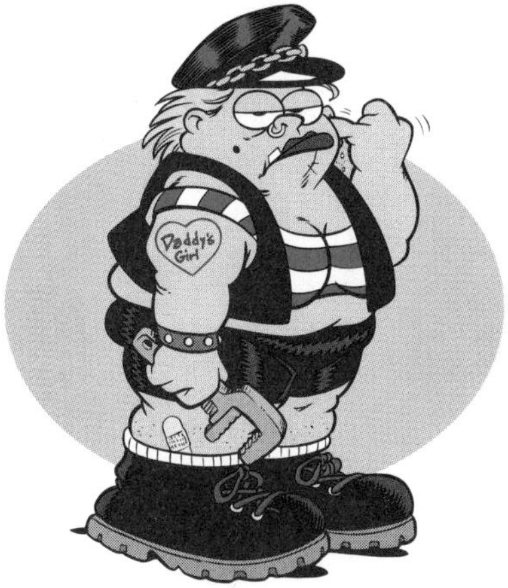
Daddy's Girl

Annie Axelrod, Harley mechanic

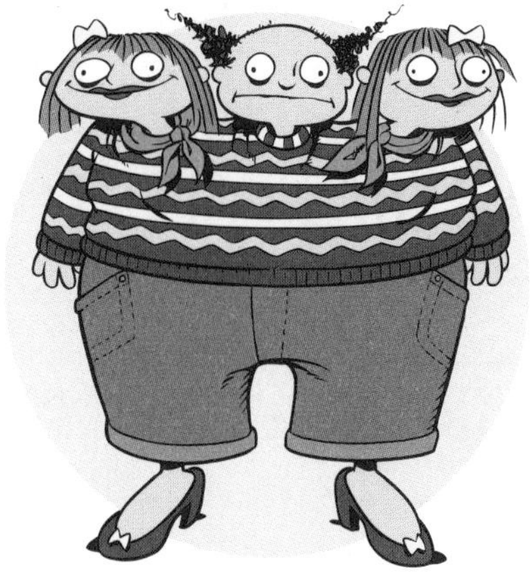

Gertie, Greta,
and Bob, Siamese Triplets

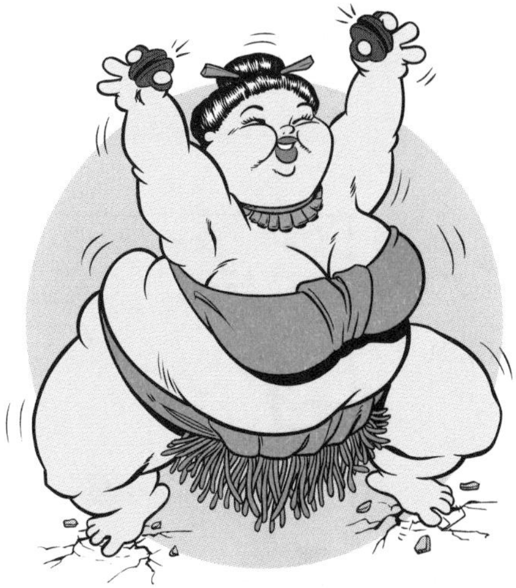

Suki the Sumo Belly Dancer

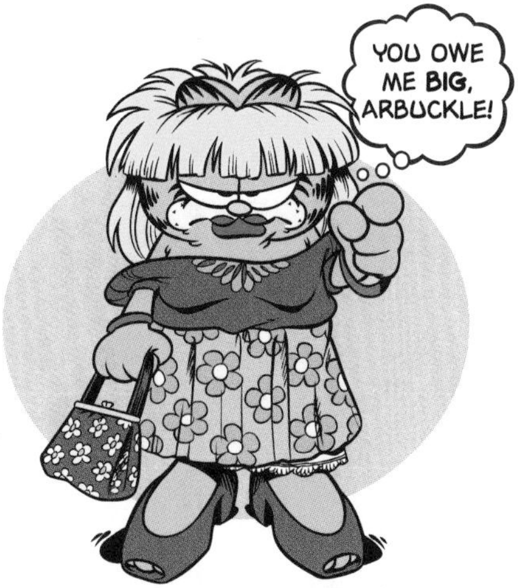
YOU OWE ME BIG, ARBUCKLE!

Garfield

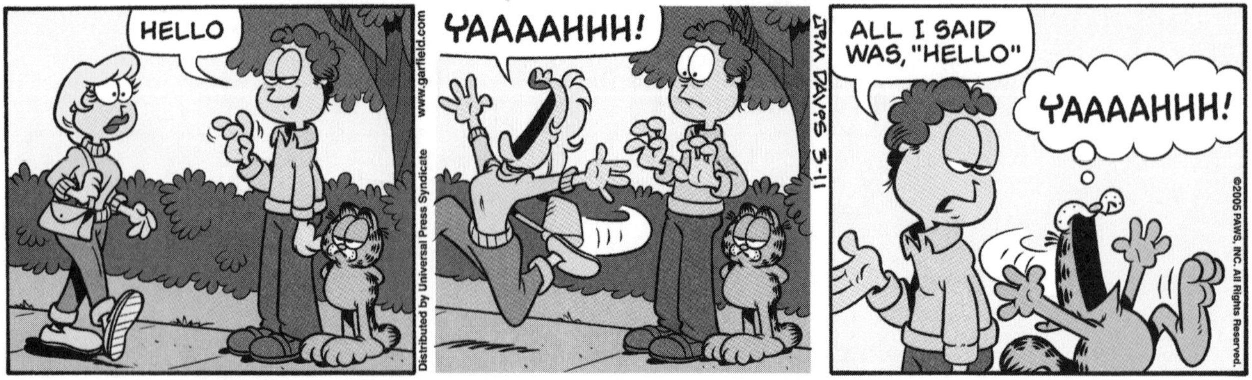
HELLO
www.garfield.com
Distributed by Universal Press Syndicate
YAAAAHHH!
JIM DAVIS 3-11
ALL I SAID WAS, "HELLO"
YAAAAHHH!
©2005 PAWS, INC. All Rights Reserved.

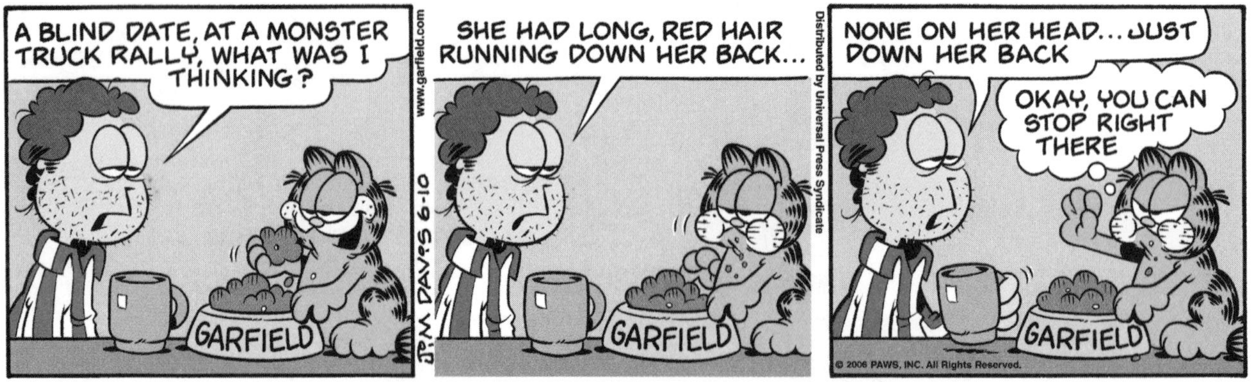
A BLIND DATE, AT A MONSTER TRUCK RALLY, WHAT WAS I THINKING?
GARFIELD
www.garfield.com
JIM DAVIS 6-10
SHE HAD LONG, RED HAIR RUNNING DOWN HER BACK...
GARFIELD
Distributed by Universal Press Syndicate
NONE ON HER HEAD... JUST DOWN HER BACK
OKAY, YOU CAN STOP RIGHT THERE
GARFIELD
© 2006 PAWS, INC. All Rights Reserved.

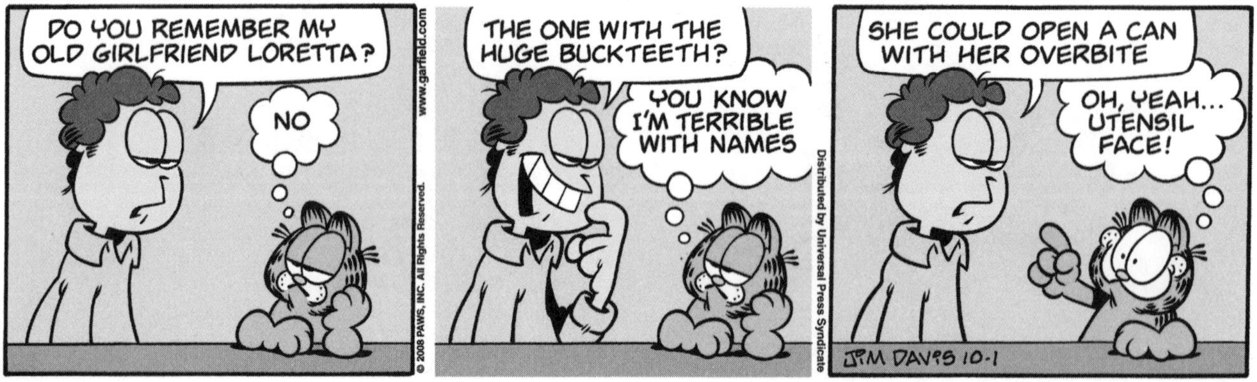
DO YOU REMEMBER MY OLD GIRLFRIEND LORETTA?
NO
www.garfield.com
© 2008 PAWS, INC. All Rights Reserved.
THE ONE WITH THE HUGE BUCKTEETH?
YOU KNOW I'M TERRIBLE WITH NAMES
Distributed by Universal Press Syndicate
SHE COULD OPEN A CAN WITH HER OVERBITE
OH, YEAH... UTENSIL FACE!
JIM DAVIS 10-1

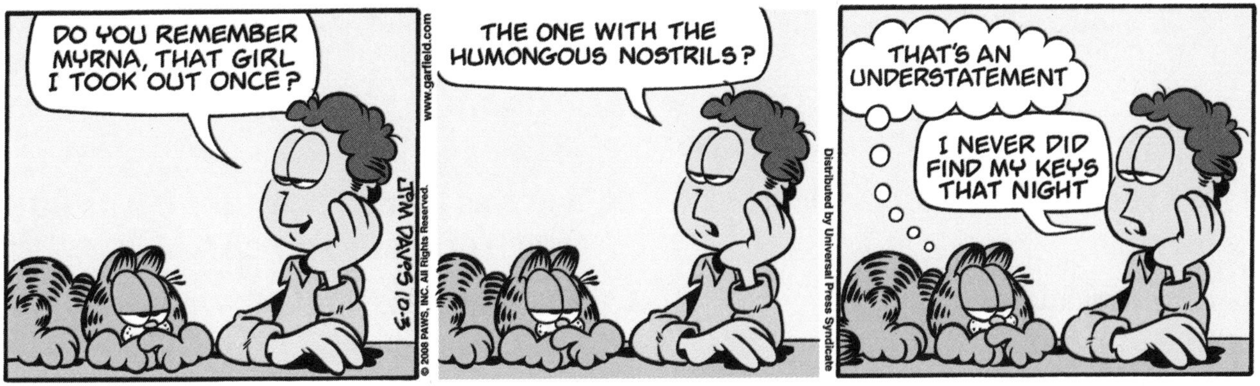
DO YOU REMEMBER MYRNA, THAT GIRL I TOOK OUT ONCE?
JIM DAVIS 10-3
© 2008 PAWS, INC. All Rights Reserved. www.garfield.com
THE ONE WITH THE HUMONGOUS NOSTRILS?
Distributed by Universal Press Syndicate
THAT'S AN UNDERSTATEMENT
I NEVER DID FIND MY KEYS THAT NIGHT

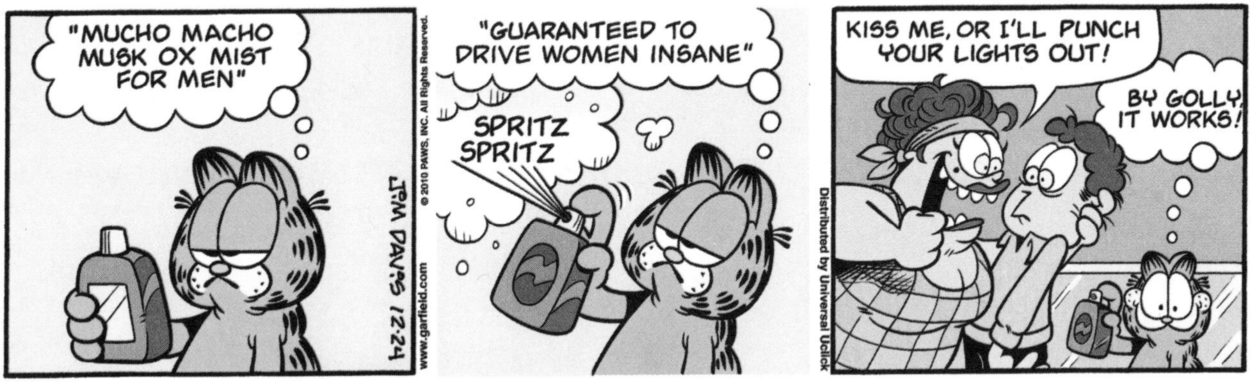
"MUCHO MACHO MUSK OX MIST FOR MEN"
JIM DAVIS 12-24
© 2010 PAWS, INC. All Rights Reserved. www.garfield.com
"GUARANTEED TO DRIVE WOMEN INSANE"
SPRITZ SPRITZ
Distributed by Universal Uclick
KISS ME, OR I'LL PUNCH YOUR LIGHTS OUT!
BY GOLLY, IT WORKS!

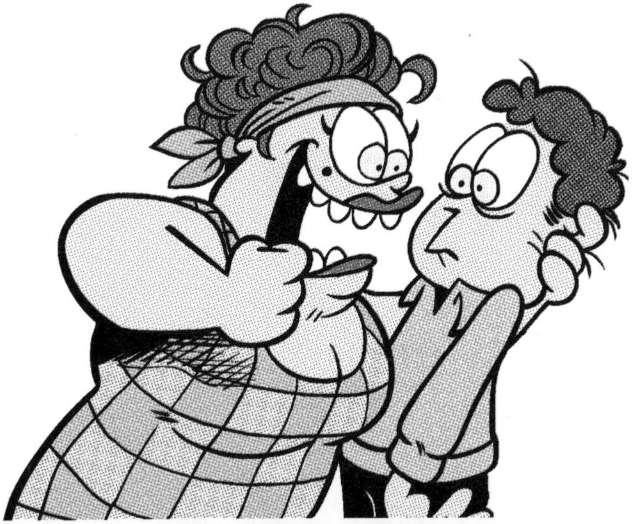

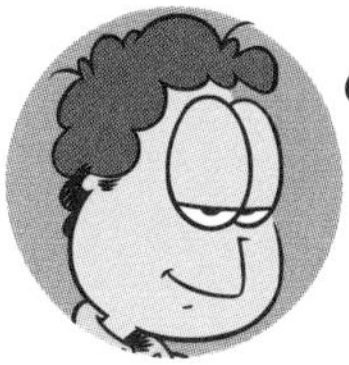

"Actually, this was one of my *better* dates."

ARE YOU A JON TRIVIA GEEK?

Take this quirky quiz and find out!

1. **What does Jon Arbuckle do for a living?**

   A. Ventriloquist
   B. Cartoonist
   C. Bassoonist
   D. Unicyclist

2. **Jon shares the same birthday (July 28) with which of the following famous people?**

   A. LeBron James
   B. Henry James
   C. James Brown
   D. Jim Davis

3. **What was the name of Jon's high school sweetheart?**

   A. Amy Farrah Fowler
   B. Lorna Grubsky
   C. Moms Mabley
   D. Marilyn Manson

4. **Jon was turned down for a date by which of these women?**

   A. Gap-toothed Gretta, the distance-spitting queen
   B. Daisy, the scullery maid
   C. Morticia, who raised flesh-eating houseplants
   D. Baby Jane, the bad caregiver

5. **What's the first thing Liz the vet remembers saying to Jon?**

   A. "Is that your face, or did your pants fall down?"
   B. "Don't make me get a restraining order."
   C. "Nice teddy bear tie."
   D. "Your cat's so fat, he sweats butter."

6. **Garfield has served in what capacity to Jon?**

   A. Pool boy
   B. Pooper-scooper
   C. Toenail trimmer
   D. Golf caddy

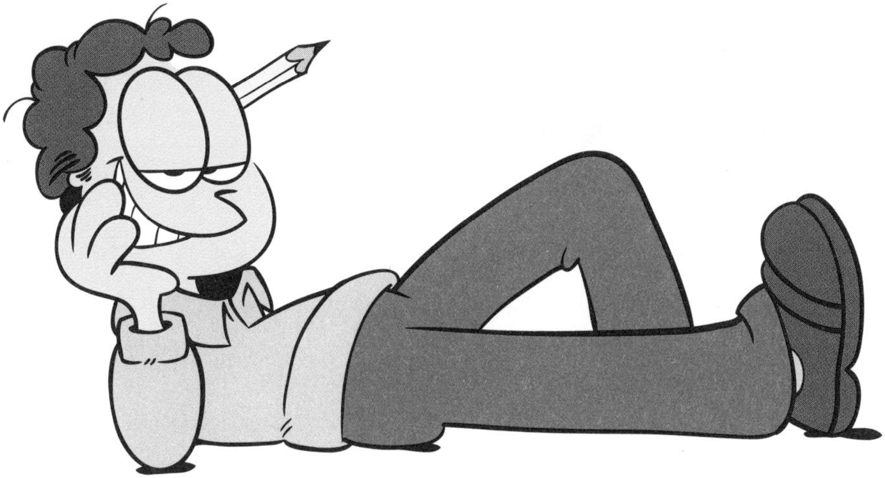

7. **From where did Jon get Odie?**
   A. A friend named Lyman
   B. A neighbor named Mrs. Feeny
   C. A clinic for chronic droolers
   D. An alien from a really dumb planet

8. **What did Doc Boy want to do when he visited Jon in the city?**
   A. Attend a rave
   B. Parallel park his tractor
   C. Watch the planes land
   D. Go to White Castle

9. **Which of the following has Jon's grandma NOT done?**
   A. Hang gliding
   B. Motorcycling
   C. Martial arts
   D. Sumo wrestling

10. **What does Jon most commonly wear?**
   A. Blue shirt
   B. Fanny pack
   C. Adult diaper
   D. Liz's high heels

11. **Jon has a T-shirt that says**
   A. Biggest Loser
   B. Paste Eater
   C. DY-NO-MITE!
   D. Cat-Whipped

12. **Which actor played Jon in the Garfield feature films?**
   A. Bill Murray
   B. Breckin Meyer
   C. Sir Laurence Olivier
   D. Divine

Answers: 1.B 2.D 3.B 4.A 5.C 6.D 7.A 8.C 9.D 10.A 11.C 12.B

LIZ, THE PET VET

In the beginning, Dr. Liz Wilson was strictly Garfield's veterinarian: She treated Garfield like a patient—and Jon like the plague. She was always putting him down because, as Garfield noted, Jon is so "putdownable."

However, Liz eventually took pity on Jon and agreed to go out with the poor sap. The romance didn't immediately click—the dates were usually disasters (often with an assist from Garfield)—because Jon suffered from "geekitis." (Alas, it's a terminal case. When he's around Liz, the lovesick spazz often drools worse than Odie. But she takes it in stride. Apparently, she's used to dealing with big dumb animals.)

Garfield, however, isn't quite as enamored with Liz. It's nothing personal; he actually thinks she's pretty nice. But she *is* a needle-wielding veterinarian, after all. And when she's not giving shots, she's poking, prodding, and (shudder) inserting things!

Despite these indignities, Garfield maintains a healthy relationship with his vet, who has earned the cat's respect with her verbal shots directed at Jon. Liz sticks it to Jon; Garfield likes that.

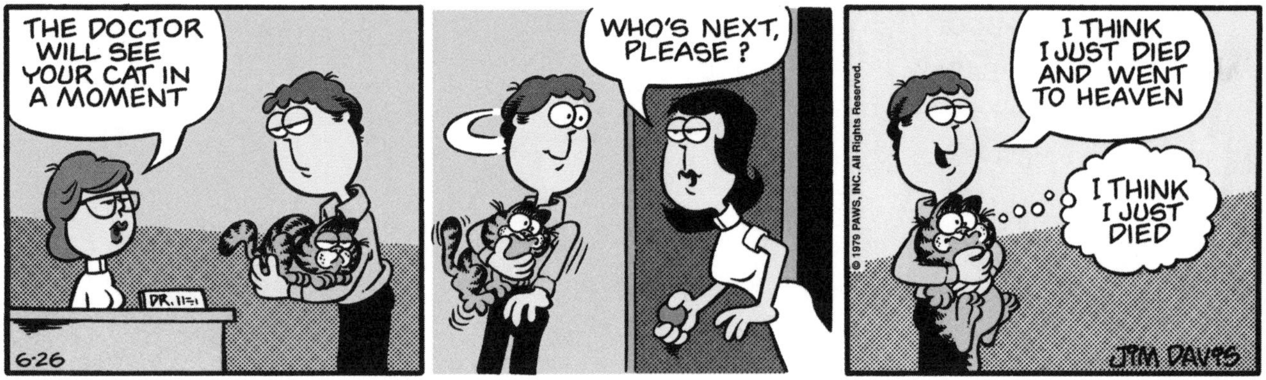
THE DOCTOR WILL SEE YOUR CAT IN A MOMENT
6-26
WHO'S NEXT, PLEASE?
© 1979 PAWS, INC. All Rights Reserved.
I THINK I JUST DIED AND WENT TO HEAVEN
I THINK I JUST DIED
JIM DAVIS

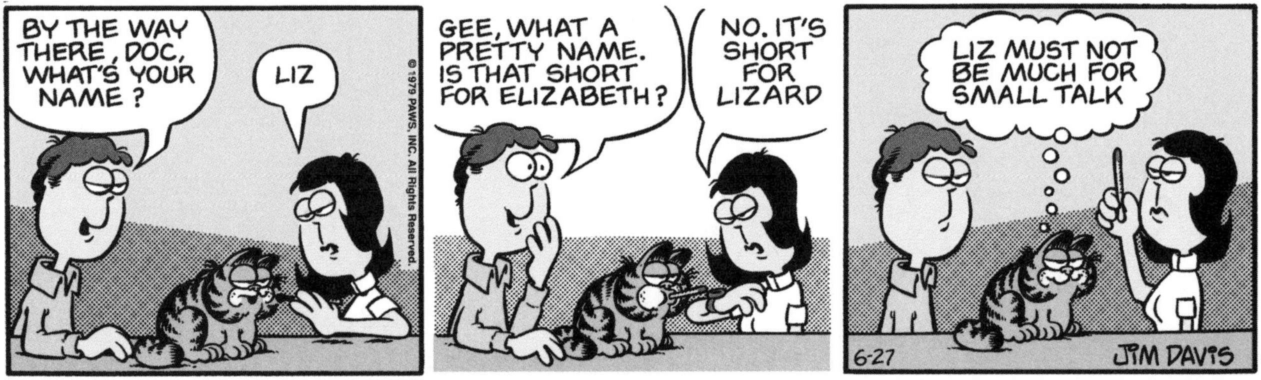
BY THE WAY THERE, DOC, WHAT'S YOUR NAME?
LIZ
© 1979 PAWS, INC. All Rights Reserved.
GEE, WHAT A PRETTY NAME. IS THAT SHORT FOR ELIZABETH?
NO. IT'S SHORT FOR LIZARD
LIZ MUST NOT BE MUCH FOR SMALL TALK
6-27
JIM DAVIS

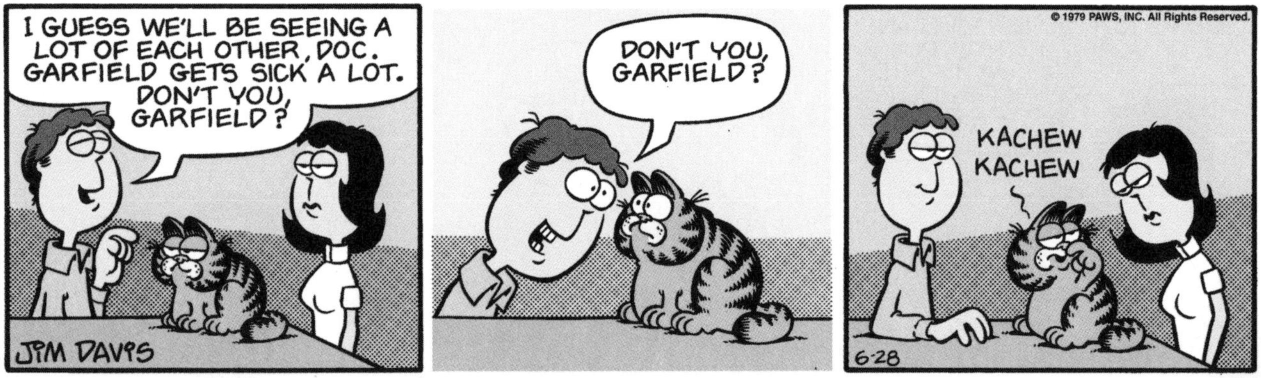
I GUESS WE'LL BE SEEING A LOT OF EACH OTHER, DOC. GARFIELD GETS SICK A LOT. DON'T YOU, GARFIELD?
JIM DAVIS
DON'T YOU, GARFIELD?
© 1979 PAWS, INC. All Rights Reserved.
KACHEW KACHEW
6-28

HOW ABOUT A DATE, SWEETHEART?
© 1979 PAWS, INC. All Rights Reserved.
JIM DAVIS
THAT'S **DOCTOR** TO YOU
7-25
OKAY, HOW ABOUT A DATE, **DOCTOR** SWEETHEART?

© 1979 PAWS, INC. All Rights Reserved.
TELL ME, DOCTOR, WHAT DO YOU SUGGEST FOR AN ANIMAL WHO'S MADLY IN LOVE?
JIM DAVIS
I USUALLY PRESCRIBE NEUTERING
7-27

YOU'RE NOT GOING TO STAND ME UP AGAIN, ARE YOU, DOC?
REALLY... WHY ARE YOU GOING OUT WITH ME?
JIM DAVIS
© 1980 PAWS, INC. All Rights Reserved.
YOU AMUSE ME
I'LL SETTLE FOR THAT
DON JUAN DAZZLES ANOTHER LOVE-STRUCK WAIF
4-22

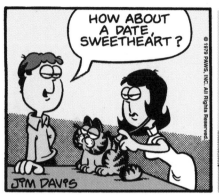

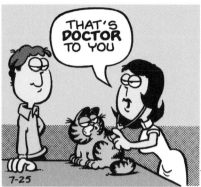

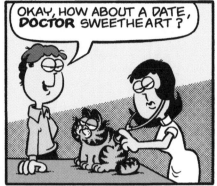

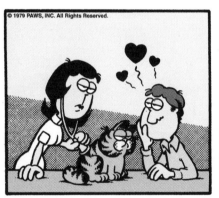

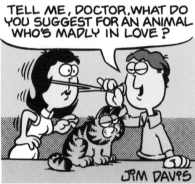

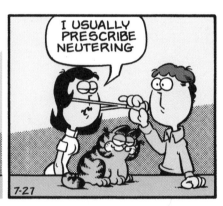

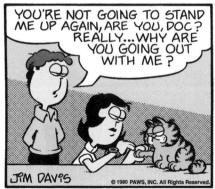

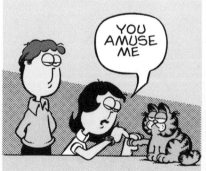

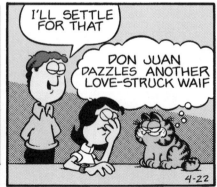

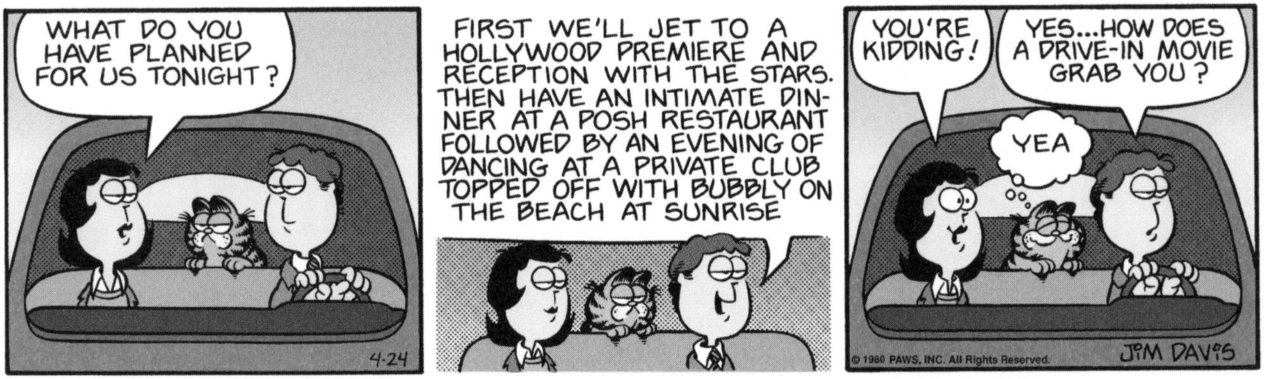
WHAT DO YOU HAVE PLANNED FOR US TONIGHT?
4-24
FIRST WE'LL JET TO A HOLLYWOOD PREMIERE AND RECEPTION WITH THE STARS. THEN HAVE AN INTIMATE DINNER AT A POSH RESTAURANT FOLLOWED BY AN EVENING OF DANCING AT A PRIVATE CLUB TOPPED OFF WITH BUBBLY ON THE BEACH AT SUNRISE
YOU'RE KIDDING!
YES...HOW DOES A DRIVE-IN MOVIE GRAB YOU?
YEA
© 1980 PAWS, INC. All Rights Reserved.
JIM DAVIS

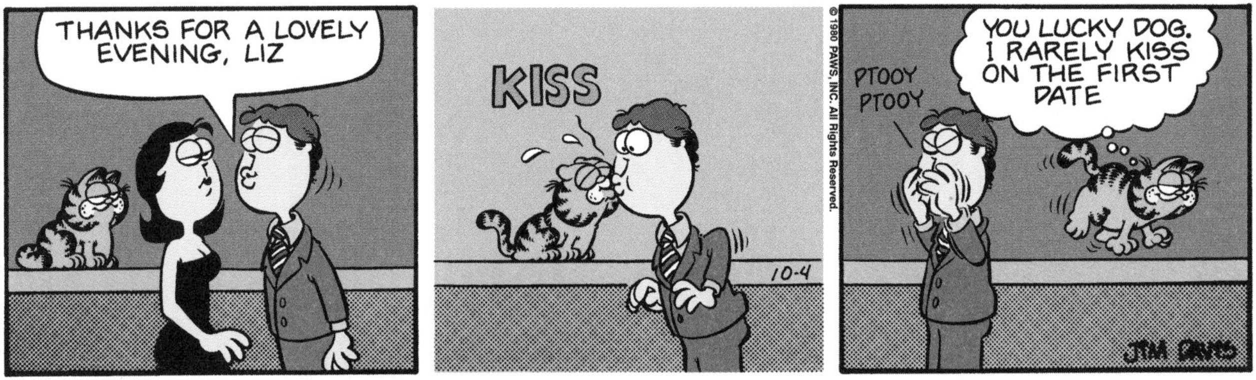
THANKS FOR A LOVELY EVENING, LIZ
KISS
10-4
© 1980 PAWS, INC. All Rights Reserved.
PTOOY PTOOY
YOU LUCKY DOG. I RARELY KISS ON THE FIRST DATE
JIM DAVIS

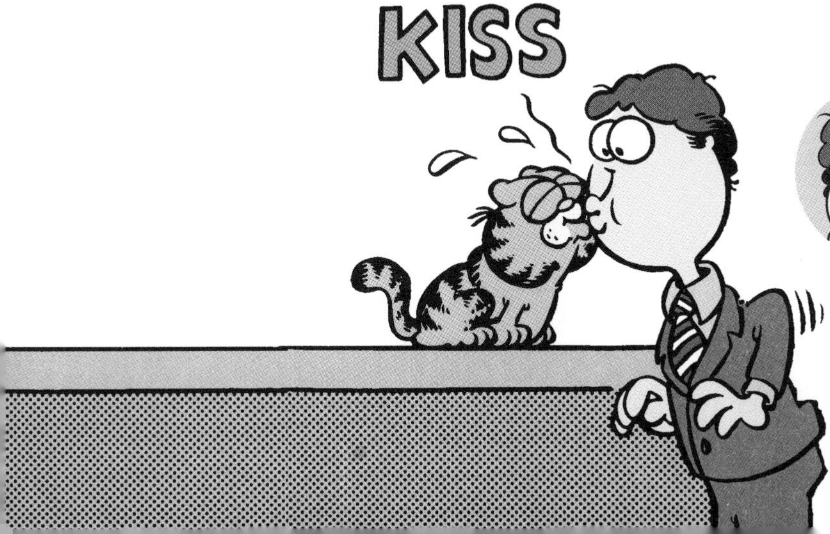
KISS

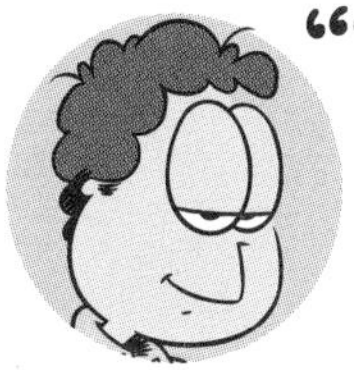

"The worst part about the kiss was that I've had *worse!*"

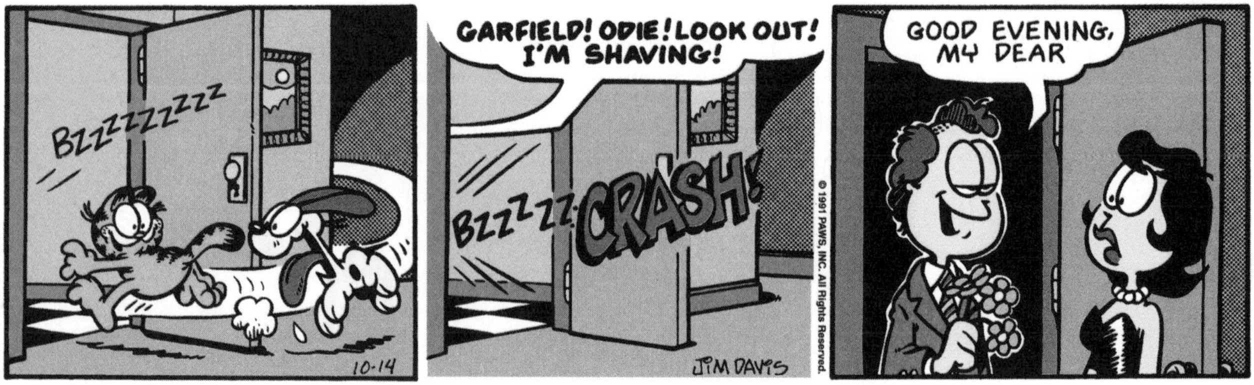
BZZZZZZZZZ
10-14
GARFIELD! ODIE! LOOK OUT! I'M SHAVING!
BZZZZZ
CRASH!
JIM DAVIS
© 1991 PAWS, INC. All Rights Reserved.
GOOD EVENING, MY DEAR

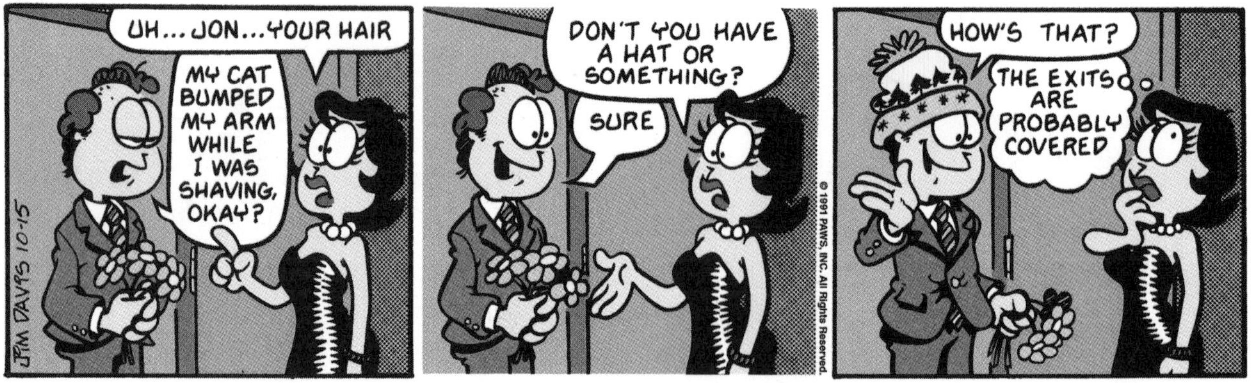
UH... JON... YOUR HAIR
MY CAT BUMPED MY ARM WHILE I WAS SHAVING, OKAY?
JIM DAVIS 10-15
DON'T YOU HAVE A HAT OR SOMETHING?
SURE
© 1991 PAWS, INC. All Rights Reserved.
HOW'S THAT?
THE EXITS ARE PROBABLY COVERED

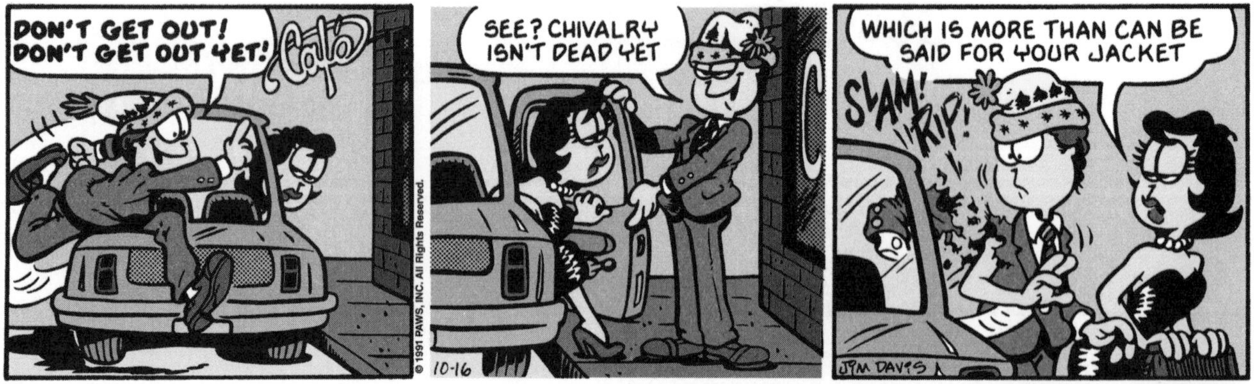
DON'T GET OUT! DON'T GET OUT YET!
© 1991 PAWS, INC. All Rights Reserved.
SEE? CHIVALRY ISN'T DEAD YET
10-16
WHICH IS MORE THAN CAN BE SAID FOR YOUR JACKET
SLAM!
RIP!
JIM DAVIS

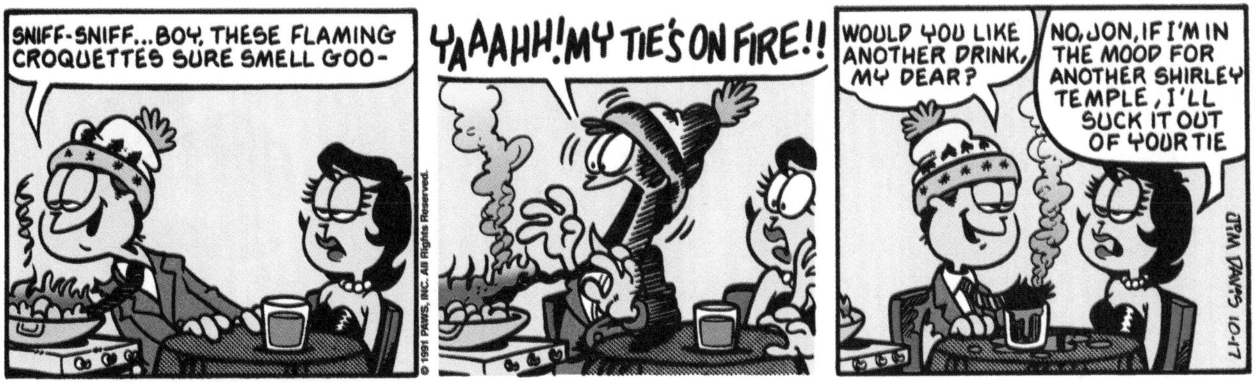
SNIFF-SNIFF...BOY, THESE FLAMING CROQUETTES SURE SMELL GOO-
YAAAHH! MY TIE'S ON FIRE!!
WOULD YOU LIKE ANOTHER DRINK, MY DEAR?
NO, JON, IF I'M IN THE MOOD FOR ANOTHER SHIRLEY TEMPLE, I'LL SUCK IT OUT OF YOUR TIE
© 1991 PAWS, INC. All Rights Reserved.
JIM DAVIS 10-17

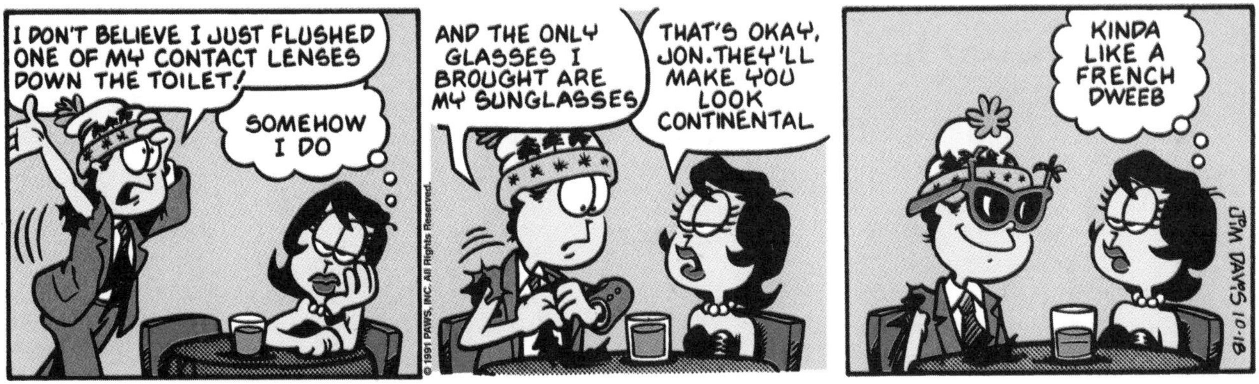
I DON'T BELIEVE I JUST FLUSHED ONE OF MY CONTACT LENSES DOWN THE TOILET!
SOMEHOW I DO
AND THE ONLY GLASSES I BROUGHT ARE MY SUNGLASSES
THAT'S OKAY, JON. THEY'LL MAKE YOU LOOK CONTINENTAL
KINDA LIKE A FRENCH DWEEB
© 1991 PAWS, INC. All Rights Reserved.
JIM DAVIS 10-18

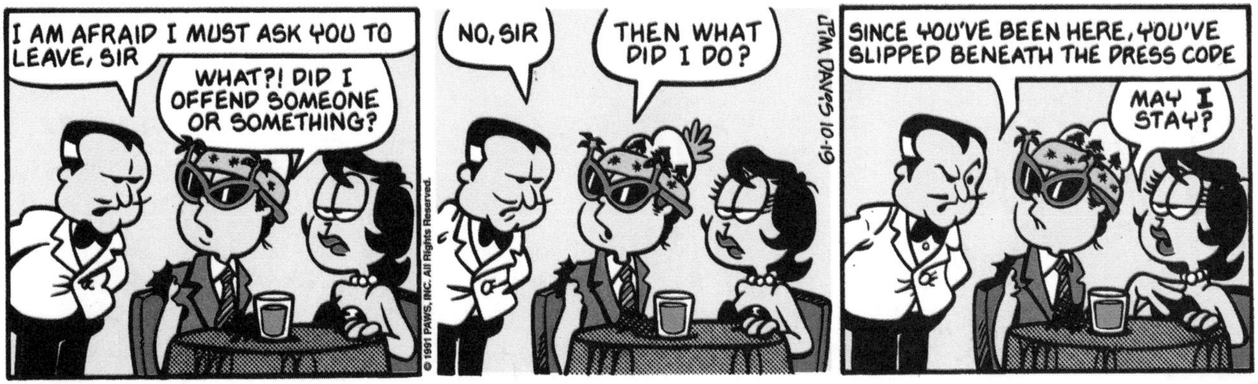
I AM AFRAID I MUST ASK YOU TO LEAVE, SIR
WHAT?! DID I OFFEND SOMEONE OR SOMETHING?
NO, SIR
THEN WHAT DID I DO?
SINCE YOU'VE BEEN HERE, YOU'VE SLIPPED BENEATH THE DRESS CODE
MAY I STAY?
© 1991 PAWS, INC. All Rights Reserved.
JIM DAVIS 10-19

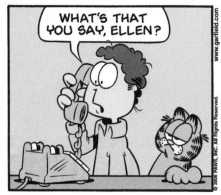

As the years passed, something surprising took place—it might even classify as a minor miracle: Liz fell for Jon. Somehow the good doctor developed immunity to Jon's "geekitis" and succumbed to his dweeby charms. Of course, she's aware that Jon's still a loser—he couldn't find his shoes, so he painted his feet black—but now he's *her* lovable loser.

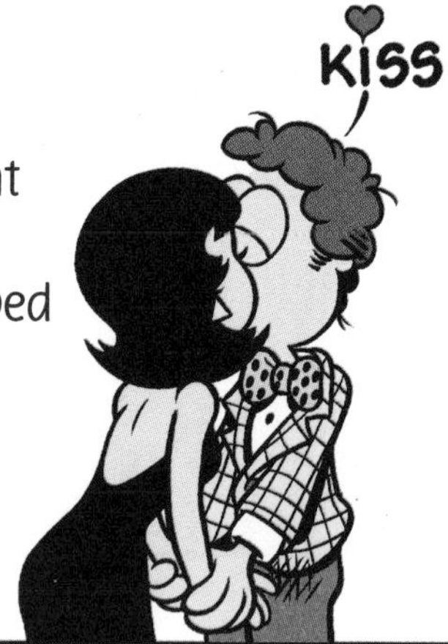

KISS

WHAT'S THAT YOU SAY, ELLEN?
YOU HAVE AMNESIA AND DON'T REMEMBER ME?
COOL!
TALK ABOUT A DARK CLOUD HAVING A SILVER LINING!
JPM DAVPS 7-17
© 2006 PAWS, INC. All Rights Reserved.
www.garfield.com
Distributed by Universal Press Syndicate

SO HOW DID YOU GET YOUR AMNESIA, ELLEN?
JPM DAVPS 7-18
SHE DOESN'T REMEMBER
I'VE HEARD THAT'S A SYMPTOM
© 2006 PAWS, INC. All Rights Reserved.
www.garfield.com
Distributed by Universal Press Syndicate

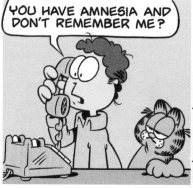

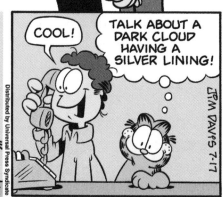

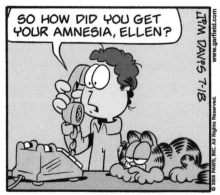

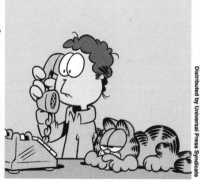

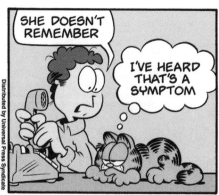

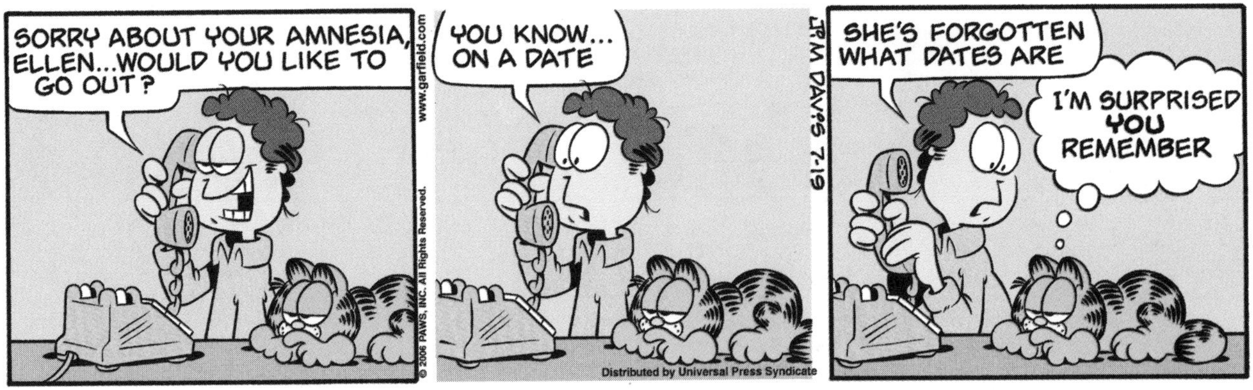
SORRY ABOUT YOUR AMNESIA, ELLEN...WOULD YOU LIKE TO GO OUT?
YOU KNOW... ON A DATE
SHE'S FORGOTTEN WHAT DATES ARE
I'M SURPRISED **YOU** REMEMBER
JIM DAVIS 7-19
© 2006 PAWS, INC. All Rights Reserved.
www.garfield.com
Distributed by Universal Press Syndicate

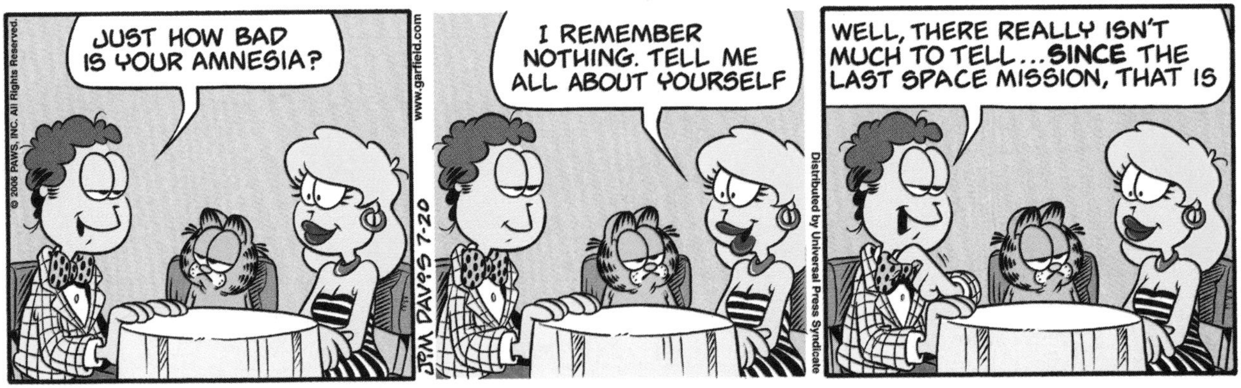
JUST HOW BAD IS YOUR AMNESIA?
I REMEMBER NOTHING. TELL ME ALL ABOUT YOURSELF
WELL, THERE REALLY ISN'T MUCH TO TELL...**SINCE** THE LAST SPACE MISSION, THAT IS
JIM DAVIS 7-20
© 2006 PAWS, INC. All Rights Reserved.
www.garfield.com
Distributed by Universal Press Syndicate

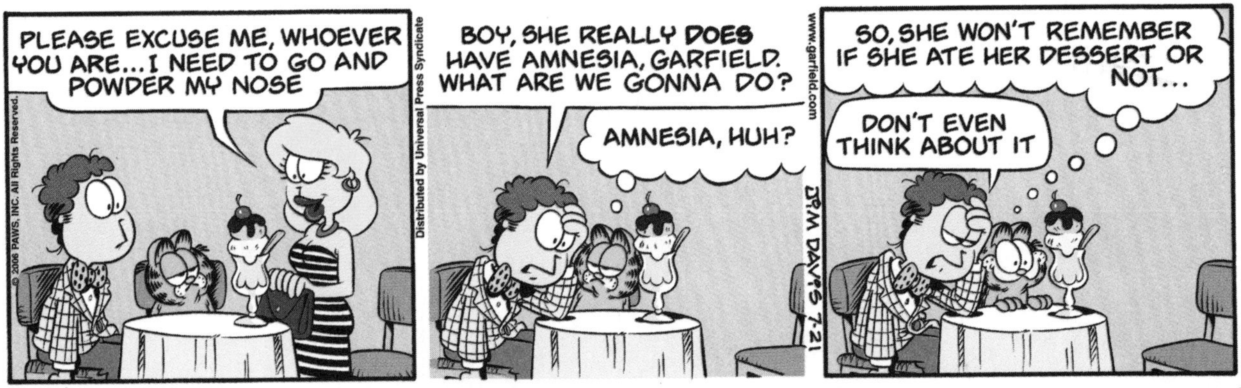
PLEASE EXCUSE ME, WHOEVER YOU ARE...I NEED TO GO AND POWDER MY NOSE
BOY, SHE REALLY **DOES** HAVE AMNESIA, GARFIELD. WHAT ARE WE GONNA DO?
AMNESIA, HUH?
SO, SHE WON'T REMEMBER IF SHE ATE HER DESSERT OR NOT...
DON'T EVEN THINK ABOUT IT
JIM DAVIS 7-21
© 2006 PAWS, INC. All Rights Reserved.
www.garfield.com
Distributed by Universal Press Syndicate

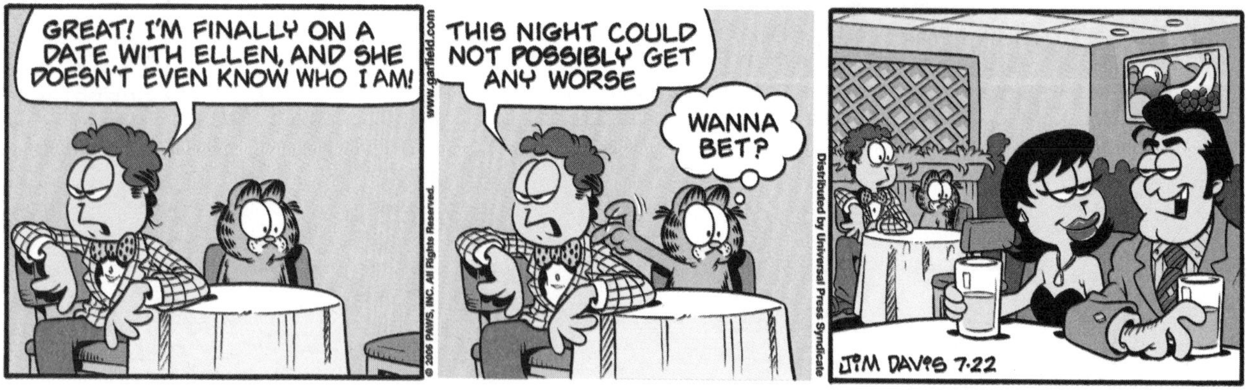
GREAT! I'M FINALLY ON A DATE WITH ELLEN, AND SHE DOESN'T EVEN KNOW WHO I AM!
© 2006 PAWS, INC. All Rights Reserved.
www.garfield.com
THIS NIGHT COULD NOT POSSIBLY GET ANY WORSE
WANNA BET?
Distributed by Universal Press Syndicate
JIM DAVIS 7-22

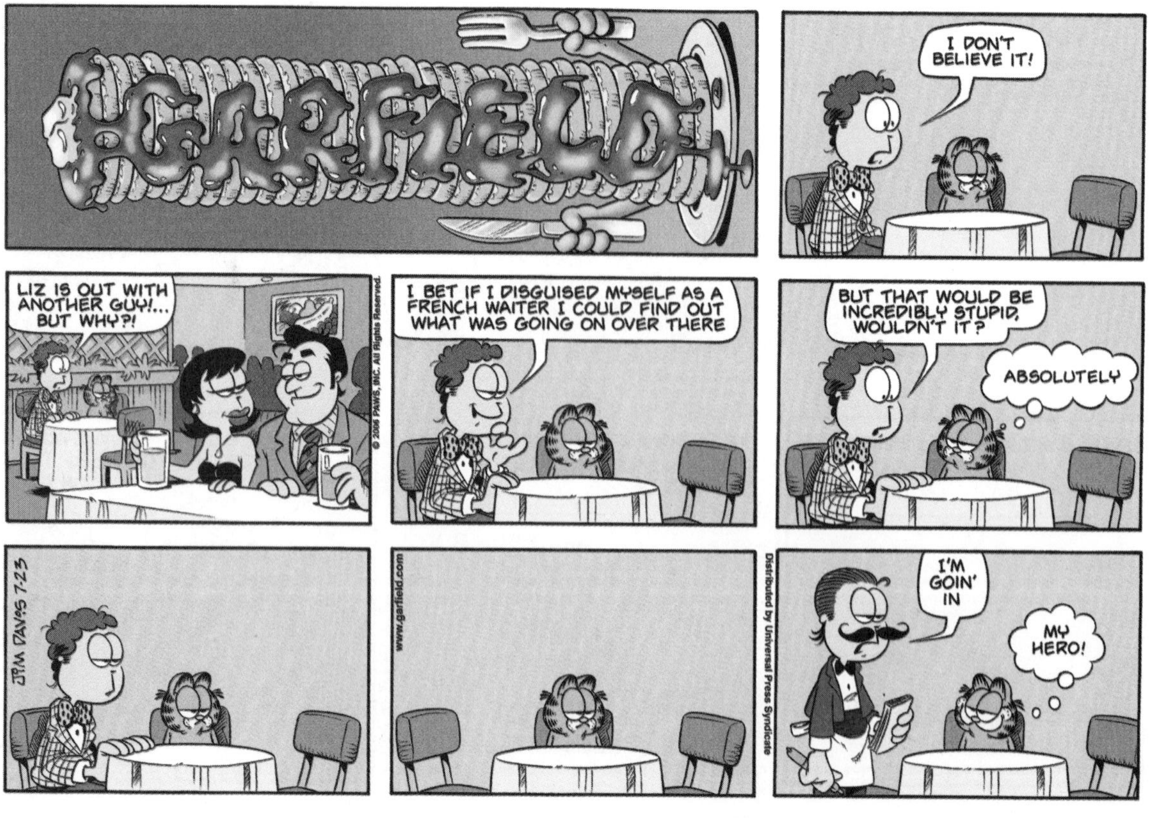
GARFIELD
I DON'T BELIEVE IT!
LIZ IS OUT WITH ANOTHER GUY!... BUT WHY?!
© 2006 PAWS, INC. All Rights Reserved.
I BET IF I DISGUISED MYSELF AS A FRENCH WAITER I COULD FIND OUT WHAT WAS GOING ON OVER THERE
BUT THAT WOULD BE INCREDIBLY STUPID, WOULDN'T IT?
ABSOLUTELY
JIM DAVIS 7-23
www.garfield.com
Distributed by Universal Press Syndicate
I'M GOIN' IN
MY HERO!

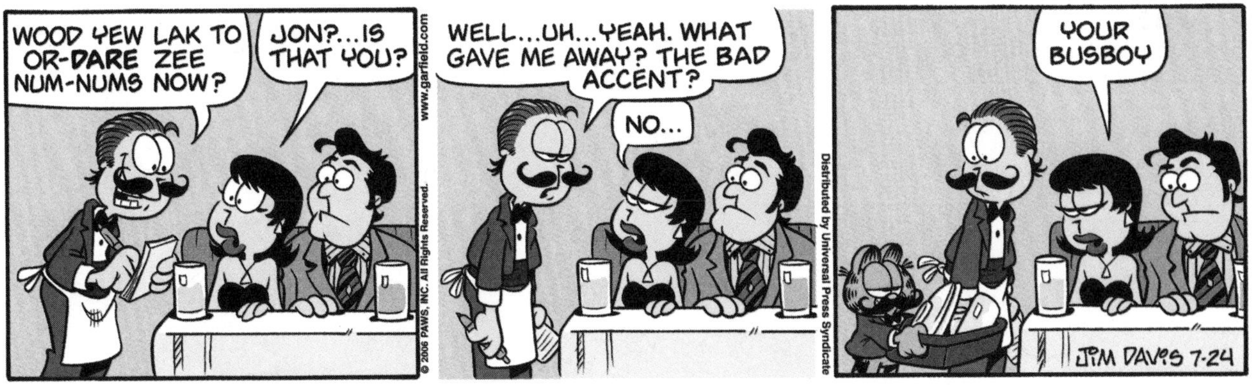
WOOD YEW LAK TO OR-**DARE** ZEE NUM-NUMS NOW?
JON?...IS THAT YOU?
www.garfield.com
© 2006 PAWS, INC. All Rights Reserved.
WELL...UH...YEAH. WHAT GAVE ME AWAY? THE BAD ACCENT?
NO...
Distributed by Universal Press Syndicate
YOUR BUSBOY
JIM DAVIS 7-24

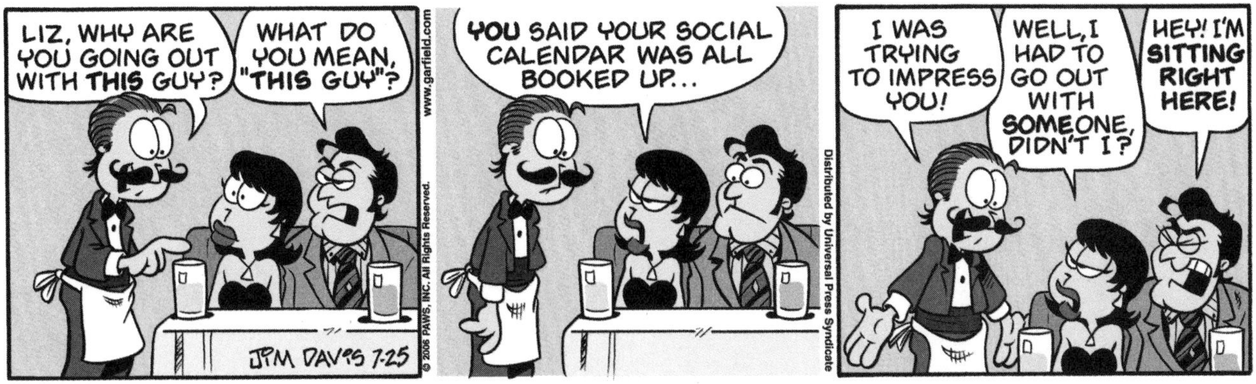
LIZ, WHY ARE YOU GOING OUT WITH **THIS** GUY?
WHAT DO YOU MEAN, "**THIS GUY**"?
JIM DAVIS 7-25
www.garfield.com
© 2006 PAWS, INC. All Rights Reserved.
YOU SAID YOUR SOCIAL CALENDAR WAS ALL BOOKED UP...
Distributed by Universal Press Syndicate
I WAS TRYING TO IMPRESS YOU!
WELL, I HAD TO GO OUT WITH **SOME**ONE, DIDN'T I?
HEY! I'M **SITTING RIGHT HERE!**

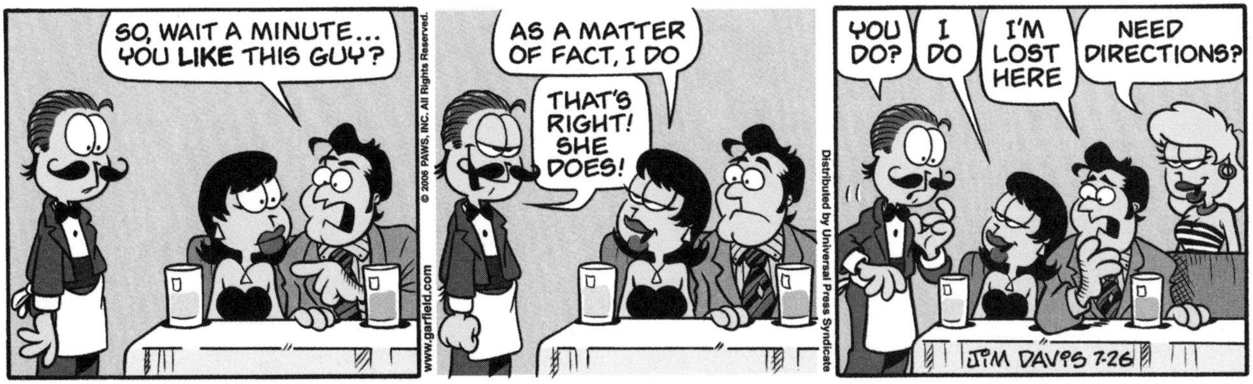
SO, WAIT A MINUTE... YOU **LIKE** THIS GUY?
www.garfield.com
© 2006 PAWS, INC. All Rights Reserved.
AS A MATTER OF FACT, I DO
THAT'S RIGHT! SHE DOES!
Distributed by Universal Press Syndicate
YOU DO?
I DO
I'M LOST HERE
NEED DIRECTIONS?
JIM DAVIS 7-26

JIM DAVIS 7-27
LOOK, SPORT, YOU TWO GO ON... SHE OBVIOUSLY HAS SOME SORT OF WEIRD ATTRACTION TO YOU
© 2006 PAWS, INC. All Rights Reserved.
www.garfield.com
AND IF THIS LOVELY LADY DOESN'T MIND, I'LL BUY HER DINNER INSTEAD!
Distributed by Universal Press Syndicate
ELLEN, I'M REALLY SORRY...
HAVE WE MET?

I HAD A WONDERFUL TIME TONIGHT, JON
SO DID I. AND IT'S MY BIRTHDAY, TOO
JIM DAVIS 7-28
© 2006 PAWS, INC. All Rights Reserved.
www.garfield.com
WELL, HAPPY BIRTHDAY!
KISS
Distributed by Universal Press Syndicate
DID YOU GET SOMETHING NICE?
I GOT A LIFE
AND THEY LIVED HAPPILY EVER AFTER

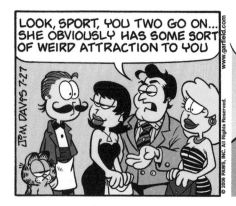

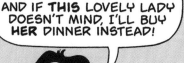

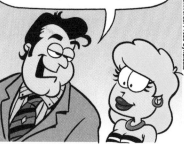

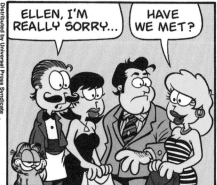

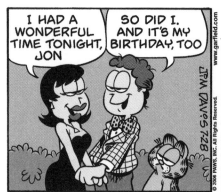

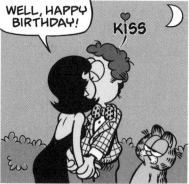

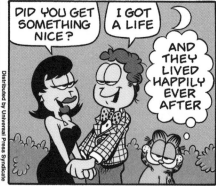

PET PEEVES OF LIZ THE VET

- Potty-mouthed parrots
- Tobacco-chewing chimps
- Horny rhinos who get fresh
- Snakes who shed their skins on her carpet
- Incontinent elephants
- Hippos with hemorrhoids

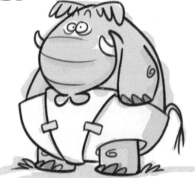

Least Likely Nicknames For Jon

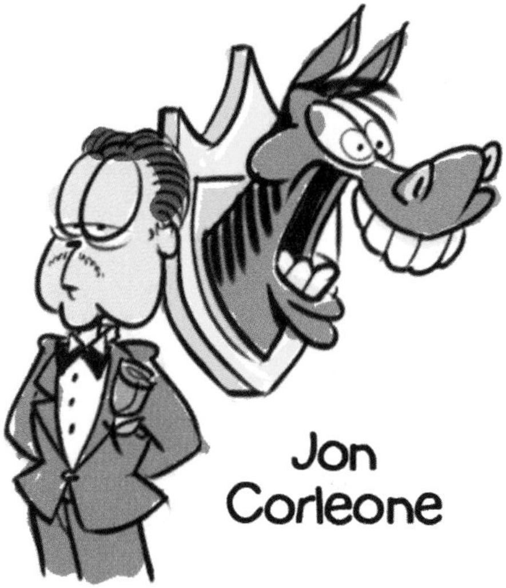

Jon Corleone

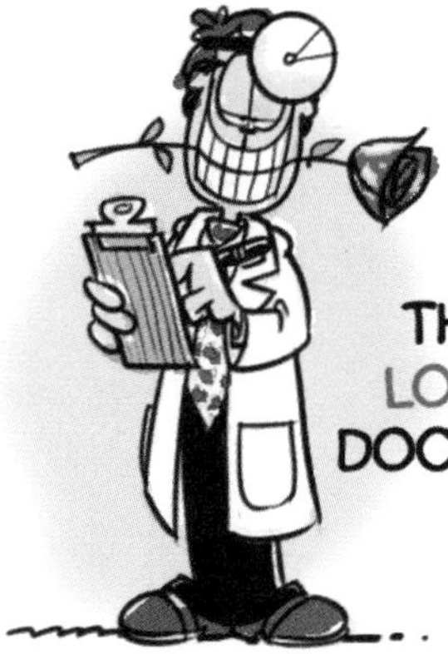

THE LOVE DOCTOR

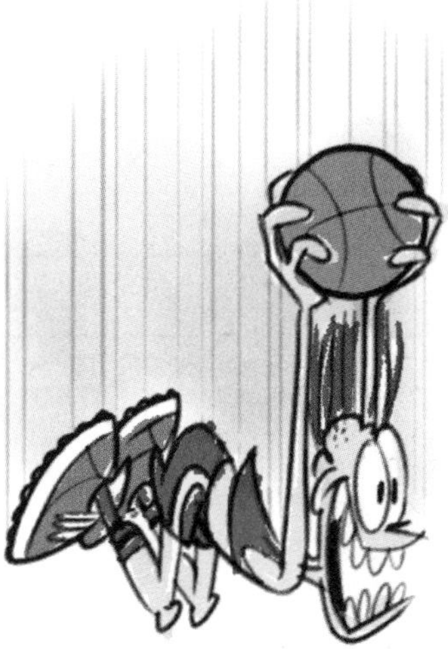

AIR ARBUCKLE

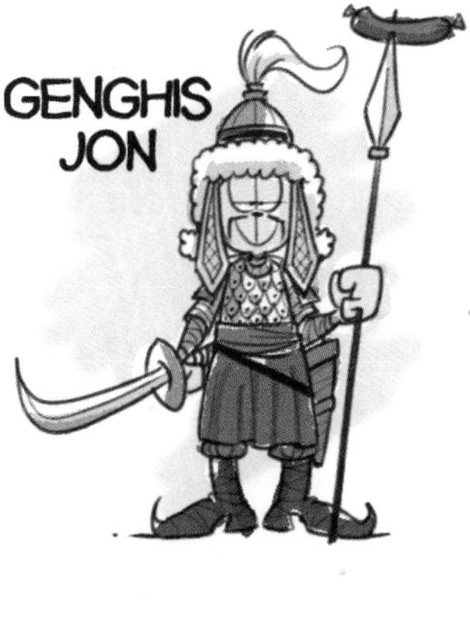

GENGHIS JON

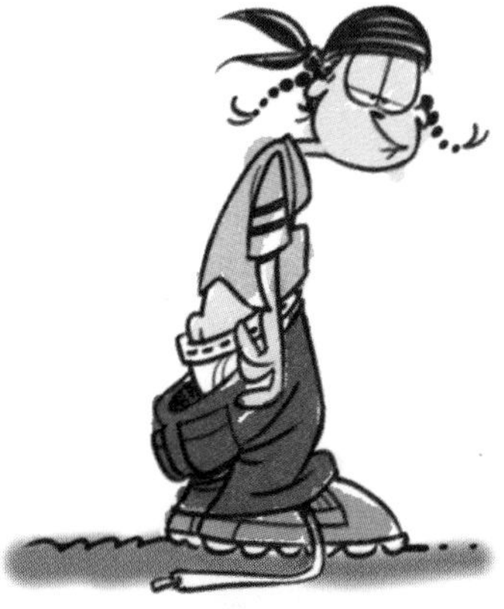

Snoop Jonny Jon

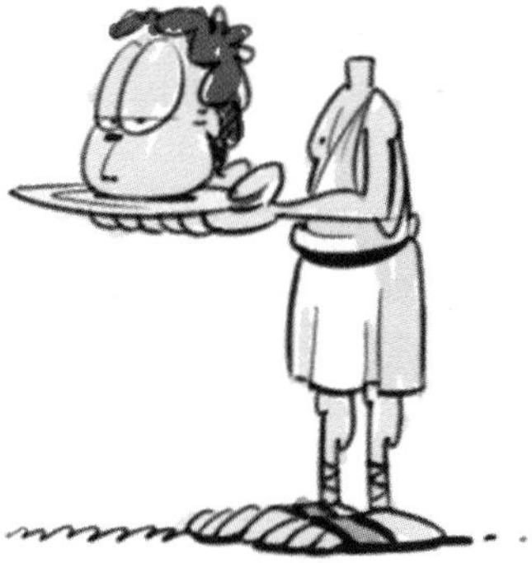

JON THE BAPTIST

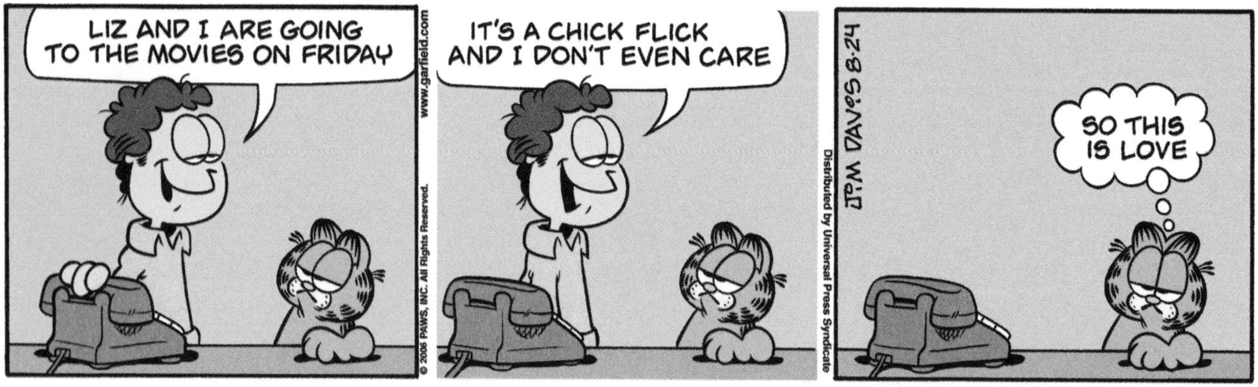
LIZ AND I ARE GOING TO THE MOVIES ON FRIDAY
IT'S A CHICK FLICK AND I DON'T EVEN CARE
SO THIS IS LOVE
www.garfield.com
© 2006 PAWS, INC. All Rights Reserved.
JPM DAVPS 8·24
Distributed by Universal Press Syndicate

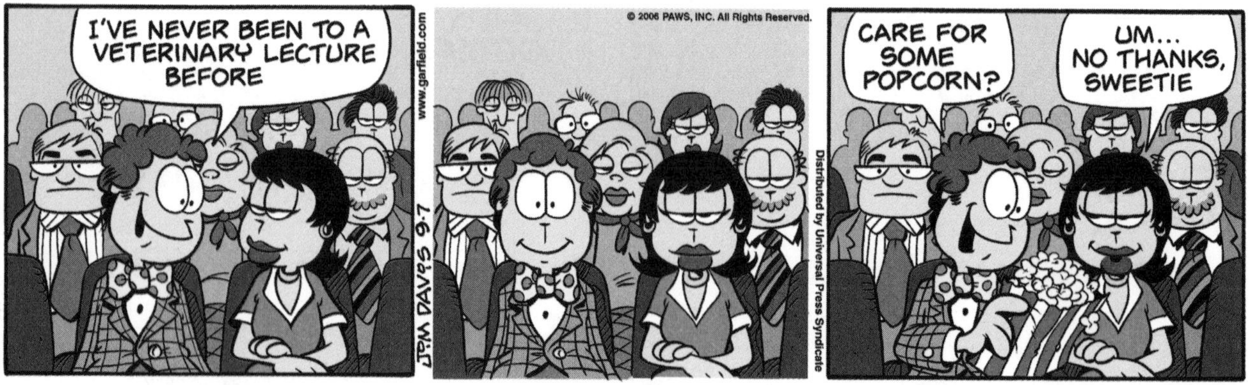
I'VE NEVER BEEN TO A VETERINARY LECTURE BEFORE
CARE FOR SOME POPCORN?
UM... NO THANKS, SWEETIE
www.garfield.com
JPM DAVPS 9·7
© 2006 PAWS, INC. All Rights Reserved.
Distributed by Universal Press Syndicate

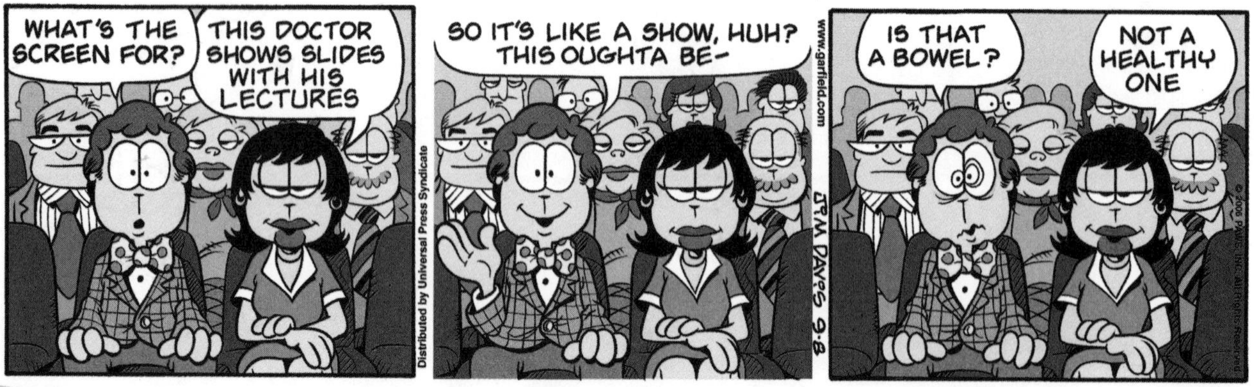
WHAT'S THE SCREEN FOR?
THIS DOCTOR SHOWS SLIDES WITH HIS LECTURES
SO IT'S LIKE A SHOW, HUH? THIS OUGHTA BE-
IS THAT A BOWEL?
NOT A HEALTHY ONE
Distributed by Universal Press Syndicate
www.garfield.com
JPM DAVPS 9·8
© 2006 PAWS, INC. All Rights Reserved.

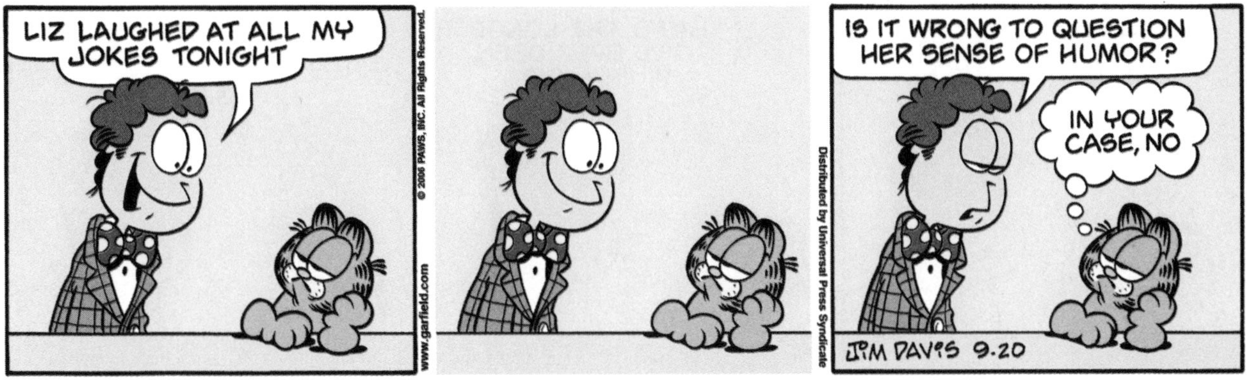
LIZ LAUGHED AT ALL MY JOKES TONIGHT
IS IT WRONG TO QUESTION HER SENSE OF HUMOR?
IN YOUR CASE, NO
JIM DAVIS 9.20
© 2006 PAWS, INC. All Rights Reserved.
www.garfield.com
Distributed by Universal Press Syndicate

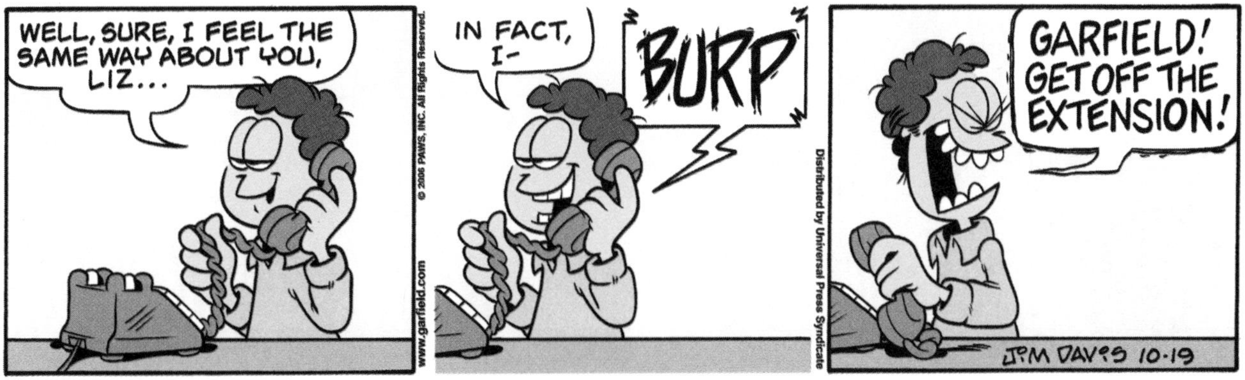
WELL, SURE, I FEEL THE SAME WAY ABOUT YOU, LIZ...
IN FACT, I-
BURP
GARFIELD! GET OFF THE EXTENSION!
JIM DAVIS 10-19
© 2006 PAWS, INC. All Rights Reserved.
www.garfield.com
Distributed by Universal Press Syndicate

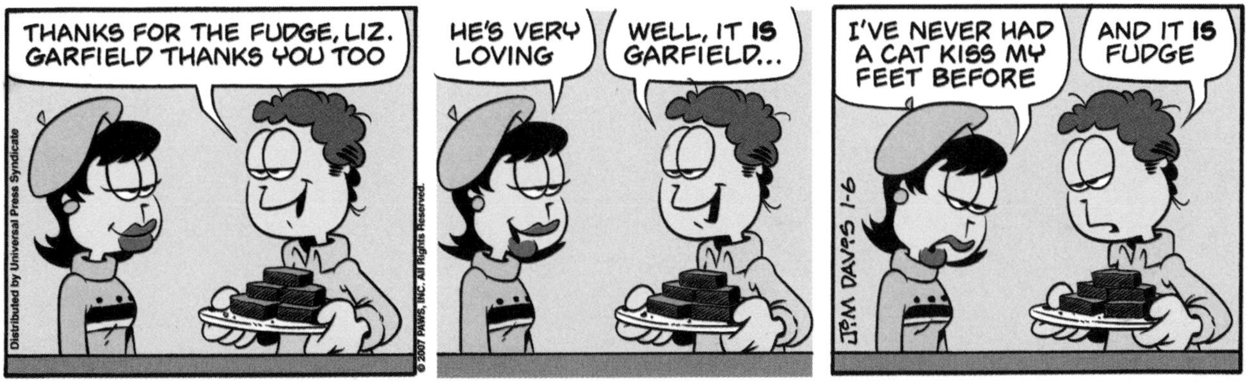
THANKS FOR THE FUDGE, LIZ. GARFIELD THANKS YOU TOO
HE'S VERY LOVING
WELL, IT IS GARFIELD...
I'VE NEVER HAD A CAT KISS MY FEET BEFORE
AND IT IS FUDGE
JIM DAVIS 1-6
Distributed by Universal Press Syndicate
© 2007 PAWS, INC. All Rights Reserved.

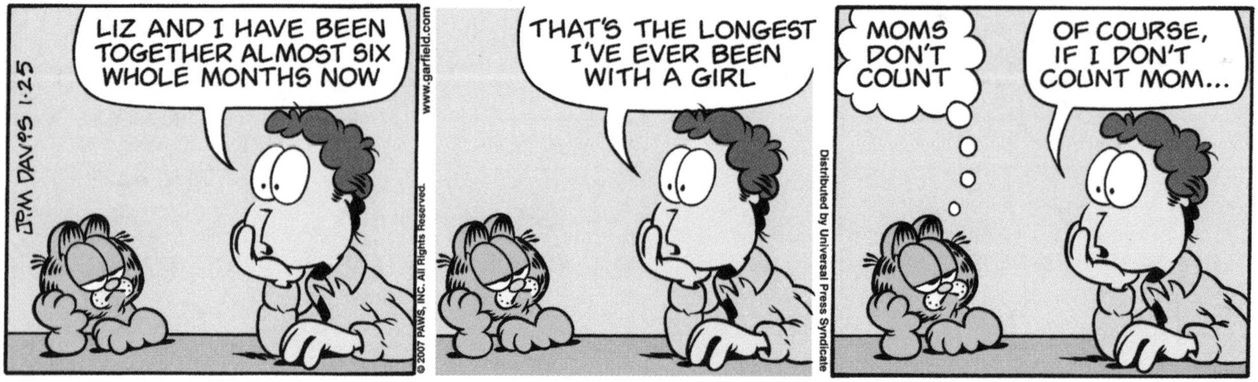
LIZ AND I HAVE BEEN TOGETHER ALMOST SIX WHOLE MONTHS NOW
THAT'S THE LONGEST I'VE EVER BEEN WITH A GIRL
MOMS DON'T COUNT
OF COURSE, IF I DON'T COUNT MOM...
www.garfield.com
© 2007 PAWS, INC. All Rights Reserved.
Distributed by Universal Press Syndicate

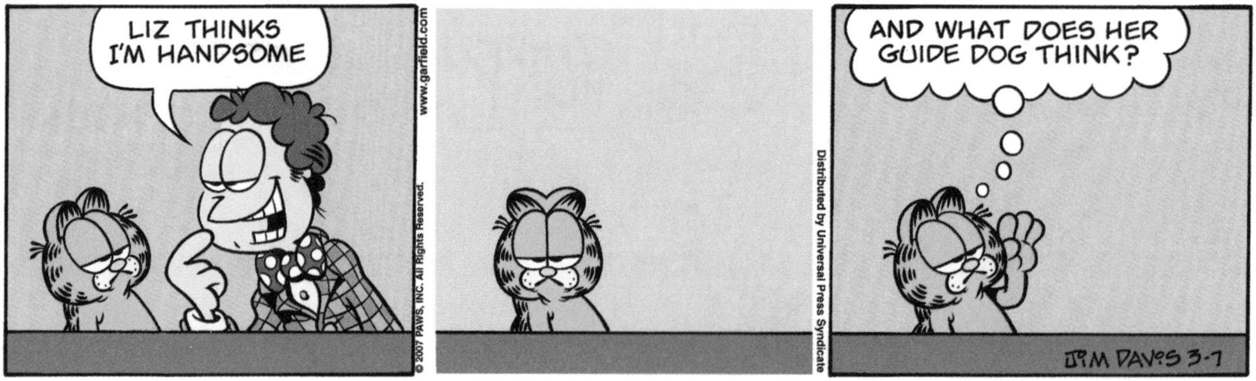
LIZ THINKS I'M HANDSOME
AND WHAT DOES HER GUIDE DOG THINK?
www.garfield.com
© 2007 PAWS, INC. All Rights Reserved.
Distributed by Universal Press Syndicate

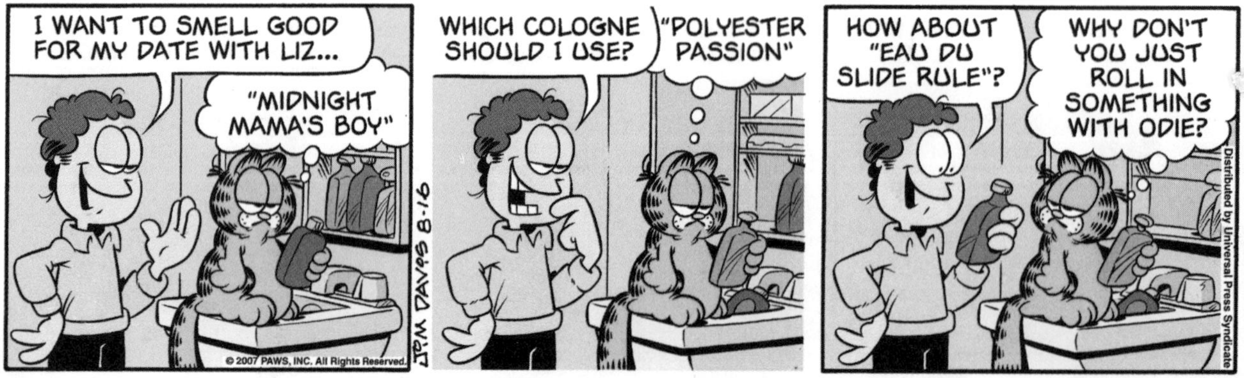
I WANT TO SMELL GOOD FOR MY DATE WITH LIZ...
"MIDNIGHT MAMA'S BOY"
WHICH COLOGNE SHOULD I USE?
"POLYESTER PASSION"
HOW ABOUT "EAU DU SLIDE RULE"?
WHY DON'T YOU JUST ROLL IN SOMETHING WITH ODIE?
© 2007 PAWS, INC. All Rights Reserved.
Distributed by Universal Press Syndicate

Garfield®
♪ DOO-DOOO DEE-DEE DUM DOO-DOOO...
♪ OOH-OOH-OOOOOOHHH BABY, BAY-BEE...
www.garfield.com
© 2011 PAWS, INC. All Rights Reserved.
UH-HUH-UH-HUH
♪ BLANG-A TWANNG-YANG!!
CHA-CONK, CHA-CONK
Distributed by Universal Uclick
JPM DAVIS 5-1
PLAY AGAIN?

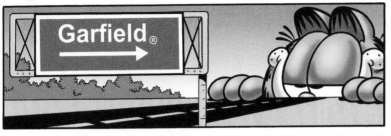

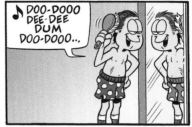

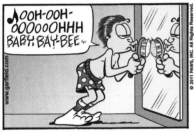

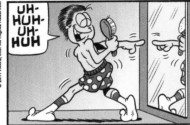

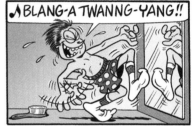

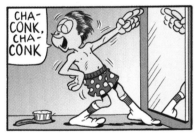

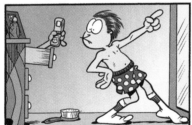

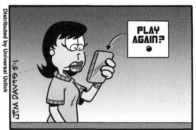

WORST NIGHTMARES OF LIZ THE VET

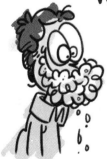

- Weasel she misdiagnosed turns out to be a lawyer
- Forced to pay full cover price for waiting room magazines
- Tarantula falls inside blouse
- Must send Lassie to that "Big Kennel in the Sky"
- She's bitten by a rabid Arbuckle
- Another Garfield checkup!

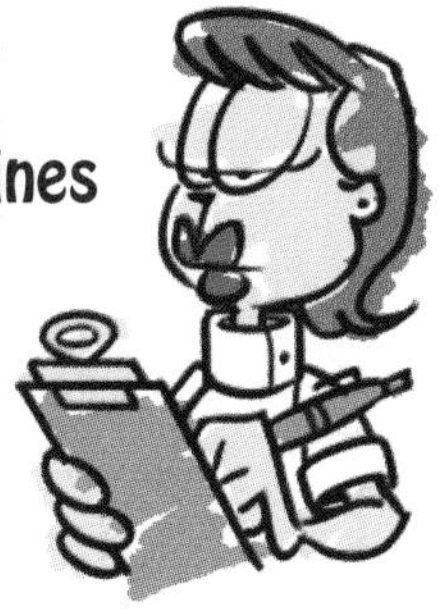

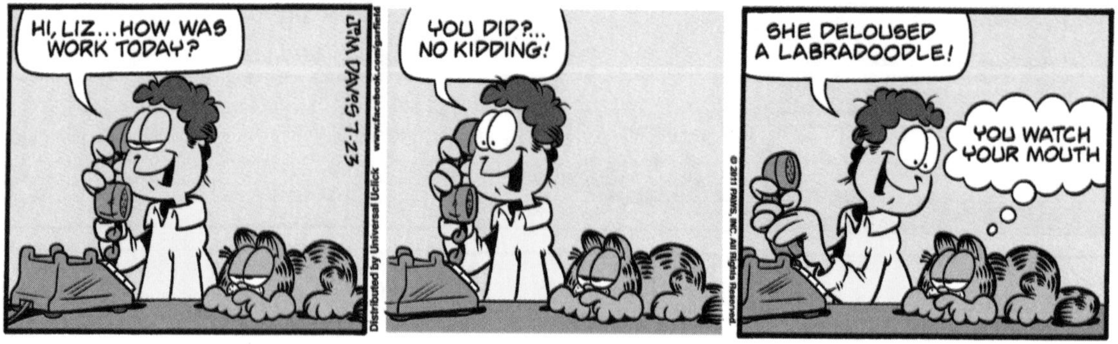
HI, LIZ... HOW WAS WORK TODAY?
JIM DAVIS 7-23
www.facebook.com/garfield
Distributed by Universal Uclick
YOU DID?... NO KIDDING!
SHE DELOUSED A LABRADOODLE!
YOU WATCH YOUR MOUTH
© 2011 PAWS, INC. All Rights Reserved.

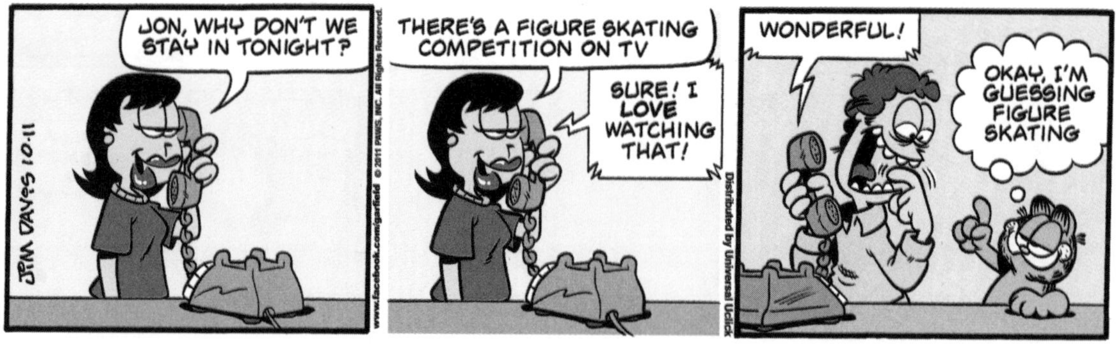
JIM DAVIS 10-11
JON, WHY DON'T WE STAY IN TONIGHT?
www.facebook.com/garfield © 2011 PAWS, INC. All Rights Reserved.
THERE'S A FIGURE SKATING COMPETITION ON TV
SURE! I LOVE WATCHING THAT!
Distributed by Universal Uclick
WONDERFUL!
OKAY, I'M GUESSING FIGURE SKATING

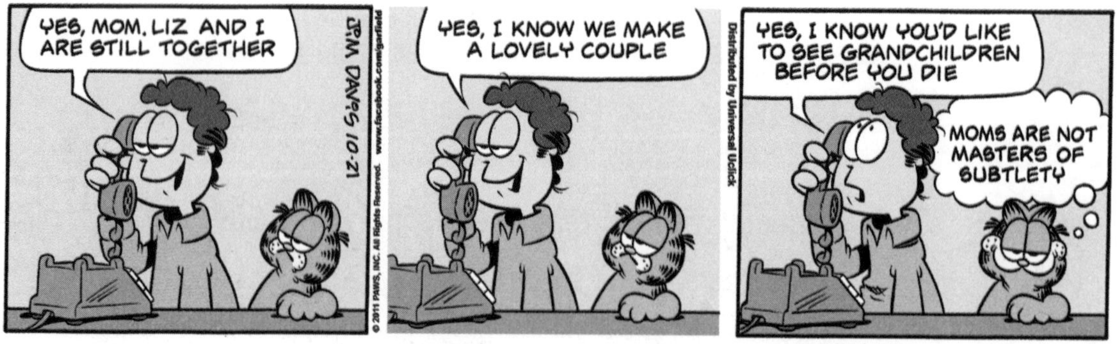
YES, MOM. LIZ AND I ARE STILL TOGETHER
JIM DAVIS 10-21
www.facebook.com/garfield
© 2011 PAWS, INC. All Rights Reserved.
YES, I KNOW WE MAKE A LOVELY COUPLE
Distributed by Universal Uclick
YES, I KNOW YOU'D LIKE TO SEE GRANDCHILDREN BEFORE YOU DIE
MOMS ARE NOT MASTERS OF SUBTLETY

GEEKS ROCK

NERD IS THE WORD

Nerd, thy name is "Arbuckle." (From the Latin *arbuculus*, "wiener-chested"; a geek; a nerd; a geeky nerd; you get the picture.) Specifically, *Jon* Arbuckle, the mega nerd whose idea of Friday night fun is yodeling . . . while wearing a kilt . . . while riding a unicycle. He's a one-man freak show!

But things have actually improved since Jon started dating Liz. His life—if you could call it that—used to be so boring, he looked forward to dental appointments. His idea of excitement was teasing his eyebrows and tweezing his ear hairs. Of course, his life was boring because *he* was boring. Even as a child, Jon was so dull, he used to make the cows yawn.

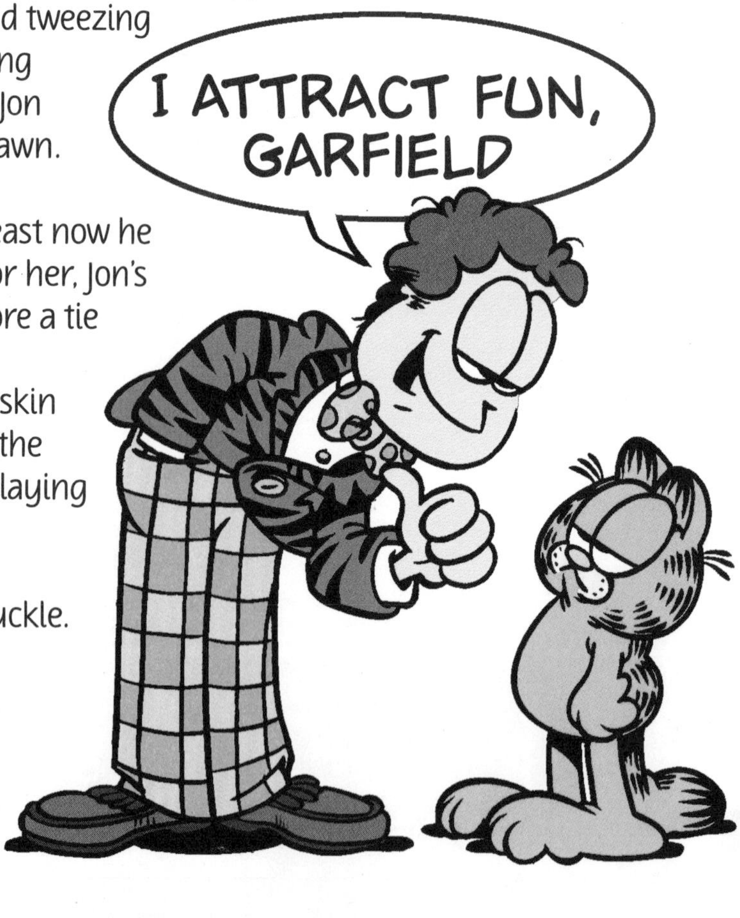
I ATTRACT FUN, GARFIELD

Actually, he's still pretty boring, but at least now he gets out more with Liz. Unfortunately for her, Jon's usually dressed like a clown. He once wore a tie so wide, he didn't wear a shirt under it. But that's nothing compared to his coonskin cap and polka-dot sport coat. (But then, the polka dots do seem apropos when he's playing polka on his trusty accordion.)

"Nerd" is definitely the word for Jon Arbuckle.

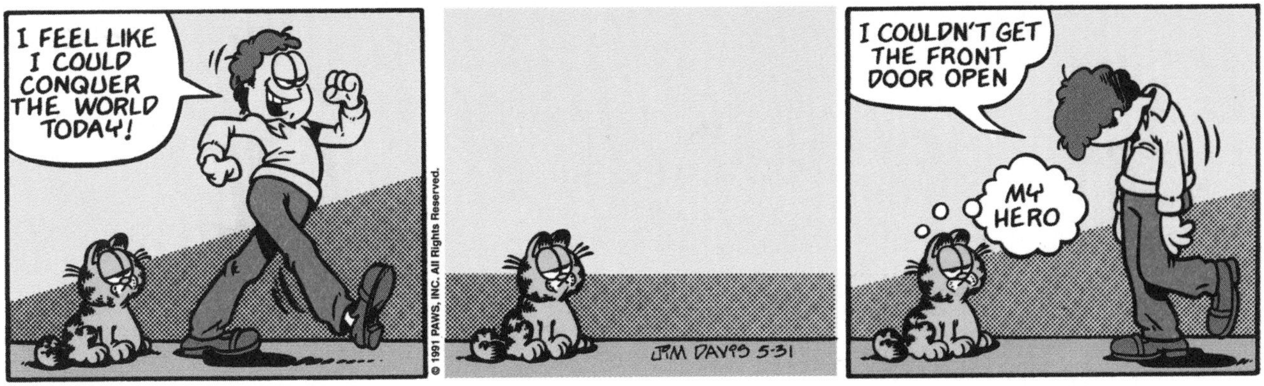
I FEEL LIKE I COULD CONQUER THE WORLD TODAY!
I COULDN'T GET THE FRONT DOOR OPEN
MY HERO
© 1991 PAWS, INC. All Rights Reserved.
JIM DAVIS 5-31

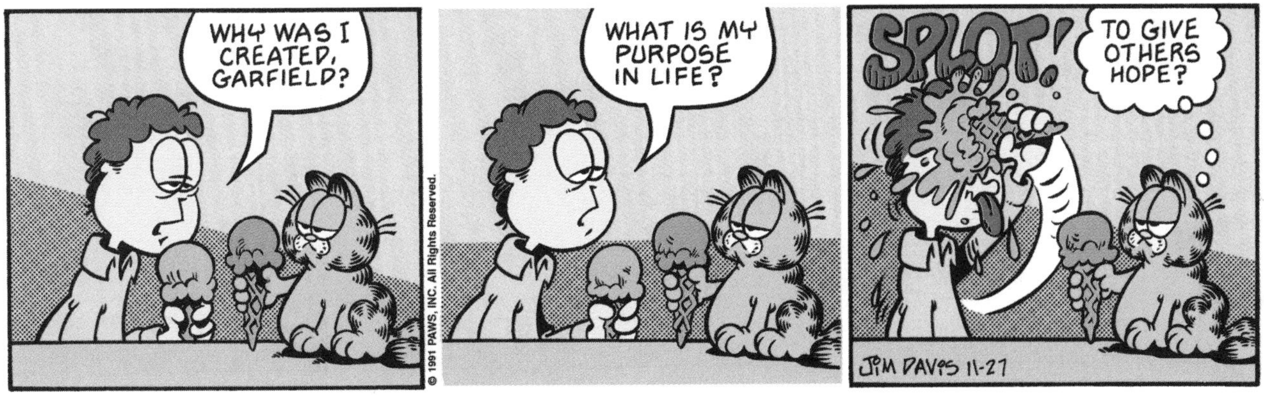
WHY WAS I CREATED, GARFIELD?
WHAT IS MY PURPOSE IN LIFE?
SPLOT!
TO GIVE OTHERS HOPE?
© 1991 PAWS, INC. All Rights Reserved.
JIM DAVIS 11-27

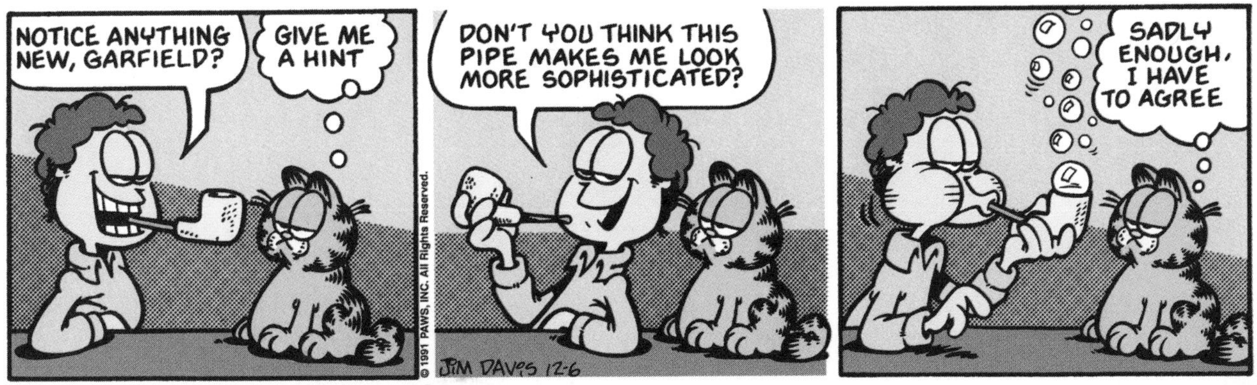
NOTICE ANYTHING NEW, GARFIELD?
GIVE ME A HINT
DON'T YOU THINK THIS PIPE MAKES ME LOOK MORE SOPHISTICATED?
SADLY ENOUGH, I HAVE TO AGREE
© 1991 PAWS, INC. All Rights Reserved.
JIM DAVIS 12-6

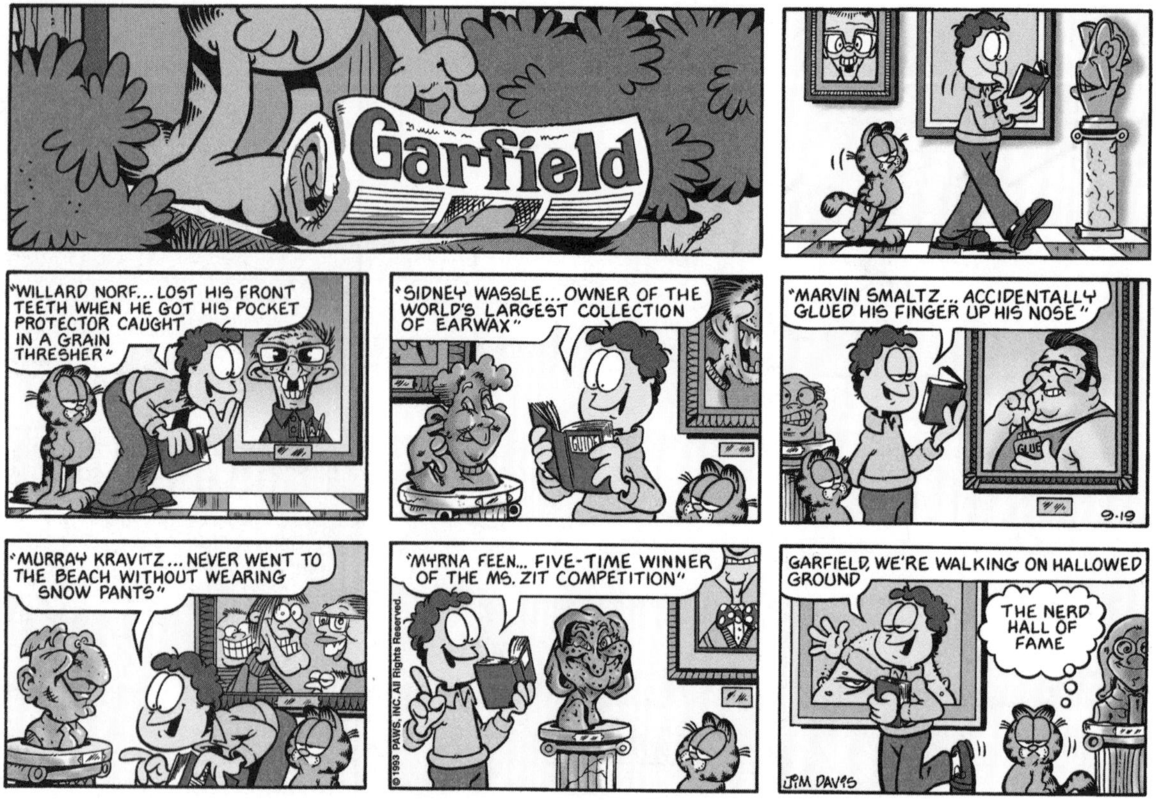

Garfield
"WILLARD NORF... LOST HIS FRONT TEETH WHEN HE GOT HIS POCKET PROTECTOR CAUGHT IN A GRAIN THRESHER"
"SIDNEY WASSLE... OWNER OF THE WORLD'S LARGEST COLLECTION OF EARWAX"
"MARVIN SMALTZ... ACCIDENTALLY GLUED HIS FINGER UP HIS NOSE"
GLUE
9·19
"MURRAY KRAVITZ... NEVER WENT TO THE BEACH WITHOUT WEARING SNOW PANTS"
"MYRNA FEEN... FIVE-TIME WINNER OF THE MS. ZIT COMPETITION"
© 1993 PAWS, INC. All Rights Reserved.
GARFIELD, WE'RE WALKING ON HALLOWED GROUND
THE NERD HALL OF FAME
JIM DAVIS

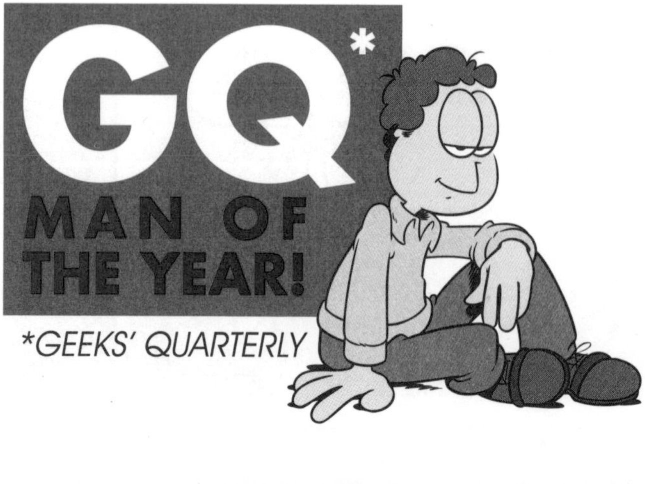

GQ*
MAN OF THE YEAR!
*GEEKS' QUARTERLY

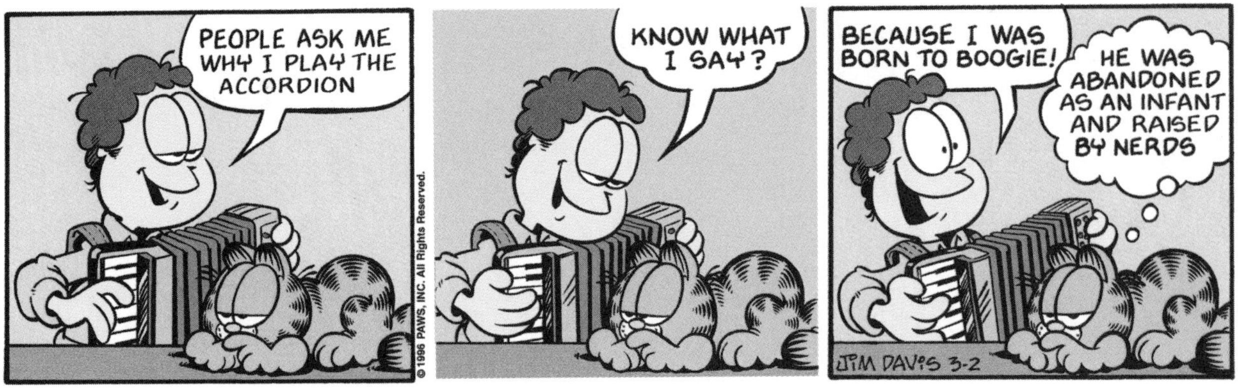
PEOPLE ASK ME WHY I PLAY THE ACCORDION
KNOW WHAT I SAY?
BECAUSE I WAS BORN TO BOOGIE!
HE WAS ABANDONED AS AN INFANT AND RAISED BY NERDS
JIM DAVIS 3-2

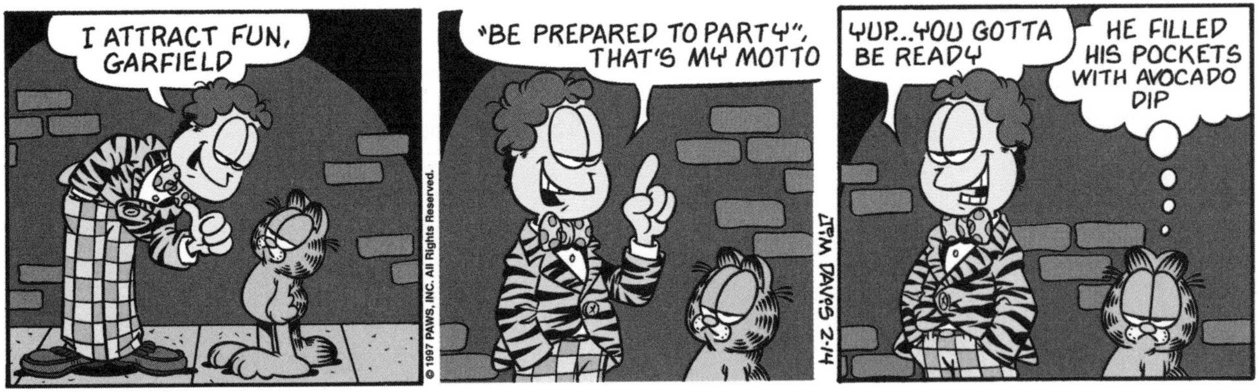
I ATTRACT FUN, GARFIELD
"BE PREPARED TO PARTY", THAT'S MY MOTTO
JIM DAVIS 2-14
YUP...YOU GOTTA BE READY
HE FILLED HIS POCKETS WITH AVOCADO DIP

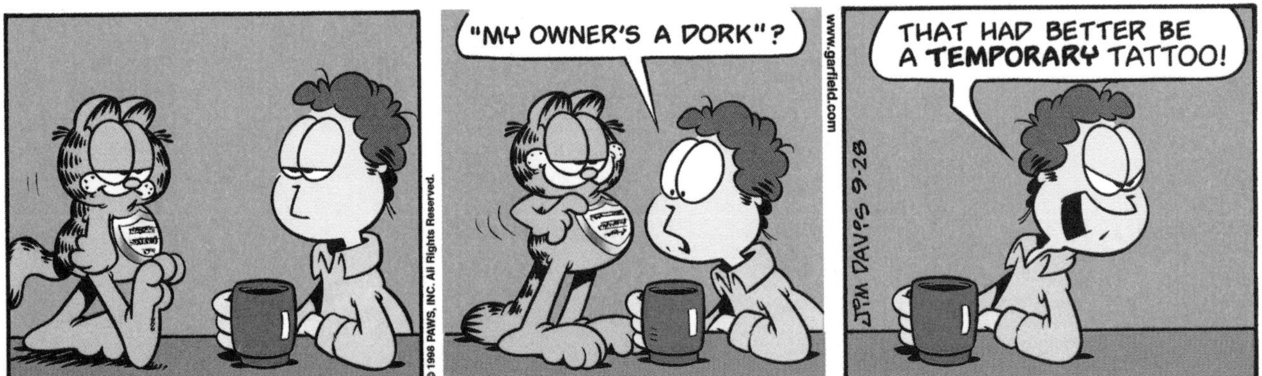
"MY OWNER'S A DORK"?
www.garfield.com
JIM DAVIS 9-28
THAT HAD BETTER BE A **TEMPORARY** TATTOO!

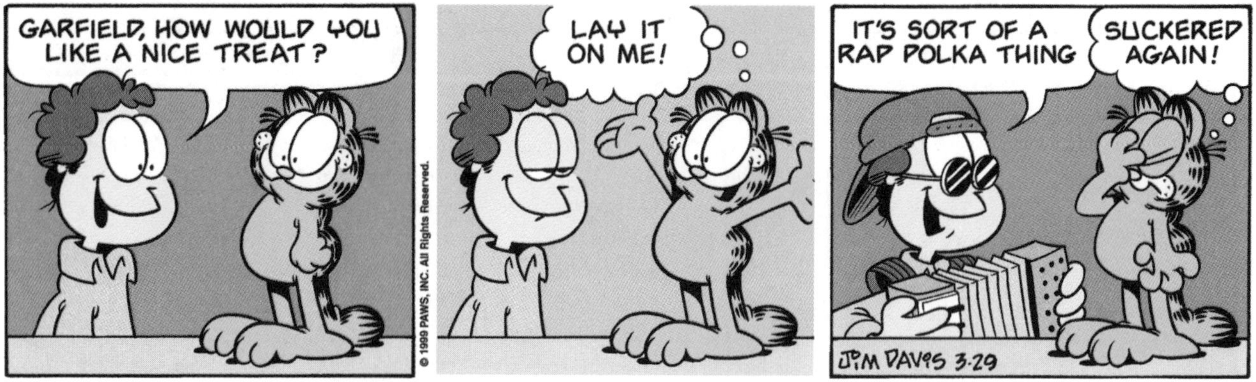
GARFIELD, HOW WOULD YOU LIKE A NICE TREAT?
LAY IT ON ME!
IT'S SORT OF A RAP POLKA THING
SUCKERED AGAIN!
JIM DAVIS 3-29

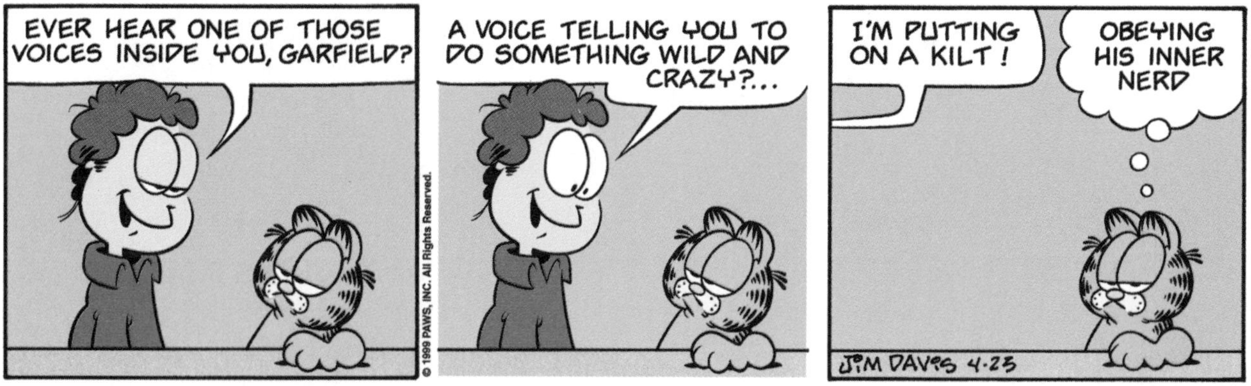
EVER HEAR ONE OF THOSE VOICES INSIDE YOU, GARFIELD?
A VOICE TELLING YOU TO DO SOMETHING WILD AND CRAZY?...
I'M PUTTING ON A KILT!
OBEYING HIS INNER NERD
JIM DAVIS 4-23

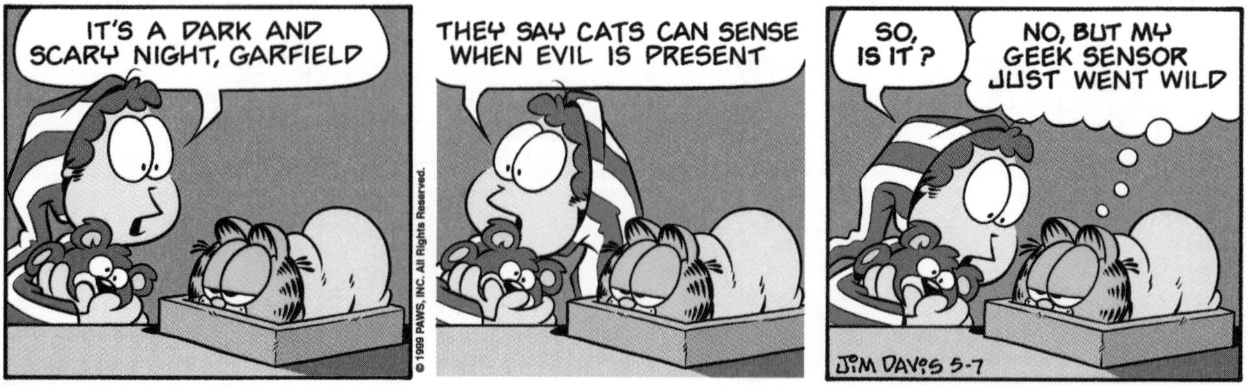
IT'S A DARK AND SCARY NIGHT, GARFIELD
THEY SAY CATS CAN SENSE WHEN EVIL IS PRESENT
SO, IS IT?
NO, BUT MY GEEK SENSOR JUST WENT WILD
JIM DAVIS 5-7

YOU KNOW YOU'RE A NERD WHEN...

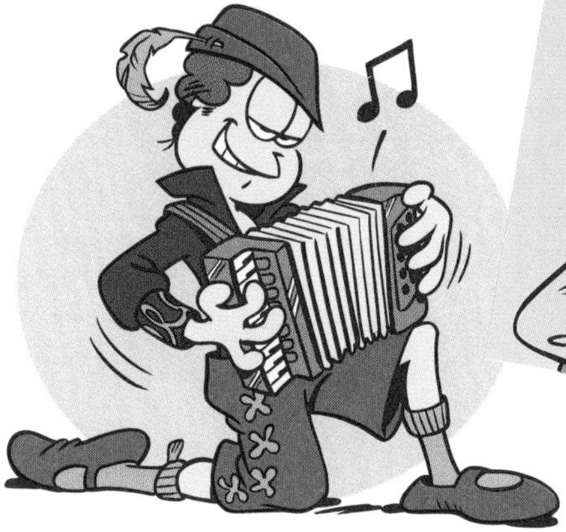

You think playing the accordion makes you look "hot"

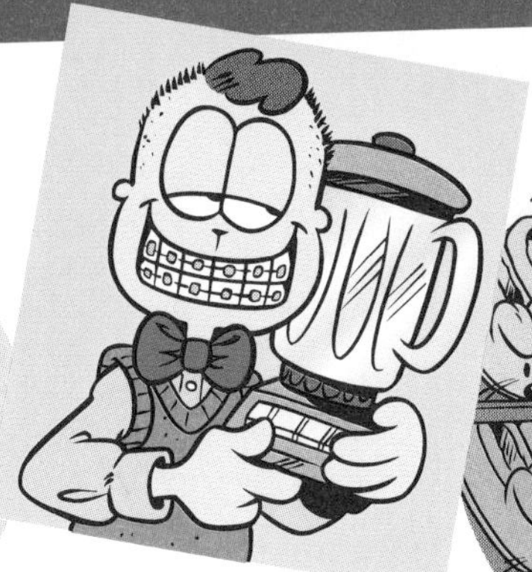

In school, you were voted "Most Likely to Marry a Kitchen Appliance"

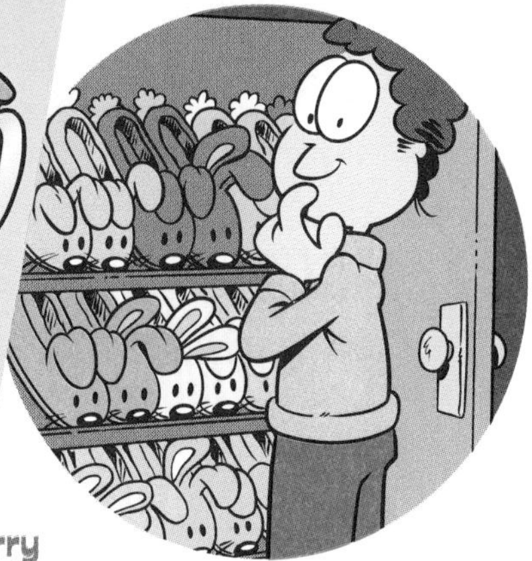

You own an extensive collection of bunny slippers

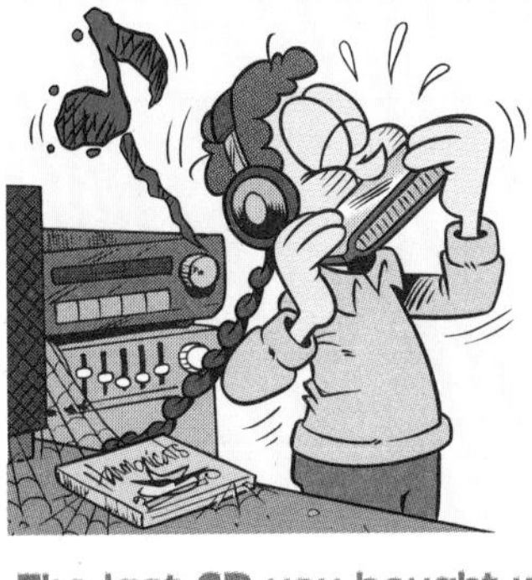
Harmonicats

The last CD you bought was "Best of the Harmonicats"

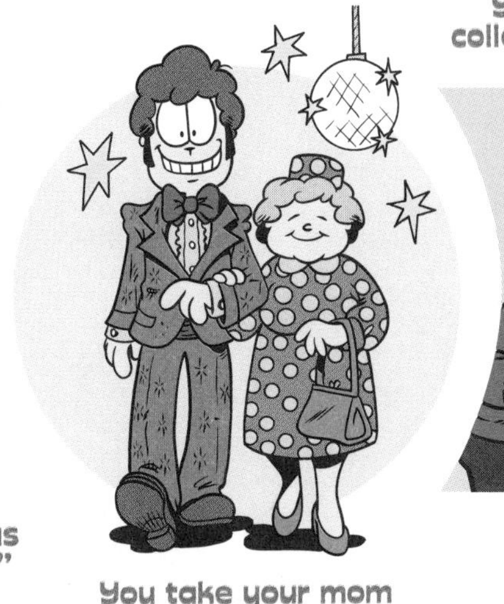

You take your mom to the prom

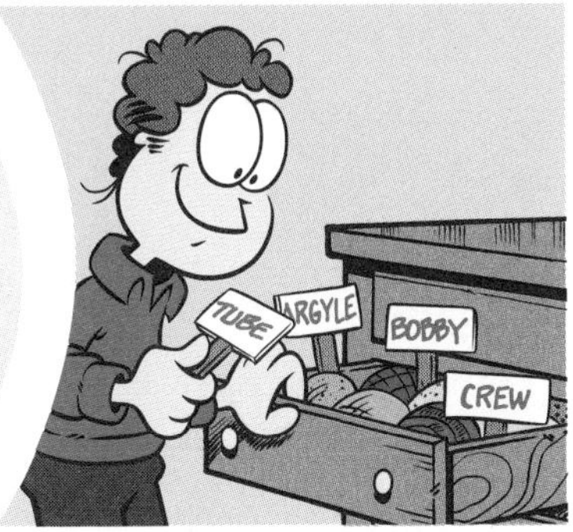
TUBE
ARGYLE
BOBBY
CREW

You alphabetize your sock drawer

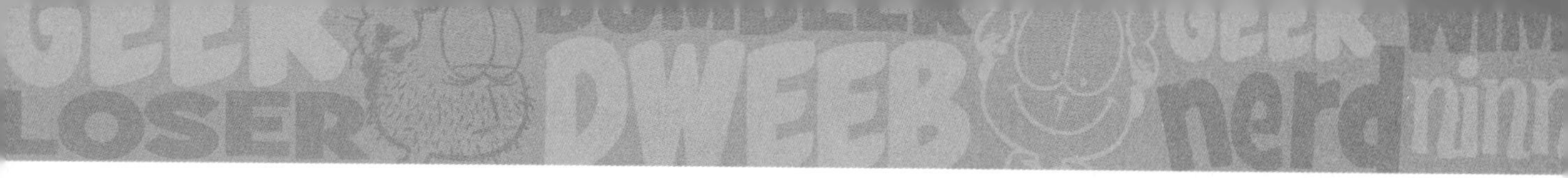
GEEK
LOSER
DWEEB
nerd

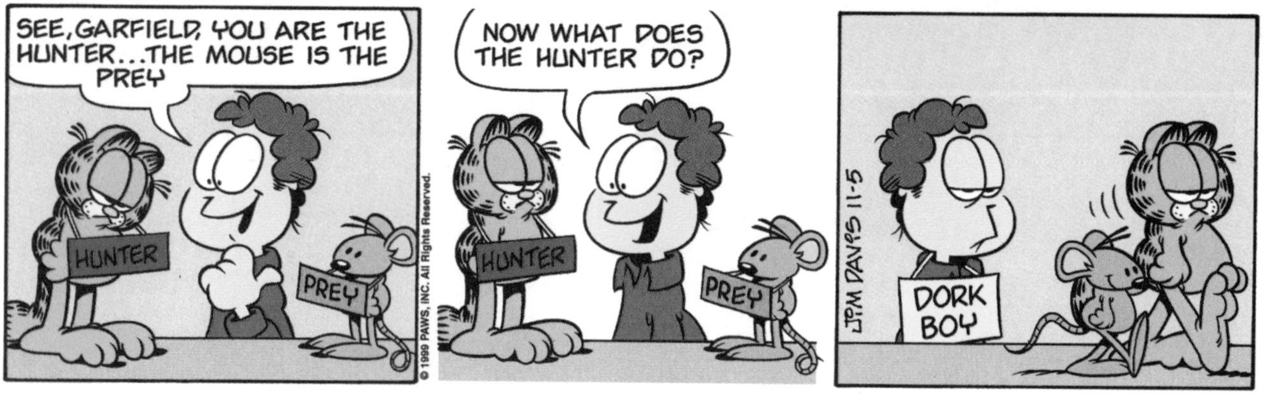
SEE, GARFIELD, YOU ARE THE HUNTER...THE MOUSE IS THE PREY
HUNTER
PREY
© 1999 PAWS, INC. All Rights Reserved.
NOW WHAT DOES THE HUNTER DO?
HUNTER
PREY
JIM DAVIS 11-5
DORK BOY

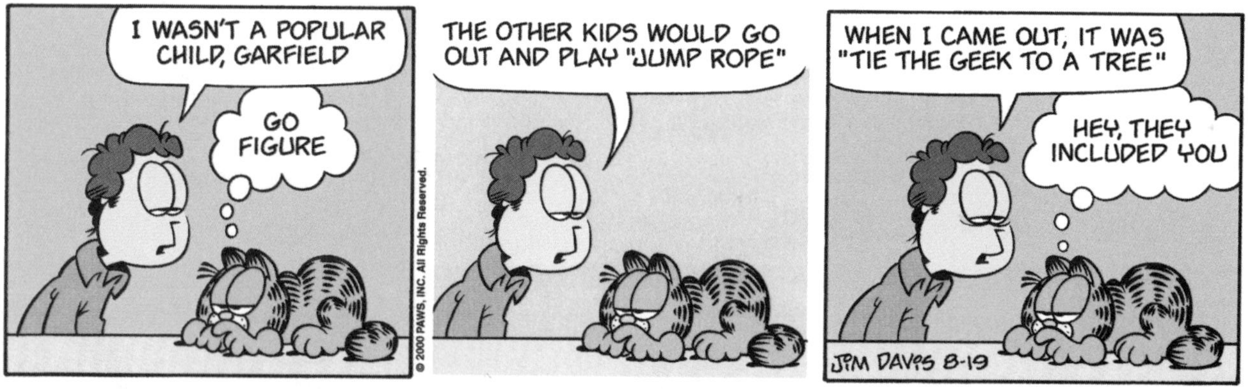
I WASN'T A POPULAR CHILD, GARFIELD
GO FIGURE
© 2000 PAWS, INC. All Rights Reserved.
THE OTHER KIDS WOULD GO OUT AND PLAY "JUMP ROPE"
WHEN I CAME OUT, IT WAS "TIE THE GEEK TO A TREE"
HEY, THEY INCLUDED YOU
JIM DAVIS 8-19

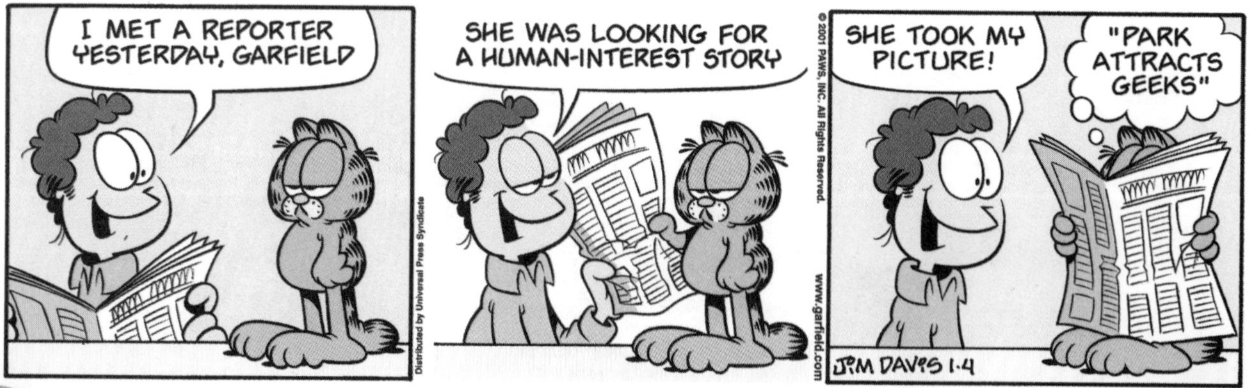
I MET A REPORTER YESTERDAY, GARFIELD
Distributed by Universal Press Syndicate
SHE WAS LOOKING FOR A HUMAN-INTEREST STORY
© 2001 PAWS, INC. All Rights Reserved.
www.garfield.com
SHE TOOK MY PICTURE!
"PARK ATTRACTS GEEKS"
JIM DAVIS 1-4

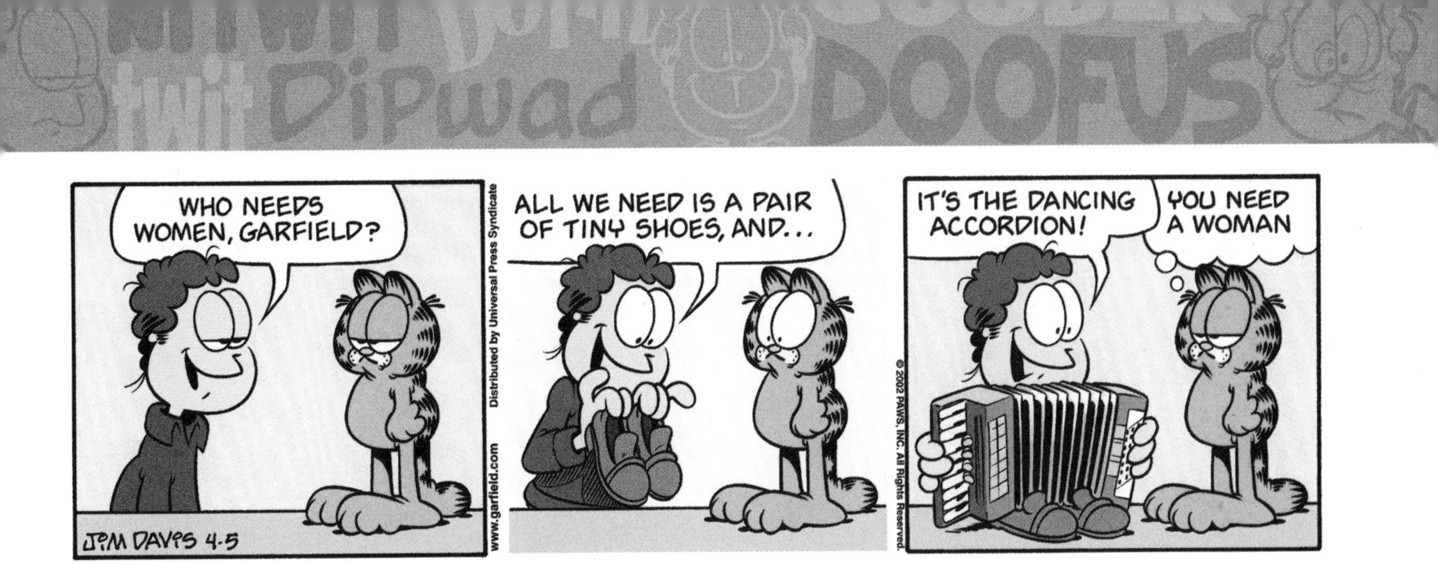
WHO NEEDS WOMEN, GARFIELD?
JIM DAVIS 4-5
www.garfield.com Distributed by Universal Press Syndicate
ALL WE NEED IS A PAIR OF TINY SHOES, AND...
IT'S THE DANCING ACCORDION!
YOU NEED A WOMAN
© 2002 PAWS, INC. All Rights Reserved.

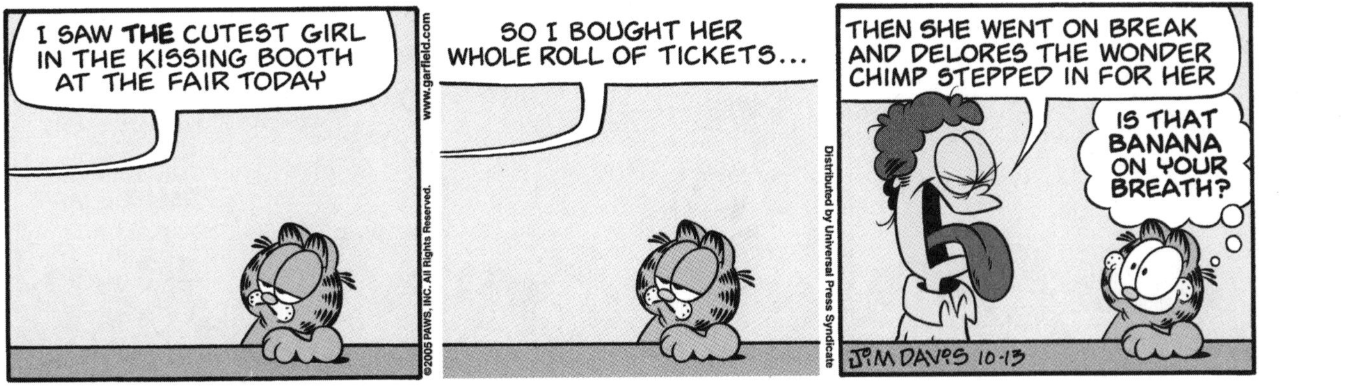
I SAW THE CUTEST GIRL IN THE KISSING BOOTH AT THE FAIR TODAY
©2005 PAWS, INC. All Rights Reserved. www.garfield.com
SO I BOUGHT HER WHOLE ROLL OF TICKETS...
THEN SHE WENT ON BREAK AND DELORES THE WONDER CHIMP STEPPED IN FOR HER
IS THAT BANANA ON YOUR BREATH?
Distributed by Universal Press Syndicate
JIM DAVIS 10-13

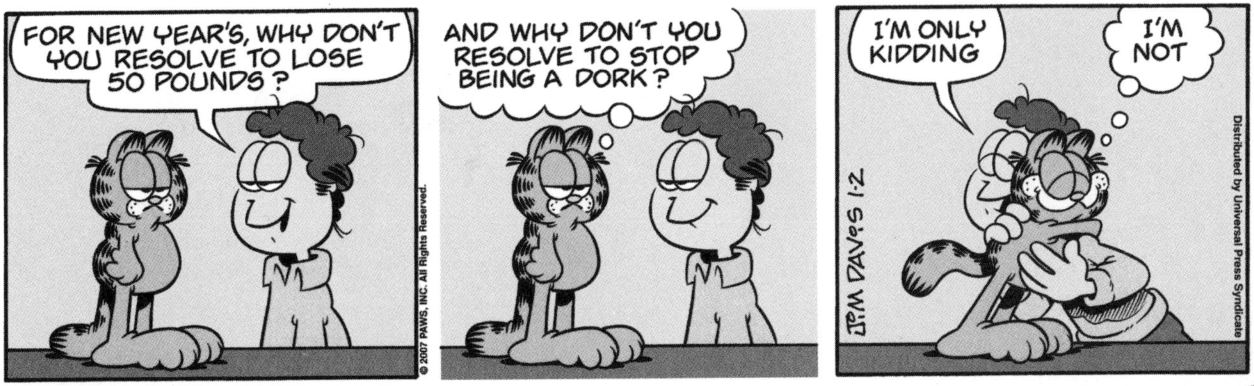
FOR NEW YEAR'S, WHY DON'T YOU RESOLVE TO LOSE 50 POUNDS?
© 2007 PAWS, INC. All Rights Reserved.
AND WHY DON'T YOU RESOLVE TO STOP BEING A DORK?
I'M ONLY KIDDING
I'M NOT
JIM DAVIS 1-2
Distributed by Universal Press Syndicate

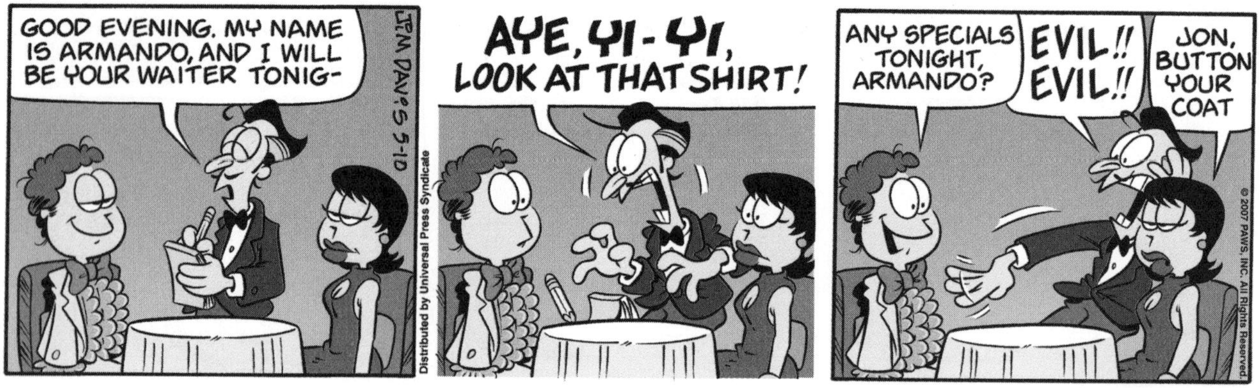
GOOD EVENING. MY NAME IS ARMANDO, AND I WILL BE YOUR WAITER TONIG-
JIM DAVIS 5-10
Distributed by Universal Press Syndicate
AYE, YI-YI, LOOK AT THAT SHIRT!
ANY SPECIALS TONIGHT, ARMANDO?
EVIL!! EVIL!!
JON, BUTTON YOUR COAT
© 2007 PAWS, INC. All Rights Reserved.

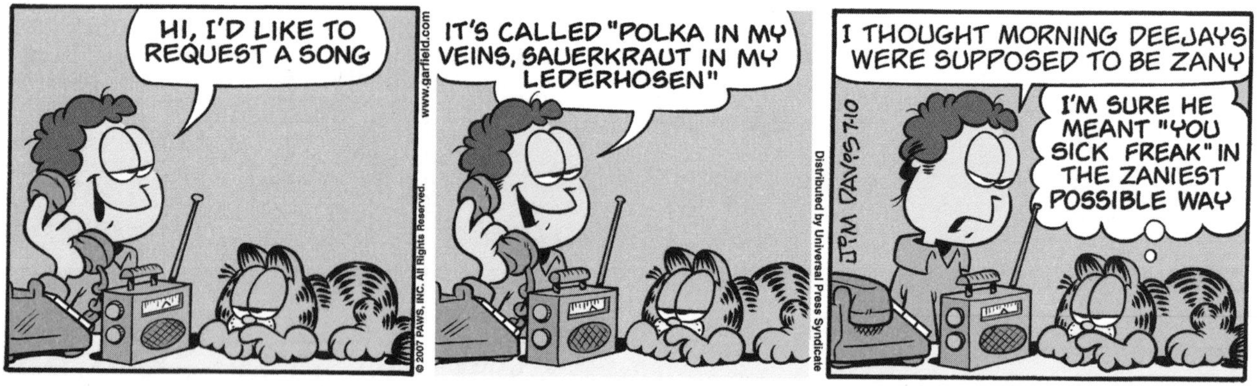
HI, I'D LIKE TO REQUEST A SONG
© 2007 PAWS, INC. All Rights Reserved.
www.garfield.com
IT'S CALLED "POLKA IN MY VEINS, SAUERKRAUT IN MY LEDERHOSEN"
Distributed by Universal Press Syndicate
I THOUGHT MORNING DEEJAYS WERE SUPPOSED TO BE ZANY
JIM DAVIS 7-10
I'M SURE HE MEANT "YOU SICK FREAK" IN THE ZANIEST POSSIBLE WAY

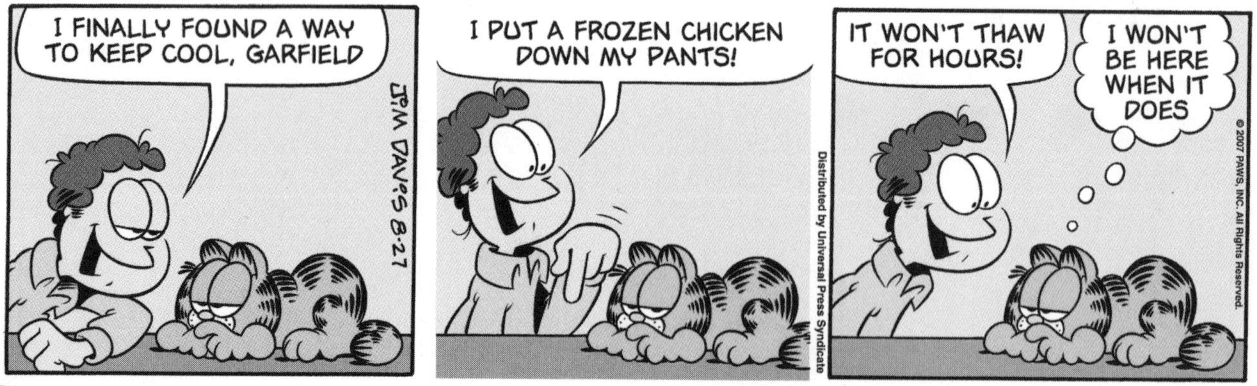
I FINALLY FOUND A WAY TO KEEP COOL, GARFIELD
JIM DAVIS 8-27
I PUT A FROZEN CHICKEN DOWN MY PANTS!
Distributed by Universal Press Syndicate
IT WON'T THAW FOR HOURS!
I WON'T BE HERE WHEN IT DOES
© 2007 PAWS, INC. All Rights Reserved.

LIFEGUARD!!!
I'M STANDING IN SEAWEED!!
LET'S GO HOME NOW
I HEAR THAT STUFF'S GOOD FOR YOUR COMPLEXION
JIM DAVIS 8·31
Distributed by Universal Press Syndicate
© 2007 PAWS, INC. All Rights Reserved.

Jon GONE WILD!

ECK'S
Angels
CHESS RULES
POLKA POWER!
BORN TO WHINE
SE 2 XY
4 MY
DISCO DADDY
I HOBBITS

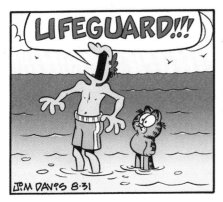

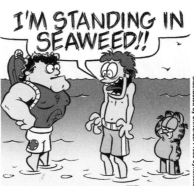

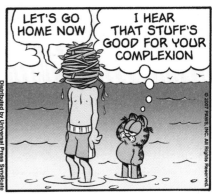

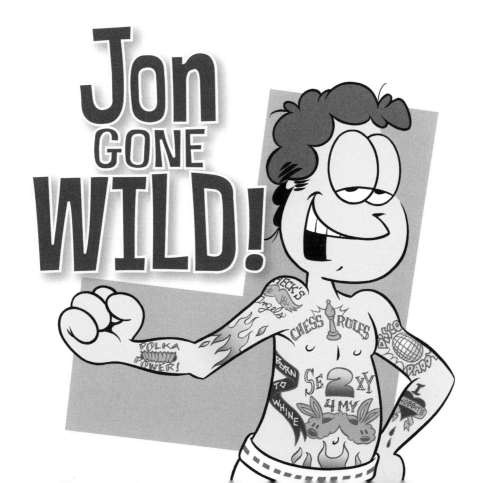

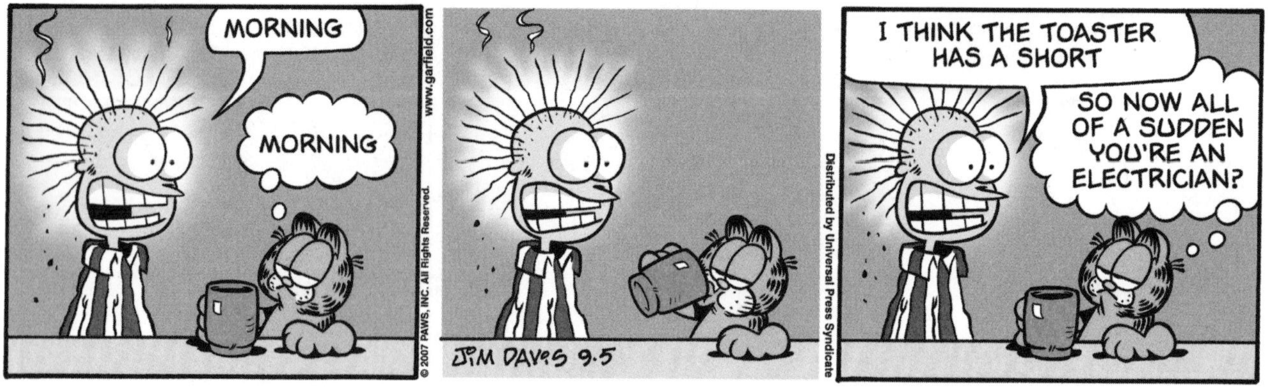
MORNING
MORNING
© 2007 PAWS, INC. All Rights Reserved. www.garfield.com
JIM DAVIS 9-5
Distributed by Universal Press Syndicate
I THINK THE TOASTER HAS A SHORT
SO NOW ALL OF A SUDDEN YOU'RE AN ELECTRICIAN?

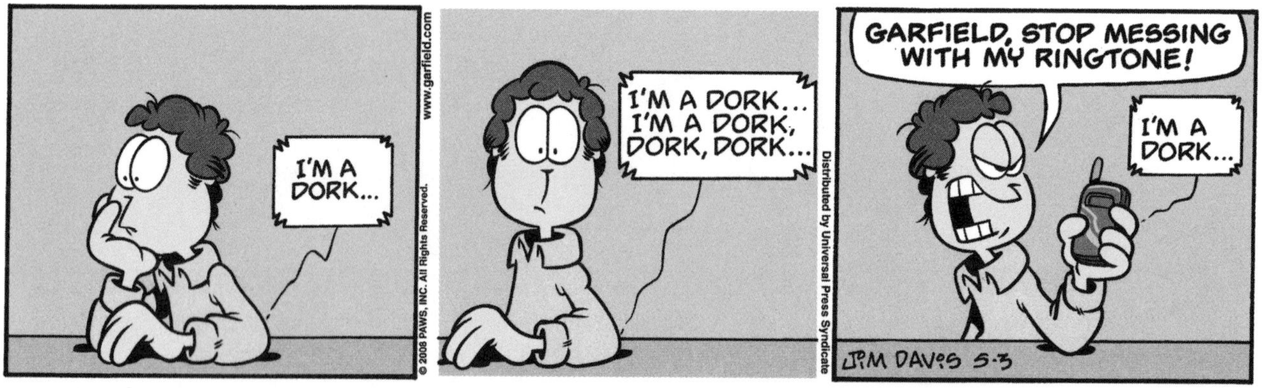
I'M A DORK...
© 2008 PAWS, INC. All Rights Reserved. www.garfield.com
I'M A DORK... I'M A DORK, DORK, DORK...
Distributed by Universal Press Syndicate
GARFIELD, STOP MESSING WITH MY RINGTONE!
I'M A DORK...
JIM DAVIS 5-3

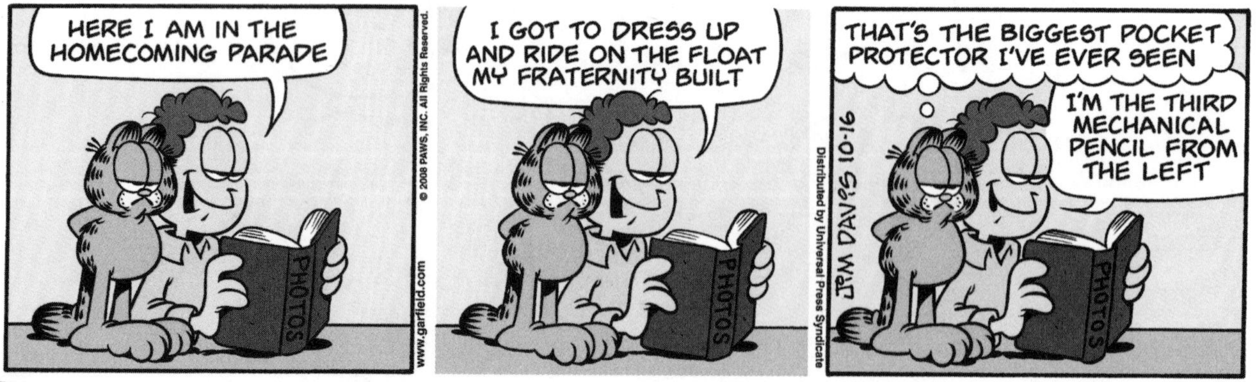
HERE I AM IN THE HOMECOMING PARADE
PHOTOS
© 2008 PAWS, INC. All Rights Reserved. www.garfield.com
I GOT TO DRESS UP AND RIDE ON THE FLOAT MY FRATERNITY BUILT
PHOTOS
JIM DAVIS 10-16
Distributed by Universal Press Syndicate
THAT'S THE BIGGEST POCKET PROTECTOR I'VE EVER SEEN
I'M THE THIRD MECHANICAL PENCIL FROM THE LEFT
PHOTOS

GEEKZILLA

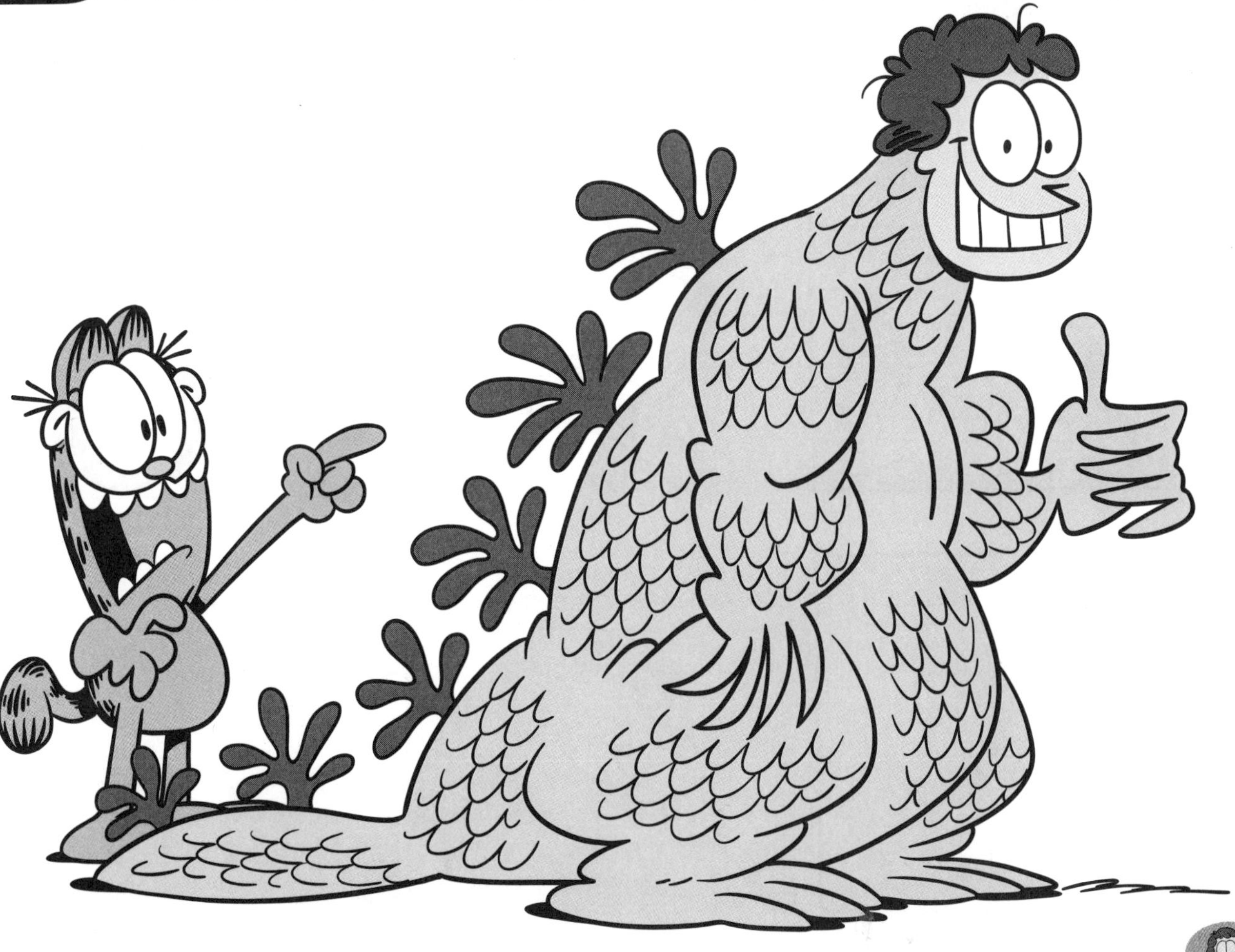

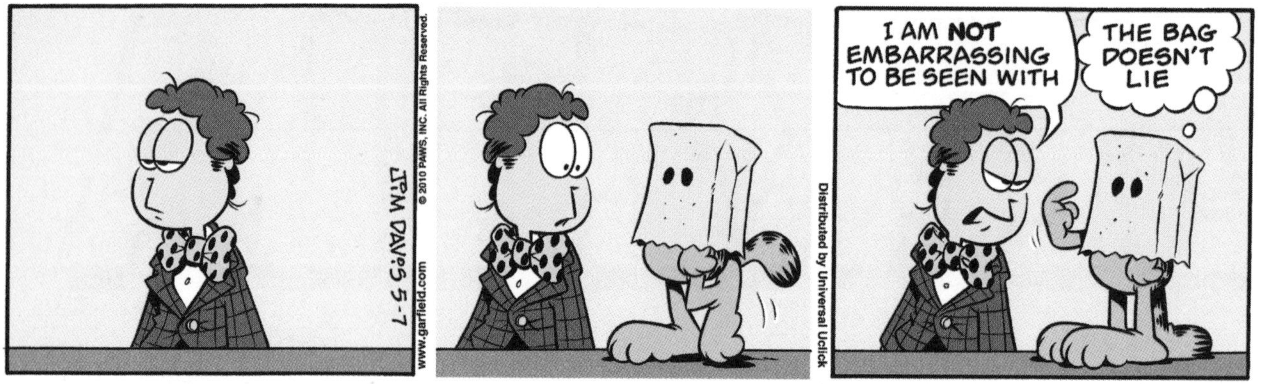
I AM **NOT** EMBARRASSING TO BE SEEN WITH
THE BAG DOESN'T LIE
JIM DAVIS 5-7
© 2010 PAWS, INC. All Rights Reserved.
www.garfield.com
Distributed by Universal Uclick

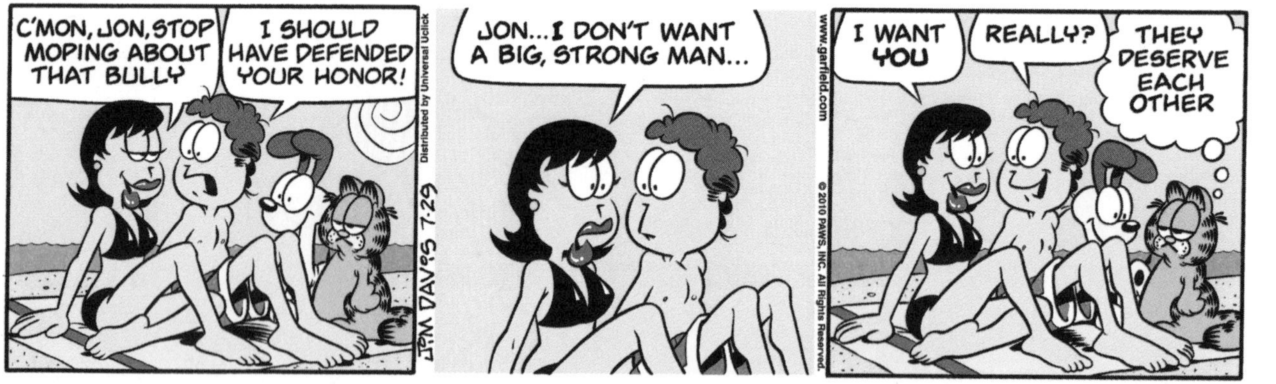
C'MON, JON, STOP MOPING ABOUT THAT BULLY
I SHOULD HAVE DEFENDED YOUR HONOR!
JON... I DON'T WANT A BIG, STRONG MAN...
I WANT **YOU**
REALLY?
THEY DESERVE EACH OTHER
JIM DAVIS 7-29
Distributed by Universal Uclick
www.garfield.com
© 2010 PAWS, INC. All Rights Reserved.

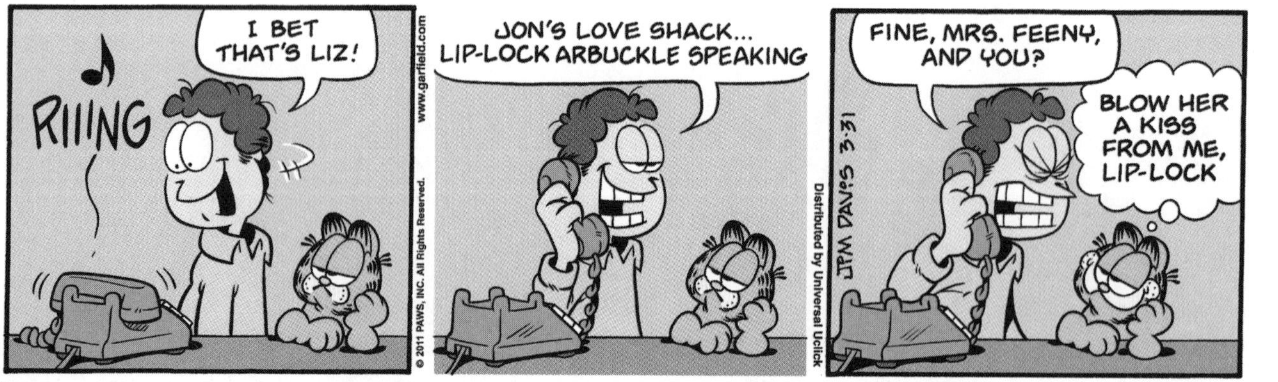
RIIING
I BET THAT'S LIZ!
JON'S LOVE SHACK... LIP-LOCK ARBUCKLE SPEAKING
FINE, MRS. FEENY, AND YOU?
BLOW HER A KISS FROM ME, LIP-LOCK
JIM DAVIS 3-31
© 2011 PAWS, INC. All Rights Reserved.
www.garfield.com
Distributed by Universal Uclick

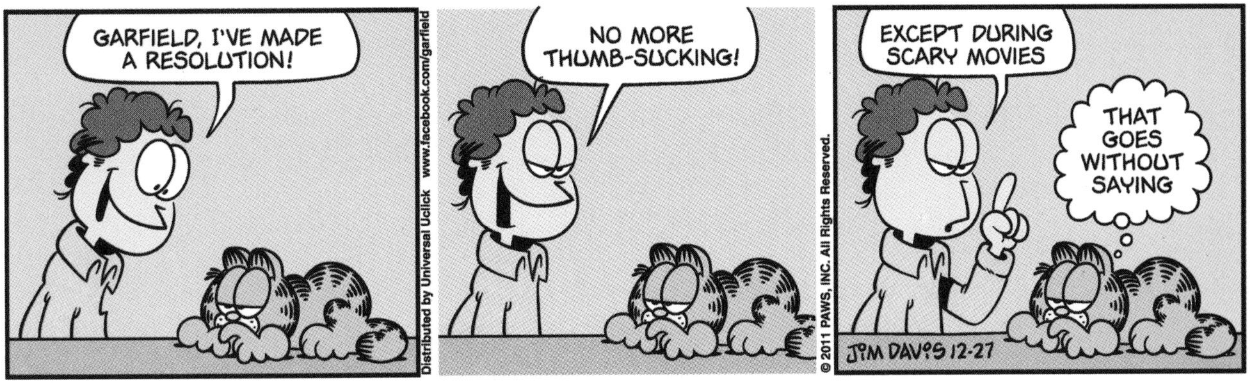
GARFIELD, I'VE MADE A RESOLUTION!
NO MORE THUMB-SUCKING!
EXCEPT DURING SCARY MOVIES
THAT GOES WITHOUT SAYING
JIM DAVIS 12-27
Distributed by Universal Uclick www.facebook.com/garfield
© 2011 PAWS, INC. All Rights Reserved.

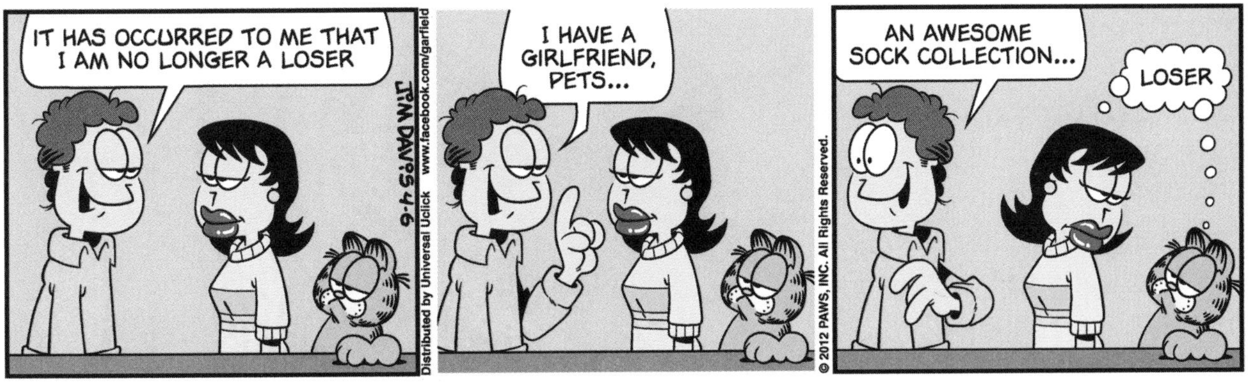
IT HAS OCCURRED TO ME THAT I AM NO LONGER A LOSER
JIM DAVIS 4-6
I HAVE A GIRLFRIEND, PETS...
AN AWESOME SOCK COLLECTION...
LOSER
Distributed by Universal Uclick www.facebook.com/garfield
© 2012 PAWS, INC. All Rights Reserved.

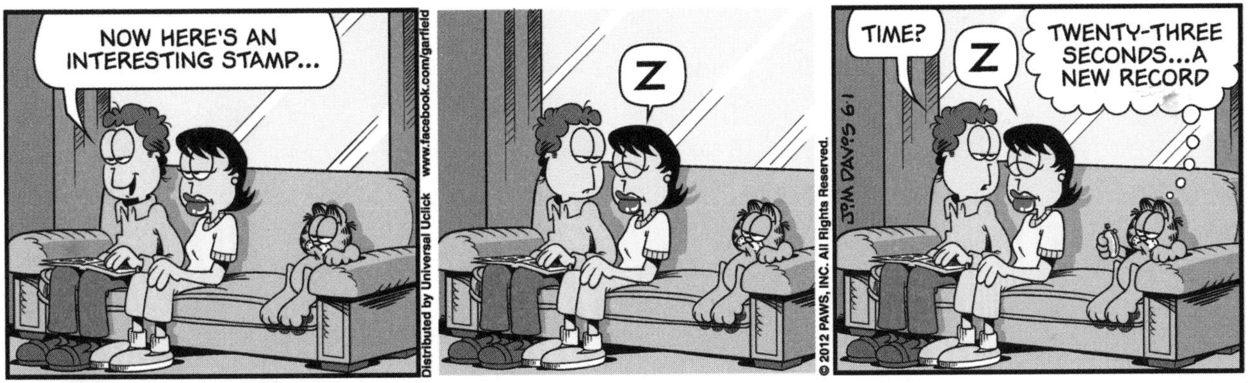
NOW HERE'S AN INTERESTING STAMP...
Z
TIME?
Z
TWENTY-THREE SECONDS...A NEW RECORD
JIM DAVIS 6-1
Distributed by Universal Uclick www.facebook.com/garfield
© 2012 PAWS, INC. All Rights Reserved.

THE JOKE'S ON JON

The great philosopher Plato said, "Comedy is pain mixed with pleasure." Jon and Garfield are proof of that. Garfield takes great pleasure inflicting pain on his poor owner.

But you can't really blame Garfield. Jon's dorky demeanor makes him the perfect target for practical jokes. Over the years, the portly prankster has battered Jon with an endless string of verbal jabs, and he's also subjected him to a lot of physical abuse. He's glued Jon's ear to the phone, greased the bottom of his shoes, poured peas down his pants, and put cat hair on his toothbrush. Garfield even tied Jon's shoestrings to a jet about to take off for Italy. Mamma mia!

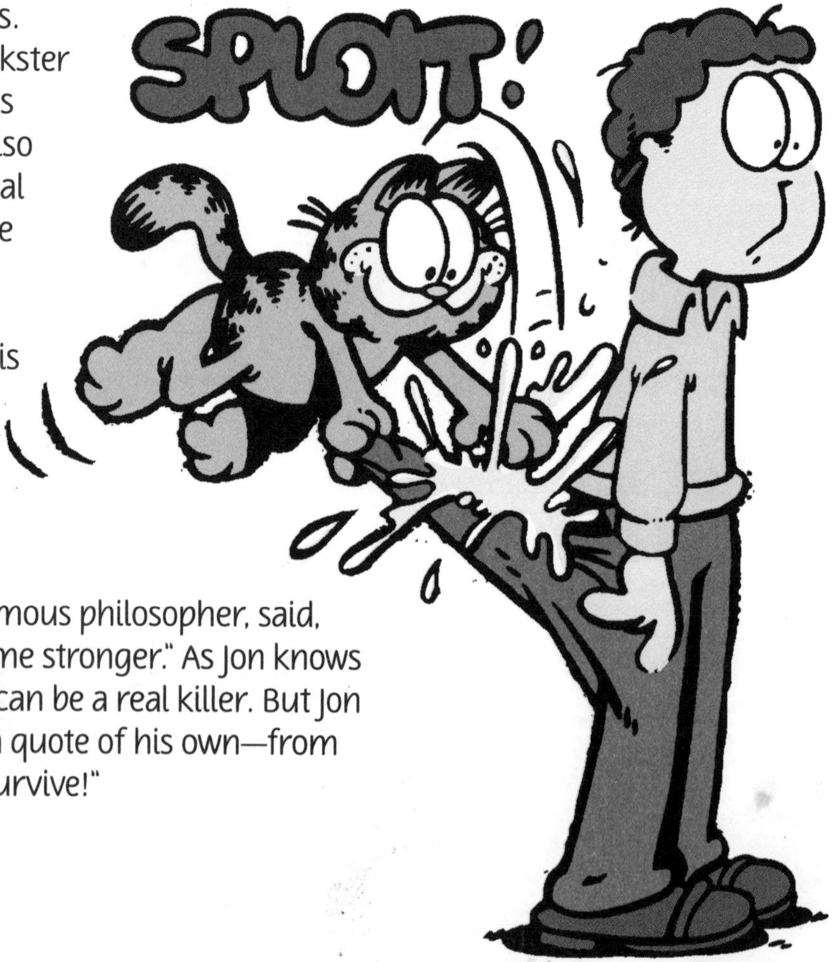
SPLOIT!

Friedrich Nietzsche, another famous philosopher, said, "What does not kill me, makes me stronger." As Jon knows all too well, living with Garfield can be a real killer. But Jon isn't worried. In fact, he offers a quote of his own—from his favorite disco song—"I will survive!"

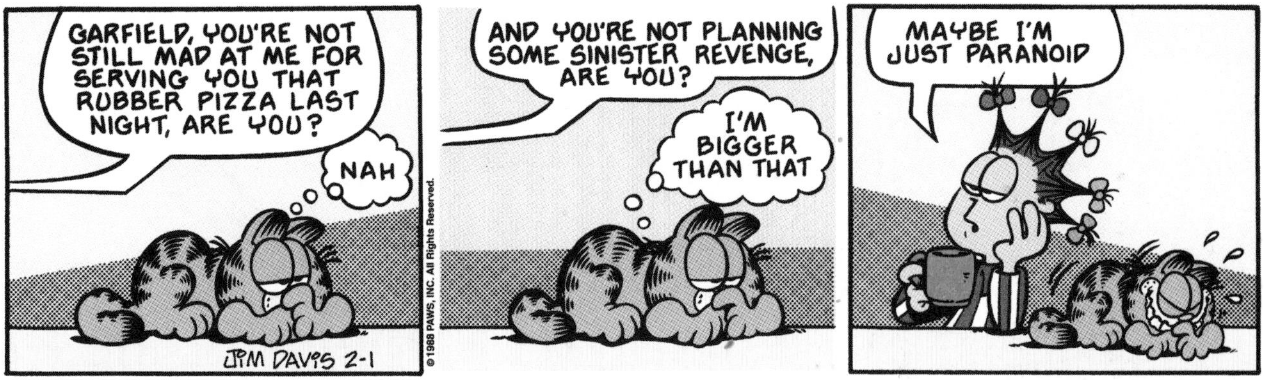
GARFIELD, YOU'RE NOT STILL MAD AT ME FOR SERVING YOU THAT RUBBER PIZZA LAST NIGHT, ARE YOU?
NAH
JIM DAVIS 2-1
© 1988 PAWS, INC. All Rights Reserved.
AND YOU'RE NOT PLANNING SOME SINISTER REVENGE, ARE YOU?
I'M BIGGER THAN THAT
MAYBE I'M JUST PARANOID

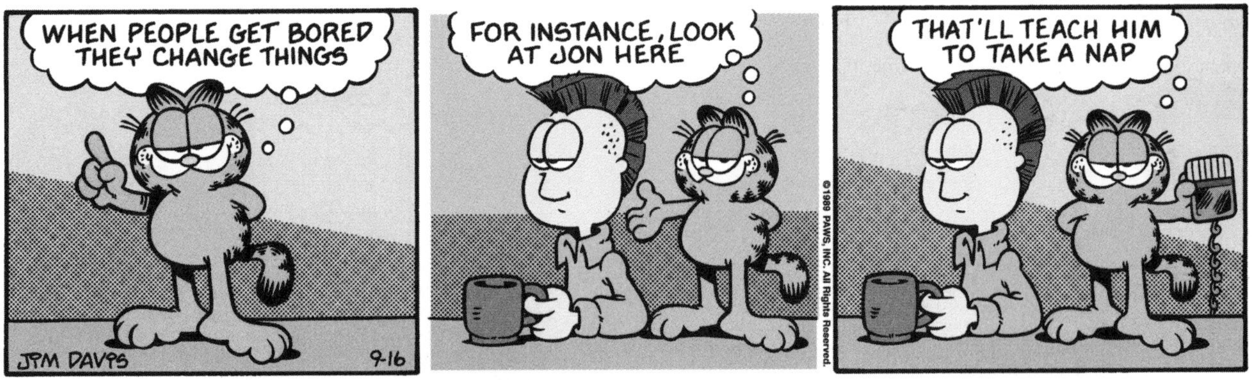
WHEN PEOPLE GET BORED THEY CHANGE THINGS
JIM DAVIS
9-16
FOR INSTANCE, LOOK AT JON HERE
©1989 PAWS, INC. All Rights Reserved.
THAT'LL TEACH HIM TO TAKE A NAP

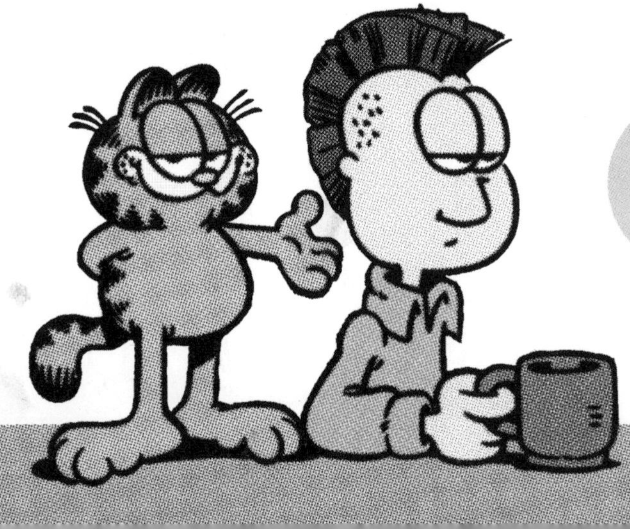

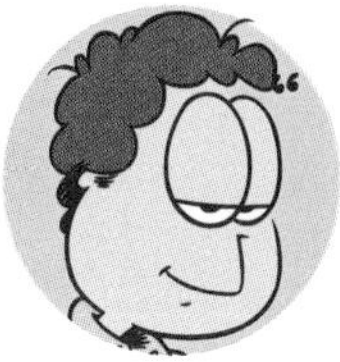

"This led to my short-lived band, Accordion Jon and the Polka Punks..."

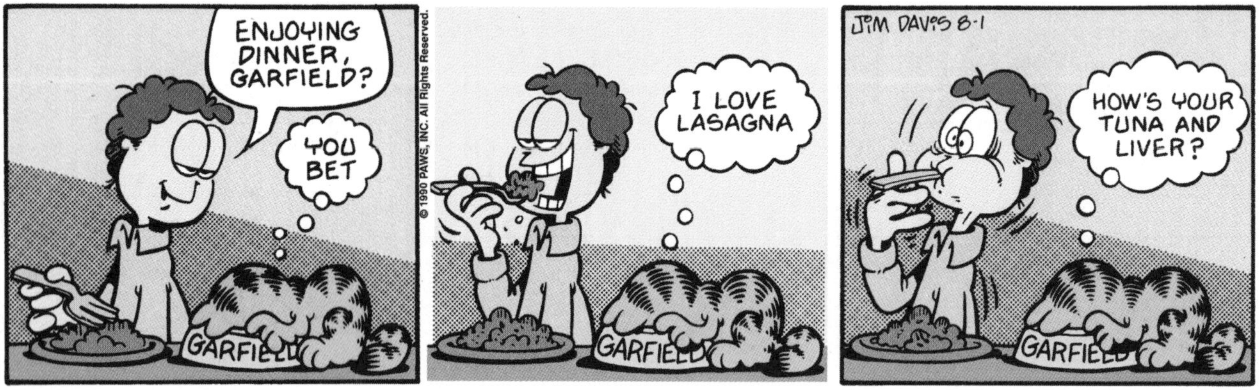
ENJOYING DINNER, GARFIELD?
YOU BET
GARFIELD
© 1990 PAWS, INC. All Rights Reserved.
I LOVE LASAGNA
GARFIELD
JIM DAVIS 8-1
HOW'S YOUR TUNA AND LIVER?
GARFIELD

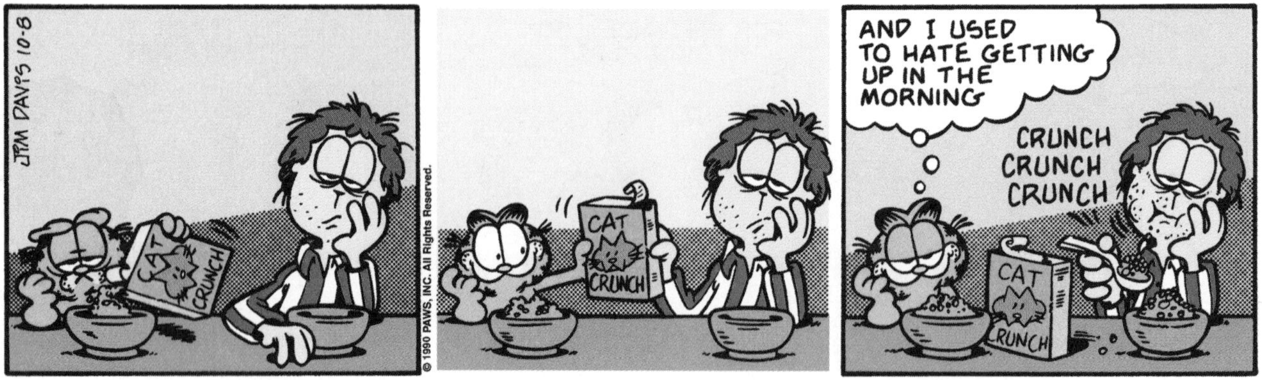
JIM DAVIS 10-8
CAT CRUNCH
© 1990 PAWS, INC. All Rights Reserved.
CAT CRUNCH
AND I USED TO HATE GETTING UP IN THE MORNING
CRUNCH CRUNCH CRUNCH
CAT CRUNCH

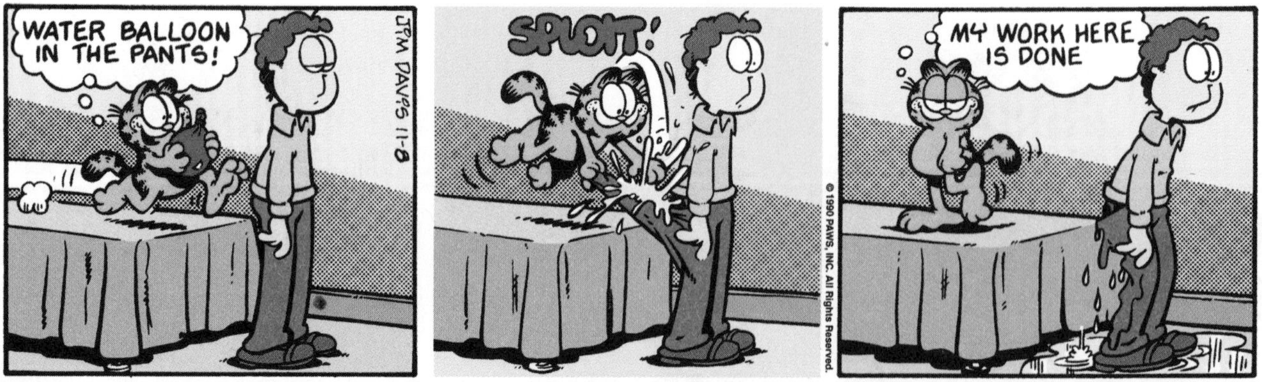
WATER BALLOON IN THE PANTS!
JIM DAVIS 11-8
SPLOIT!
© 1990 PAWS, INC. All Rights Reserved.
MY WORK HERE IS DONE

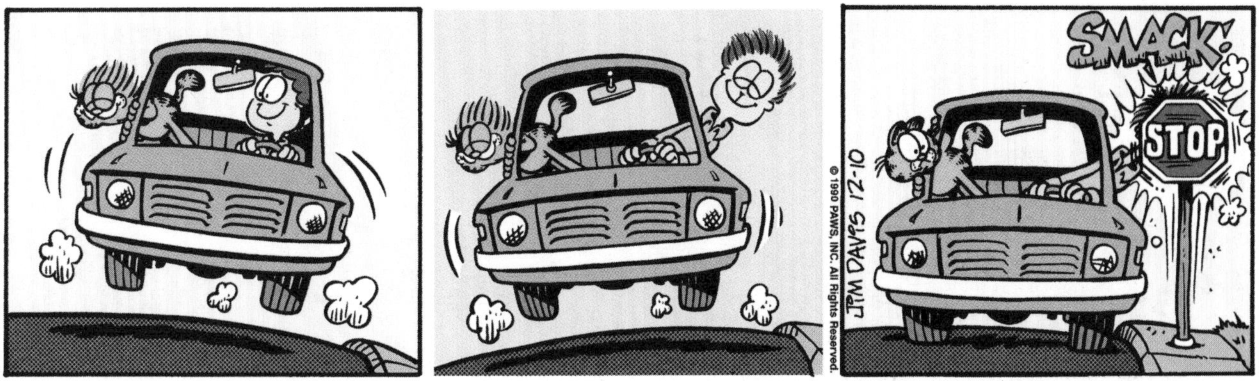
SMACK!
STOP
JIM DAVIS 12-10
© 1990 PAWS, INC. All Rights Reserved.

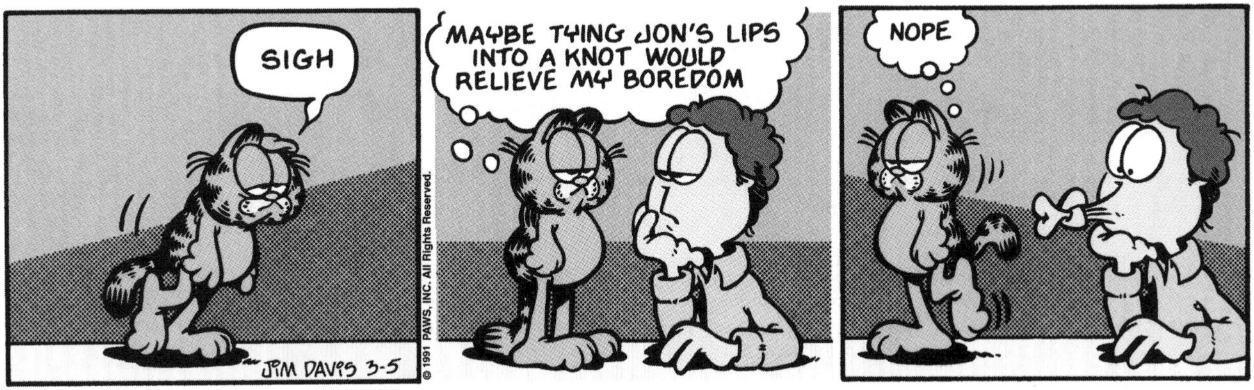
SIGH
JIM DAVIS 3-5
© 1991 PAWS, INC. All Rights Reserved.
MAYBE TYING JON'S LIPS INTO A KNOT WOULD RELIEVE MY BOREDOM
NOPE

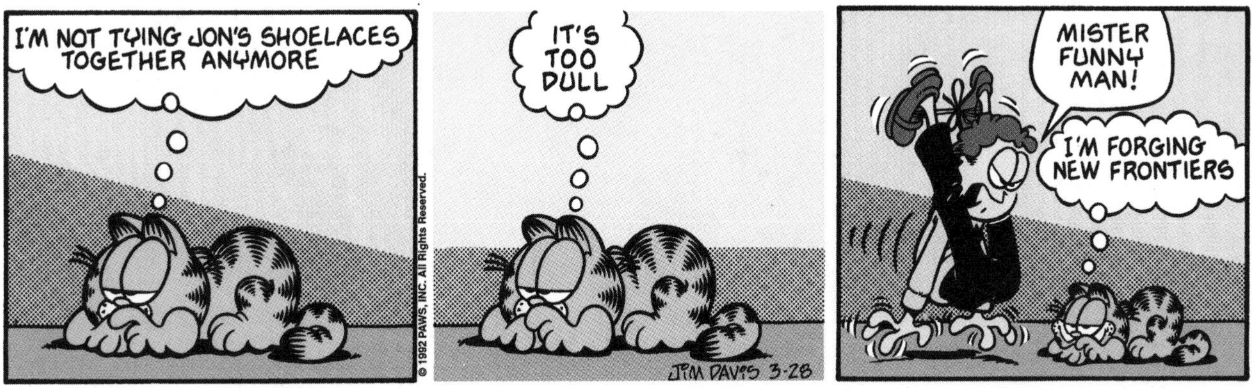
I'M NOT TYING JON'S SHOELACES TOGETHER ANYMORE
© 1992 PAWS, INC. All Rights Reserved.
IT'S TOO DULL
JIM DAVIS 3-28
MISTER FUNNY MAN!
I'M FORGING NEW FRONTIERS

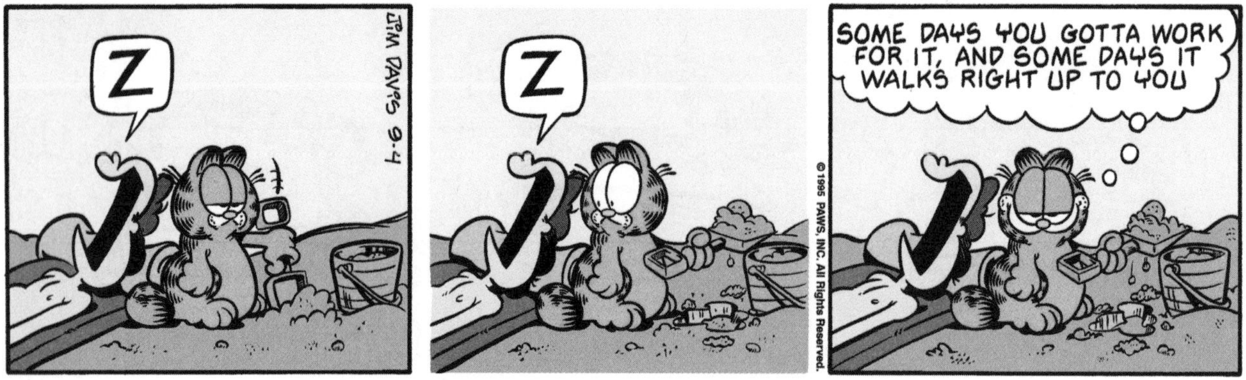
Z
JIM DAVIS 9-4
Z
SOME DAYS YOU GOTTA WORK FOR IT, AND SOME DAYS IT WALKS RIGHT UP TO YOU
© 1995 PAWS, INC. All Rights Reserved.

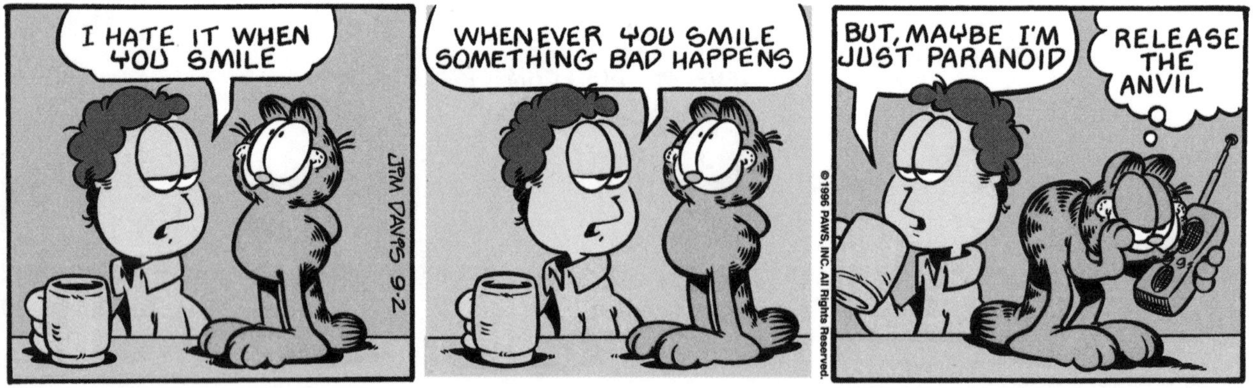
I HATE IT WHEN YOU SMILE
JIM DAVIS 9-2
WHENEVER YOU SMILE SOMETHING BAD HAPPENS
BUT, MAYBE I'M JUST PARANOID
RELEASE THE ANVIL
© 1996 PAWS, INC. All Rights Reserved.

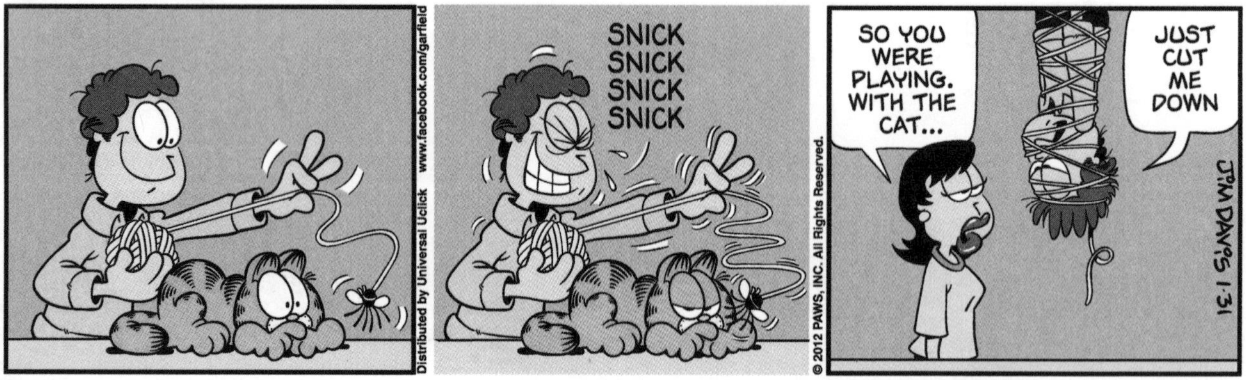
Distributed by Universal Uclick www.facebook.com/garfield
SNICK
SNICK
SNICK
SNICK
© 2012 PAWS, INC. All Rights Reserved.
SO YOU WERE PLAYING. WITH THE CAT...
JUST CUT ME DOWN
JIM DAVIS 1-31

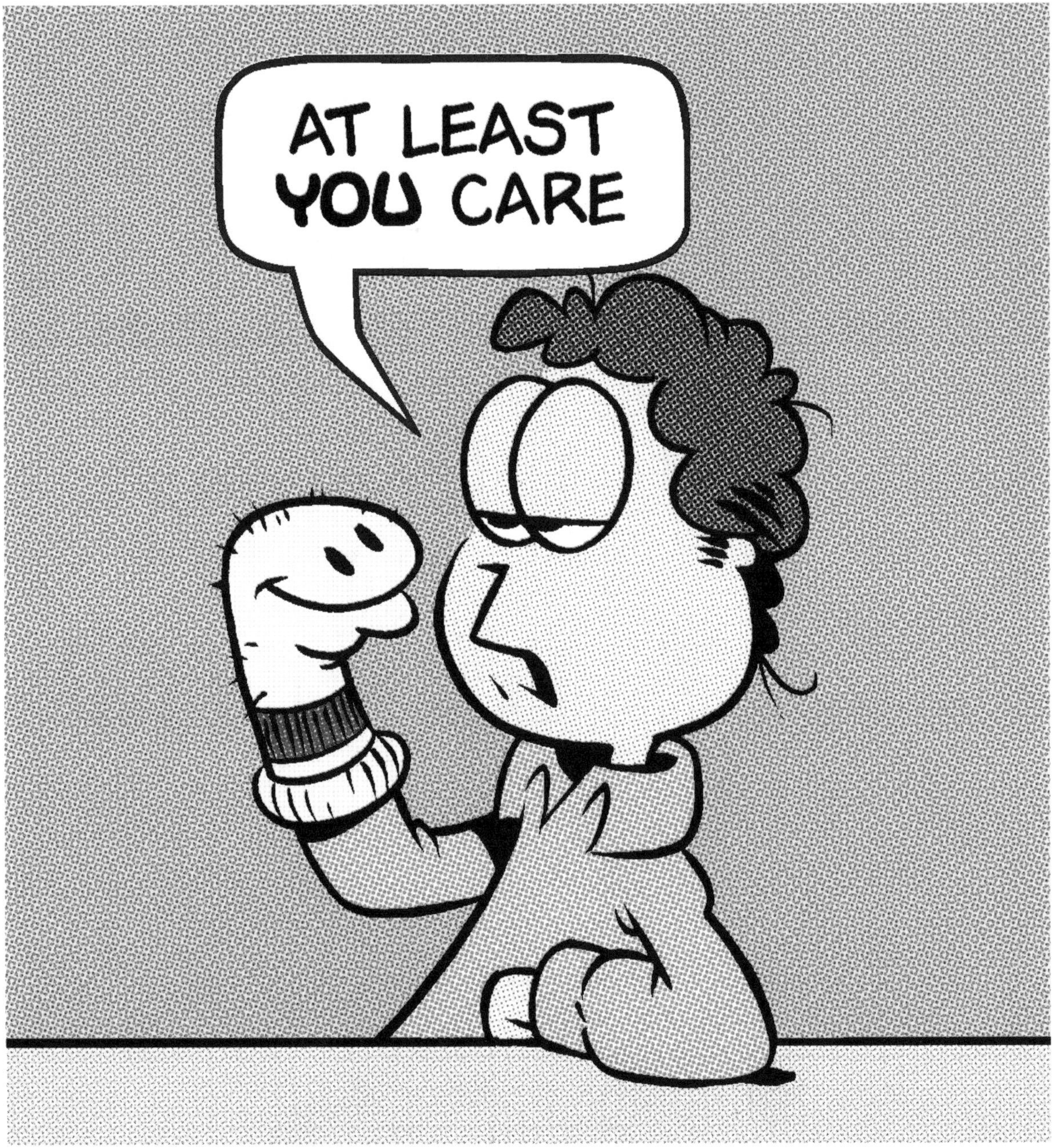
AT LEAST YOU CARE

HELLO?...NO, I JUST WOKE UP
Distributed by Universal Uclick www.facebook.com/garfield
OKAY, I'LL LOOK FOR IT
© 2012 PAWS, INC. All Rights Reserved.
LIZ CAN'T FIND HER MAKEUP CASE
HAVEN'T SEEN IT!!!
JIM DAVIS 4-13

Geekend Warrior

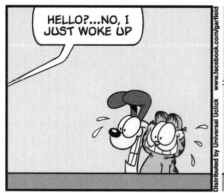

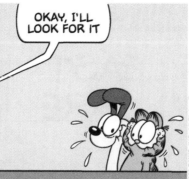

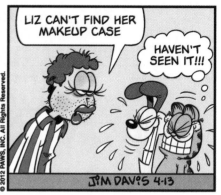

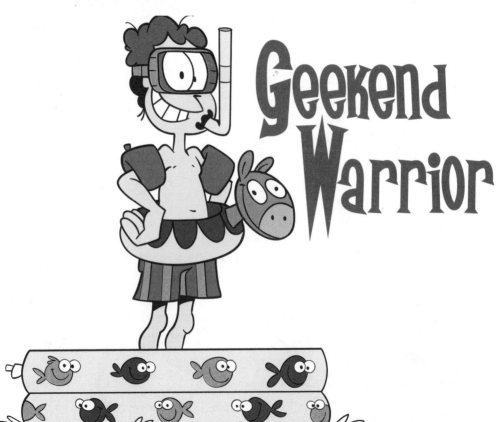

JON ARBUCKLE'S TOP TEN FAVORITE TALK SHOW TOPICS

10. **Vulcan Mating Rituals**

9. **Disco Dorks**

8. **Celebrity Bedwetters**

7. **Superpowers: Flying vs. Invisibility**

6. **Fear of Beards**

5. **Fun with Cheese**

4. **Women Who Love Men Who Love Bunny Slippers**

3. **101 Uses for Dental Floss**

2. **Chubby Chasers**

1. **Geeks Gone Wild!**

TOP TEN PLACES JON BUYS HIS CLOTHES

10. **Ace's Bodacious Bodywear**

9. **Tacky Shack**

8. **Geeks "R" Us**

7. **The Guy Sty**

6. **Nerd & Tailor**

5. **The Clown Closet**

4. **Bowtie Boutique**

3. **Saps Fifth Avenue**

2. **Beanies for Weenies**

1. **Dweeb Barn**

TRAVELS WITH GARFIELD

Jon's not exactly what you'd call a world traveler. His idea of going someplace exotic is breakfast at the International House of Pancakes. But Jon has had his share of (mis)adventures with Garfield and Odie.

Garfield *hates* camping with Jon. As far as the fat cat's concerned, there's nothing great about the "great outdoors." But Jon doesn't seem to mind the bugs, snakes, critters, potential bear attacks, and lousy weather. Maybe it's better than spending another dull Friday night counting the hairs on his arm (17,890, officially), drawing faces on all the pillows, or waxing the dishes (what else do you do after you wash them?).

If camping is bad, vacations are worse. The "Tightwad Tourist" (as Garfield calls Jon) always seems to end up on the most excruciating excursions imaginable. One time, Jon and Garfield flew third class (that's where they seat you under the landing gear).

Then there was the time Jon booked something "tropical and cheap" and wound up on the island of Guano-Guano. Not only was the weather hot and sticky (think 115% humidity), the hotel didn't have room service (or even a decent vending machine), and Jon's underwear became infested with leaf weasels (don't ask!).

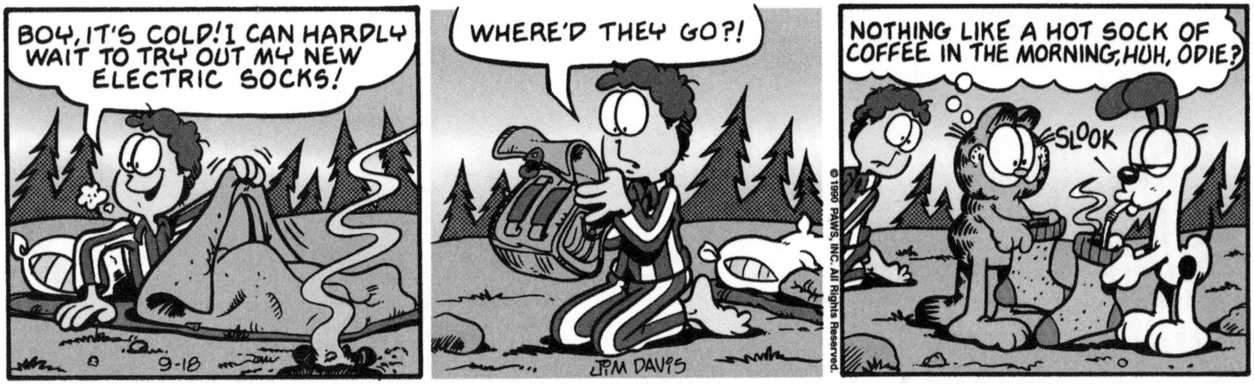
BOY, IT'S COLD! I CAN HARDLY WAIT TO TRY OUT MY NEW ELECTRIC SOCKS!
9-18
WHERE'D THEY GO?!
JIM DAVIS
NOTHING LIKE A HOT SOCK OF COFFEE IN THE MORNING, HUH, ODIE?
SLOOK
© 1990 PAWS, INC. All Rights Reserved.

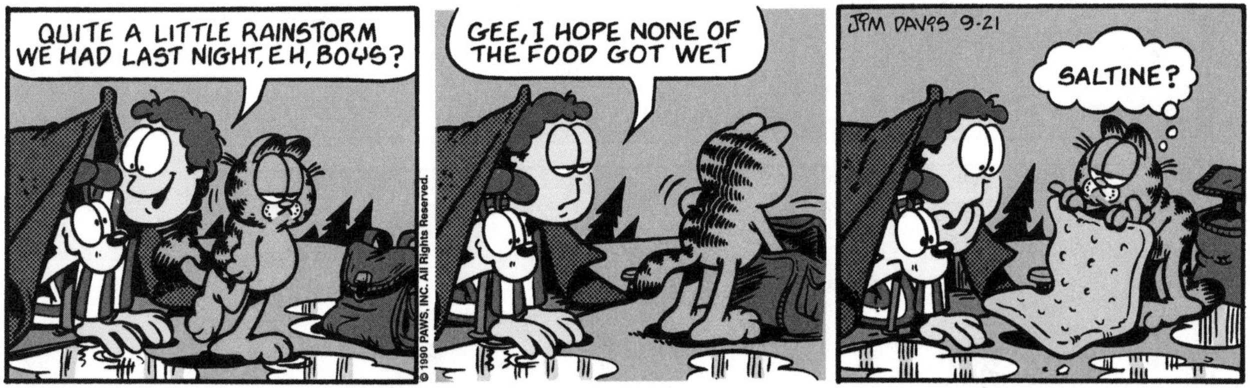
QUITE A LITTLE RAINSTORM WE HAD LAST NIGHT, EH, BOYS?
© 1990 PAWS, INC. All Rights Reserved.
GEE, I HOPE NONE OF THE FOOD GOT WET
JIM DAVIS 9-21
SALTINE?

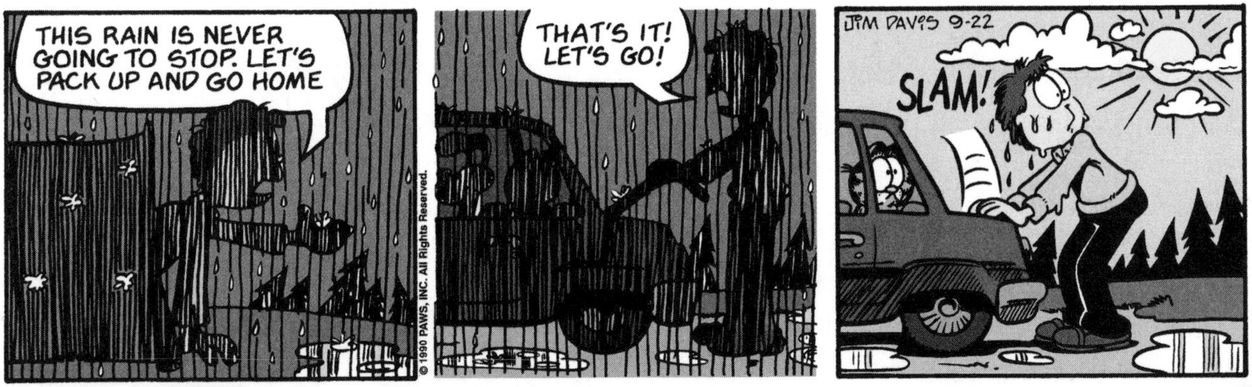
THIS RAIN IS NEVER GOING TO STOP. LET'S PACK UP AND GO HOME
© 1990 PAWS, INC. All Rights Reserved.
THAT'S IT! LET'S GO!
JIM DAVIS 9-22
SLAM!

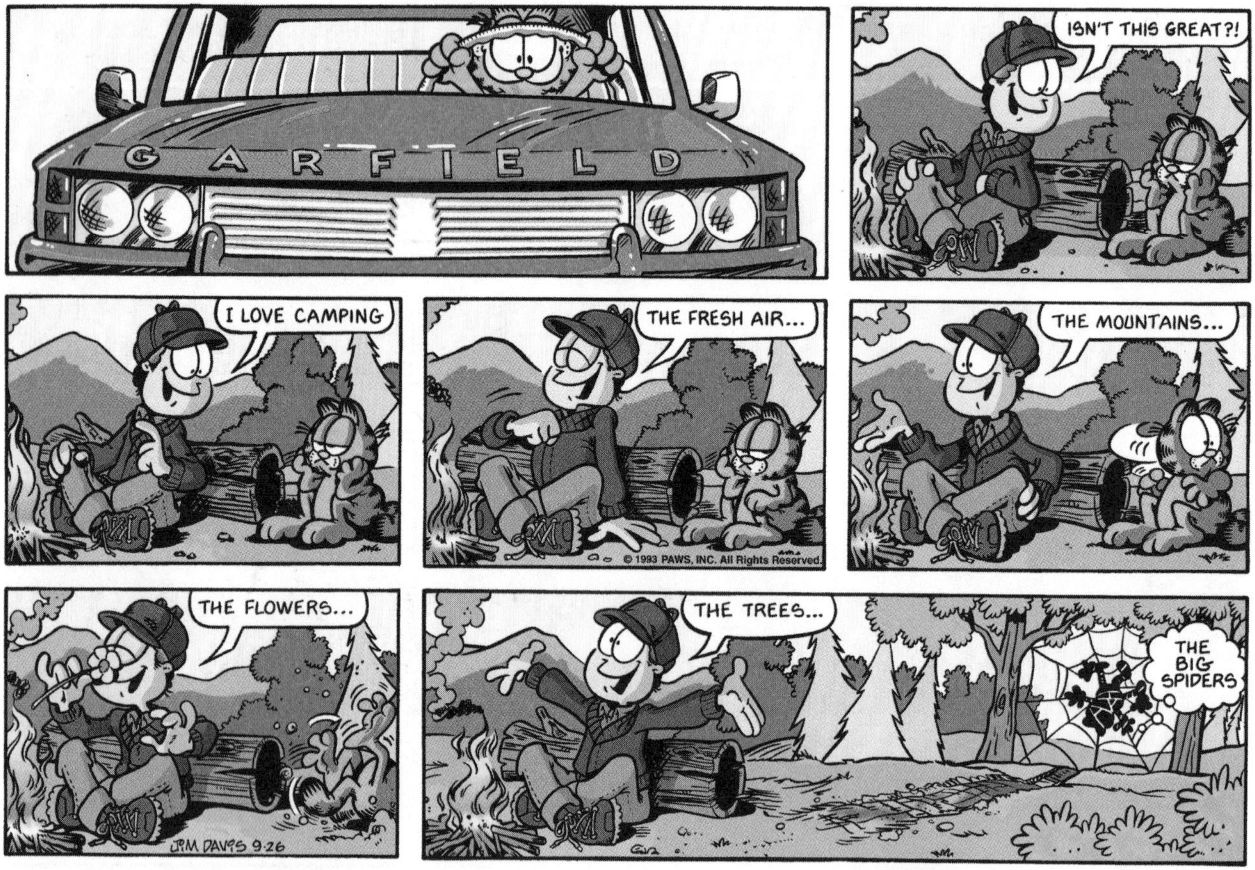
GARFIELD
ISN'T THIS GREAT?!
I LOVE CAMPING
THE FRESH AIR...
© 1993 PAWS, INC. All Rights Reserved.
THE MOUNTAINS...
THE FLOWERS...
JIM DAVIS 9·26
THE TREES...
THE BIG SPIDERS

THINGS JON DOES WHEN HE'S FEELING RECKLESS

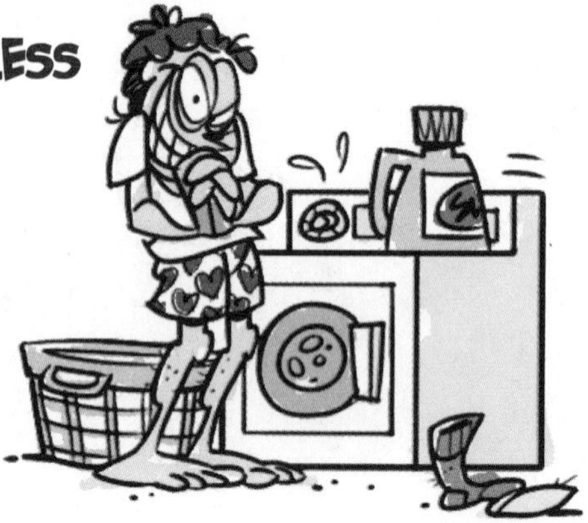

- Doesn't wash dark colors separately
- Sits too close to the TV
- Uses public restroom
- Totally disregards his gums
- Drinks milk without checking expiration date
- Wakes Garfield

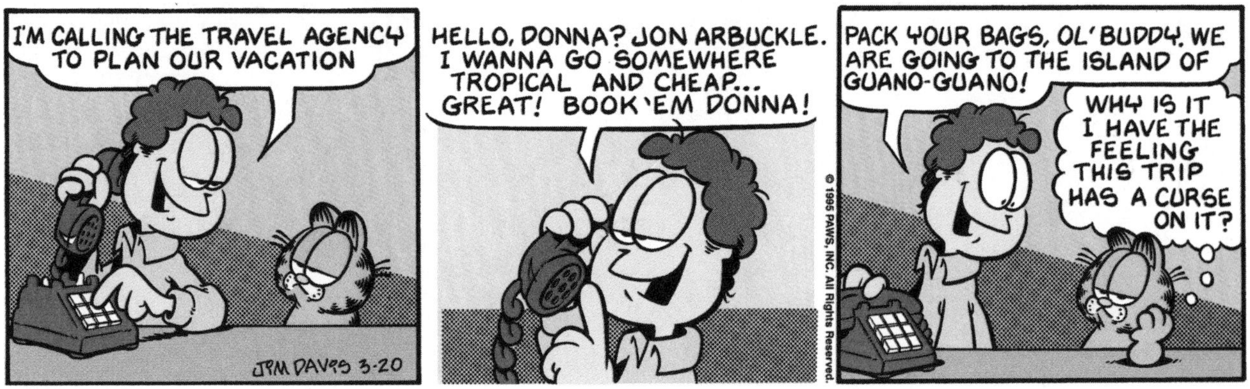
I'M CALLING THE TRAVEL AGENCY TO PLAN OUR VACATION
JPM DAVPS 3-20
HELLO, DONNA? JON ARBUCKLE. I WANNA GO SOMEWHERE TROPICAL AND CHEAP... GREAT! BOOK 'EM DONNA!
© 1995 PAWS, INC. All Rights Reserved.
PACK YOUR BAGS, OL' BUDDY. WE ARE GOING TO THE ISLAND OF GUANO-GUANO!
WHY IS IT I HAVE THE FEELING THIS TRIP HAS A CURSE ON IT?

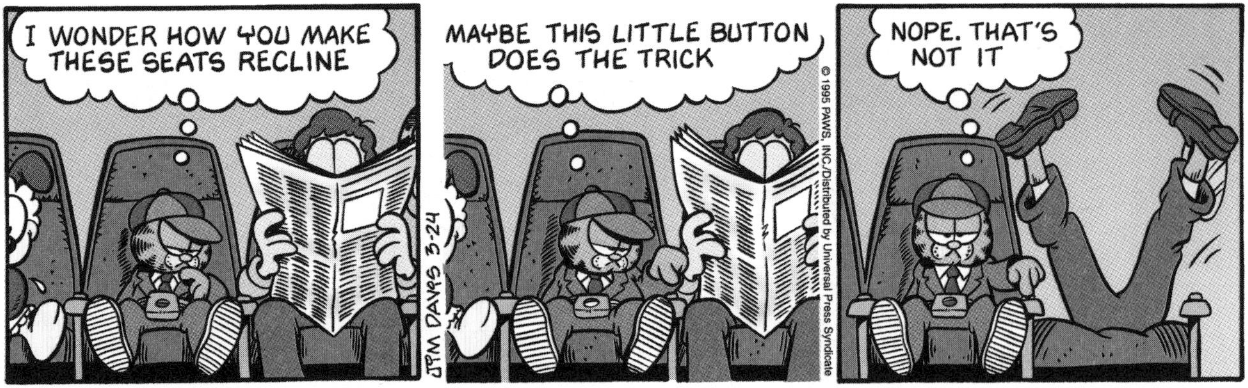
I WONDER HOW YOU MAKE THESE SEATS RECLINE
JPM DAVPS 3-24
MAYBE THIS LITTLE BUTTON DOES THE TRICK
© 1995 PAWS, INC./Distributed by Universal Press Syndicate
NOPE. THAT'S NOT IT

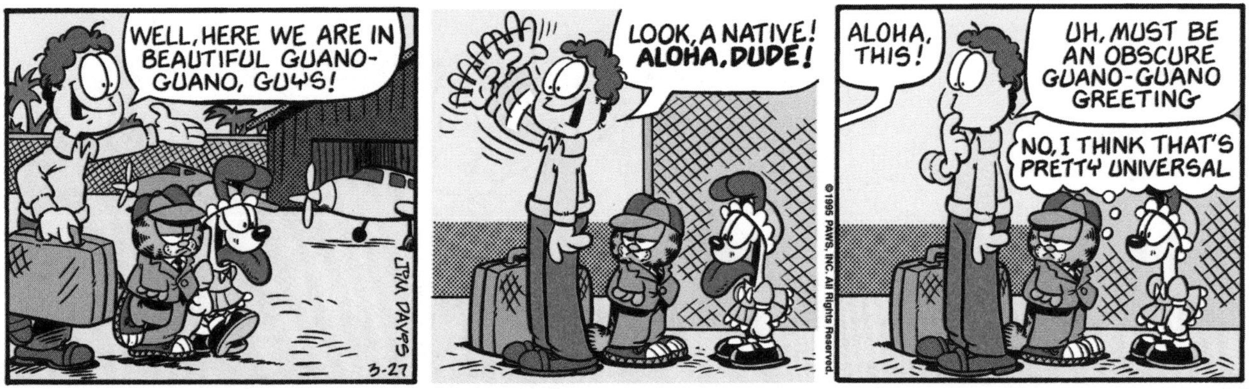
WELL, HERE WE ARE IN BEAUTIFUL GUANO-GUANO, GUYS!
JPM DAVPS 3-27
LOOK, A NATIVE! ALOHA, DUDE!
© 1995 PAWS, INC. All Rights Reserved.
ALOHA, THIS!
UH, MUST BE AN OBSCURE GUANO-GUANO GREETING
NO, I THINK THAT'S PRETTY UNIVERSAL

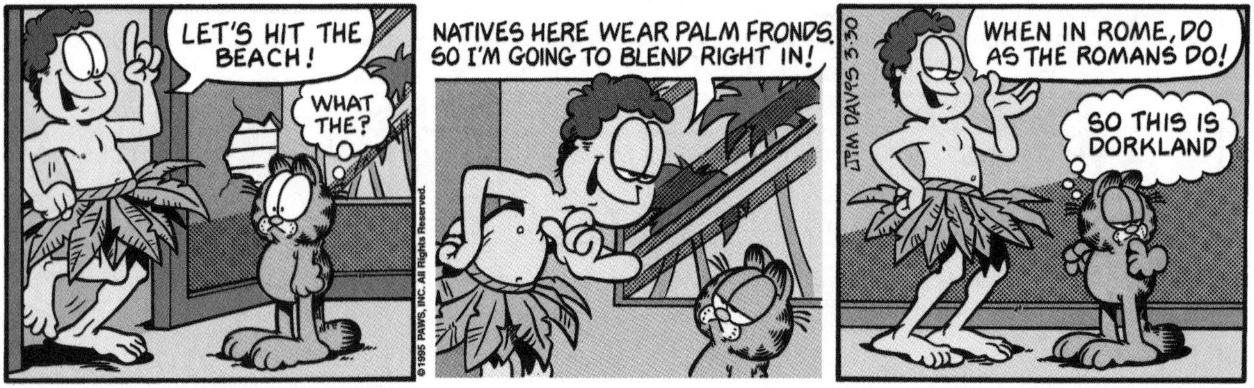
LET'S HIT THE BEACH!
WHAT THE?
© 1995 PAWS, INC. All Rights Reserved.
NATIVES HERE WEAR PALM FRONDS. SO I'M GOING TO BLEND RIGHT IN!
WHEN IN ROME, DO AS THE ROMANS DO!
SO THIS IS DORKLAND

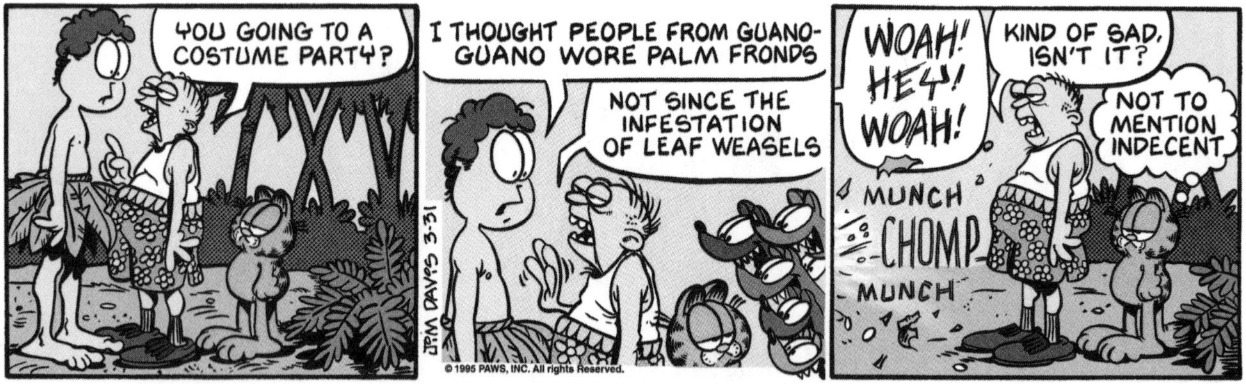
YOU GOING TO A COSTUME PARTY?
I THOUGHT PEOPLE FROM GUANO-GUANO WORE PALM FRONDS
NOT SINCE THE INFESTATION OF LEAF WEASELS
© 1995 PAWS, INC. All rights Reserved.
WOAH! HEY! WOAH!
MUNCH
CHOMP
MUNCH
KIND OF SAD, ISN'T IT?
NOT TO MENTION INDECENT

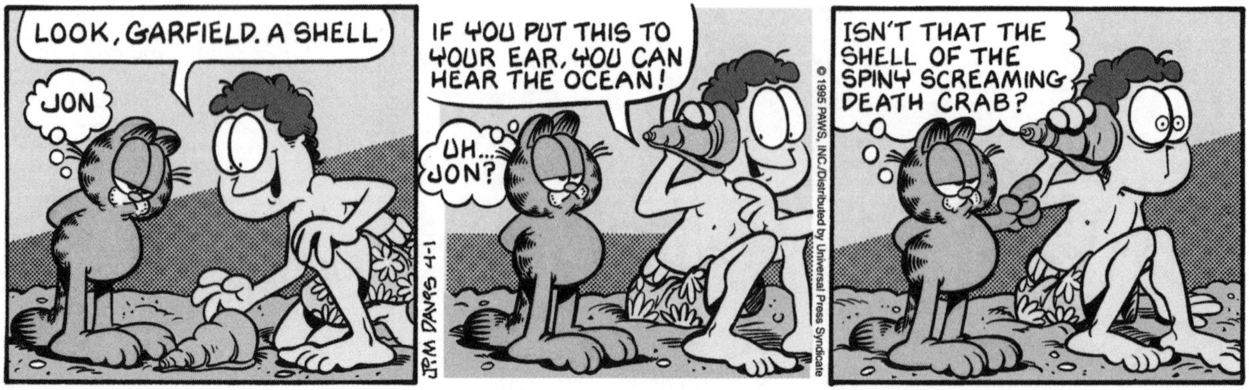
LOOK, GARFIELD. A SHELL
JON
IF YOU PUT THIS TO YOUR EAR, YOU CAN HEAR THE OCEAN!
UH... JON?
© 1995 PAWS, INC./Distributed by Universal Press Syndicate
ISN'T THAT THE SHELL OF THE SPINY SCREAMING DEATH CRAB?

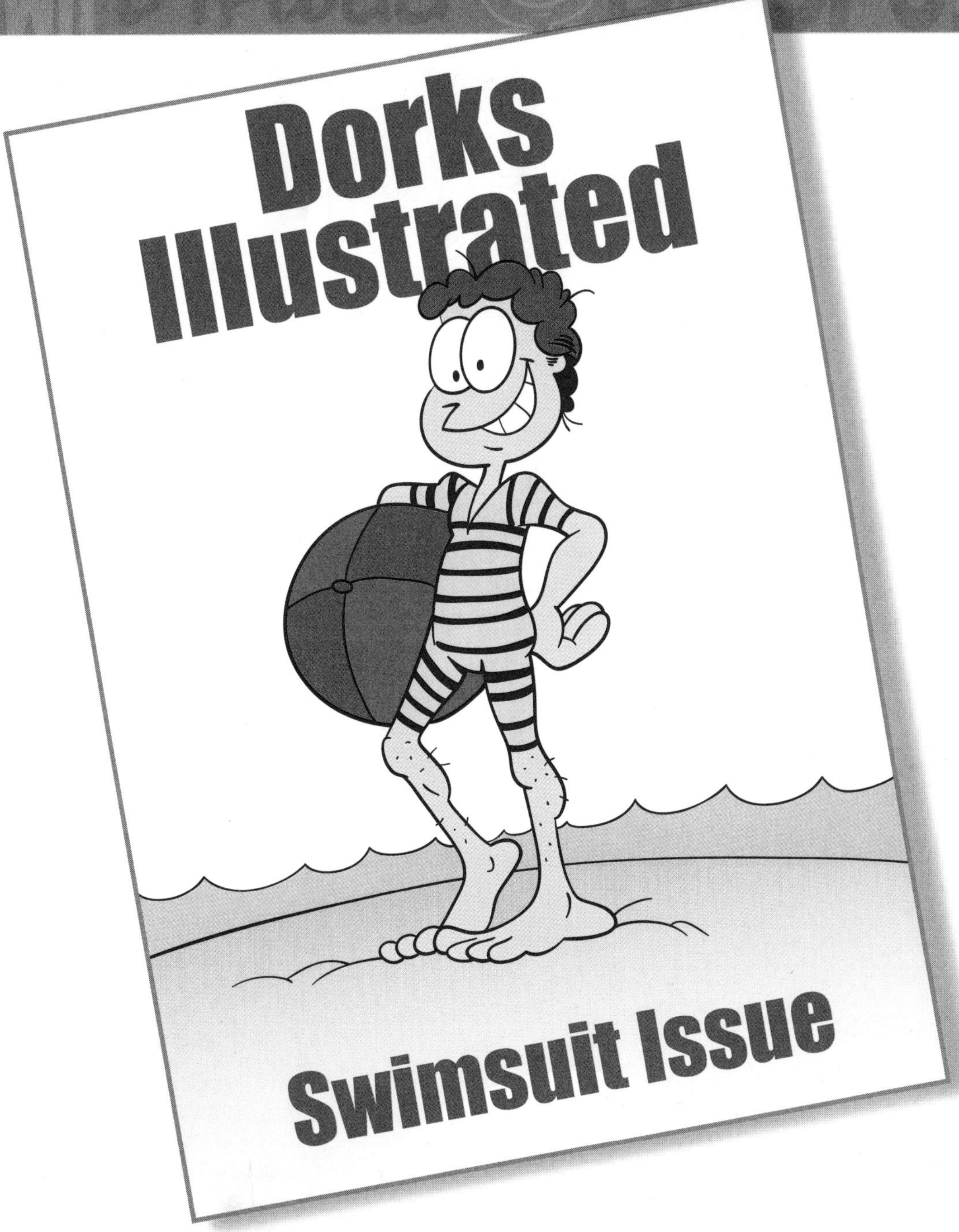
Dorks Illustrated
Swimsuit Issue

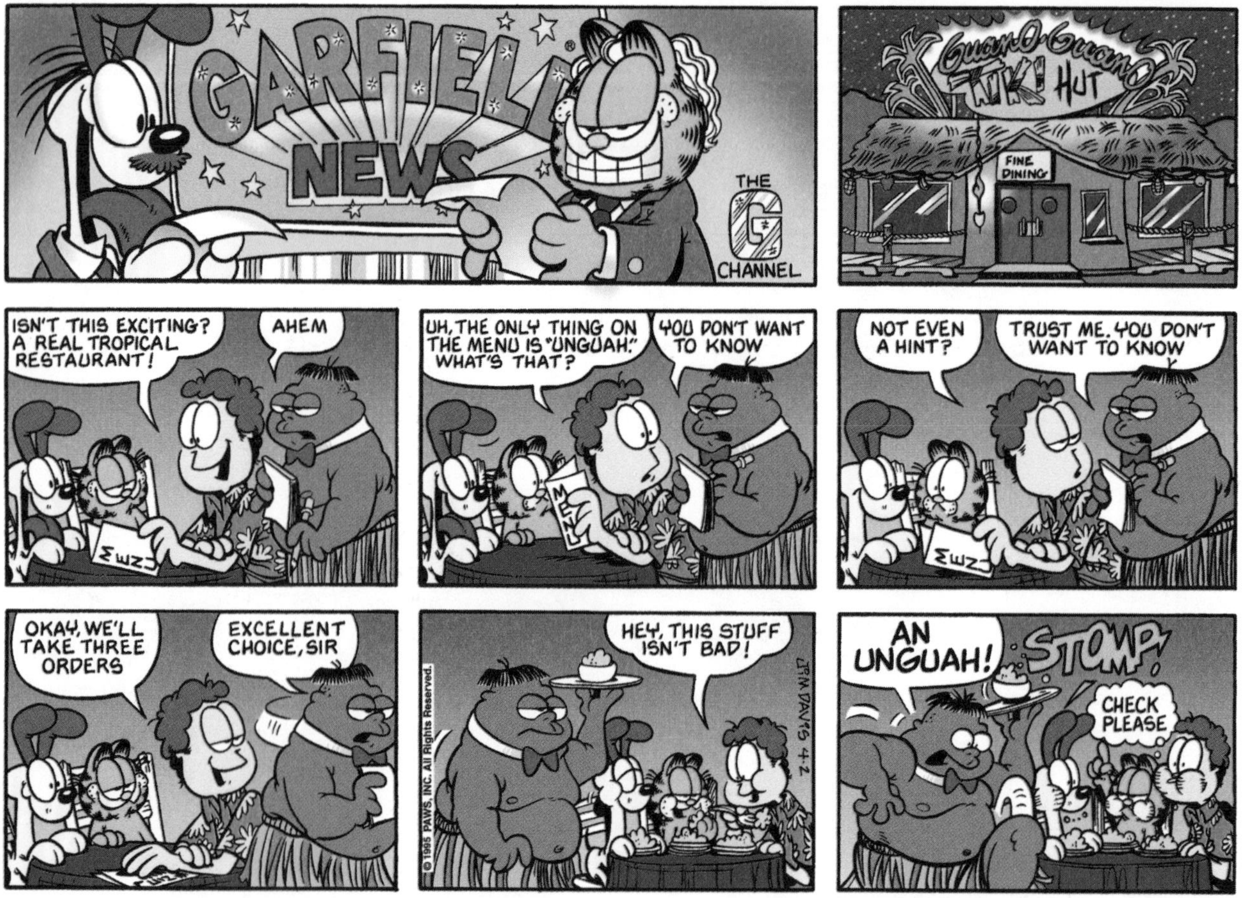
GARFIELD
NEWS
THE G CHANNEL
Guano-Guano TIKI HUT
FINE DINING
ISN'T THIS EXCITING? A REAL TROPICAL RESTAURANT!
AHEM
UH, THE ONLY THING ON THE MENU IS "UNGUAH." WHAT'S THAT?
MENU
YOU DON'T WANT TO KNOW
NOT EVEN A HINT?
TRUST ME. YOU DON'T WANT TO KNOW
OKAY, WE'LL TAKE THREE ORDERS
EXCELLENT CHOICE, SIR
© 1995 PAWS, INC. All Rights Reserved.
HEY, THIS STUFF ISN'T BAD!
JPM DAVIS 4-2
AN UNGUAH!
STOMP
CHECK PLEASE

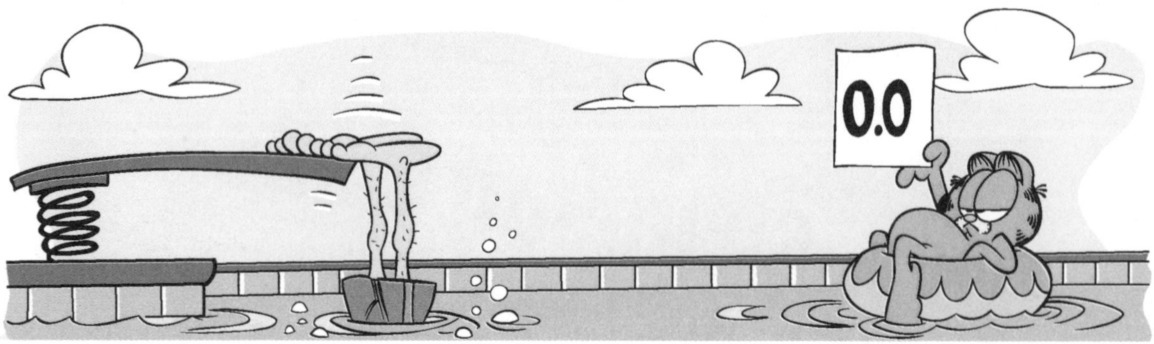
0.0

JON ARBUCKLE'S TOP TEN PICK-UP LINES

10. "EXCUSE ME, HAVE YOU SEEN MY NOBEL PRIZE AROUND HERE ANYWHERE?"

9. "I'M STILL INTO MACRAMÉ. HOW ABOUT YOU?"

8. "YOU LOOK LIKE A WOMAN WITH LOW STANDARDS."

7. "YOU'VE CERTAINLY GOT THE FIGURE FOR THAT DUMPY
   CASHIER'S OUTFIT."

6. "WHEN I SAW YOU, I LOST CONTROL OF ALL
   MY BODILY FUNCTIONS."

5. "EVER BEEN HIT ON BY A CARTOON
   CHARACTER?"

4. "ARE YOU AS LONELY AND
   DEPRESSED AS I AM?"

3. "I HAVE VERY FEW COMMUNICABLE
   DISEASES."

2. "PLEASE. I'M BEGGING YOU."

1. "UH...UH...UM...DUH...COUGH..."

GEEK CHIC

DIARY OF A DORK: JON'S BLOG

Jon used to write in his diary by hand; now he blogs on his computer. But one thing hasn't changed: He's still BOR-ING! His entries range from the mundane to the inane: from cleaning the caked-on gunk on his barbecue grill to, well. . .see for yourself what the social "twit wit" has to say. . . .

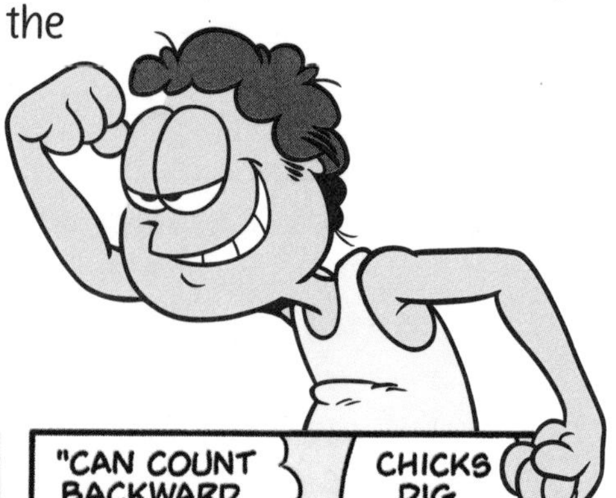

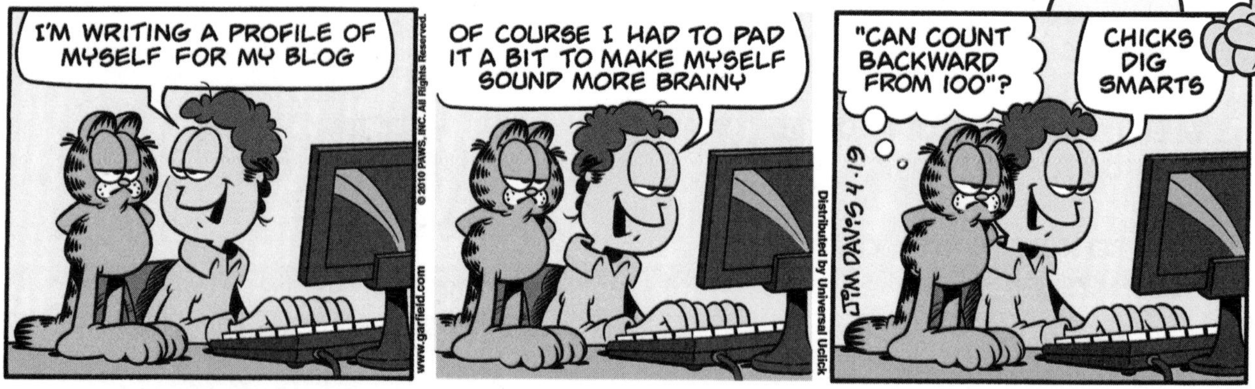

I'M WRITING A PROFILE OF MYSELF FOR MY BLOG
© 2010 PAWS, INC. All Rights Reserved.
www.garfield.com
OF COURSE I HAD TO PAD IT A BIT TO MAKE MYSELF SOUND MORE BRAINY
Distributed by Universal Uclick
"CAN COUNT BACKWARD FROM 100"?
CHICKS DIG SMARTS
JPM DAVPS 4-19

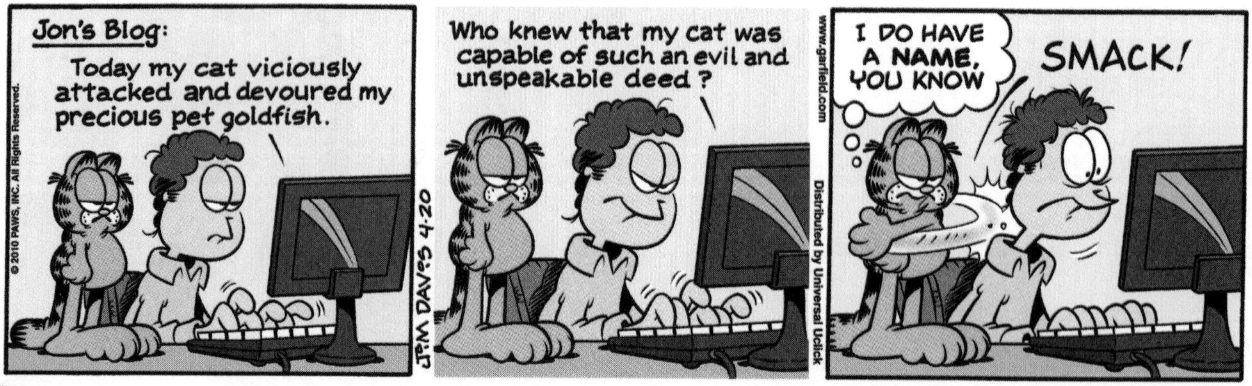

Jon's Blog:
Today my cat viciously attacked and devoured my precious pet goldfish.
© 2010 PAWS, INC. All Rights Reserved.
Who knew that my cat was capable of such an evil and unspeakable deed ?
JPM DAVPS 4-20
www.garfield.com
Distributed by Universal Uclick
I DO HAVE A NAME, YOU KNOW
SMACK!

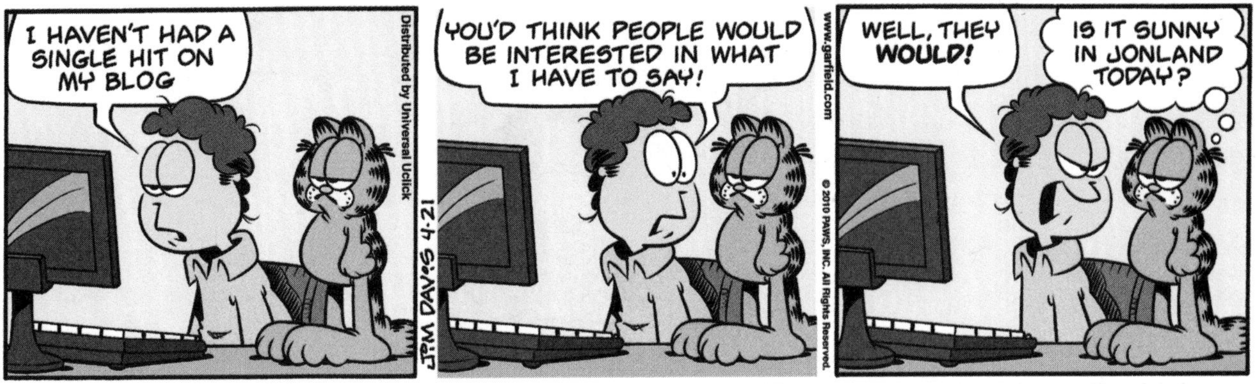
I HAVEN'T HAD A SINGLE HIT ON MY BLOG
Distributed by Universal Uclick
JIM DAVIS 4-21
YOU'D THINK PEOPLE WOULD BE INTERESTED IN WHAT I HAVE TO SAY!
www.garfield.com
© 2010 PAWS, INC. All Rights Reserved.
WELL, THEY **WOULD!**
IS IT SUNNY IN JONLAND TODAY?

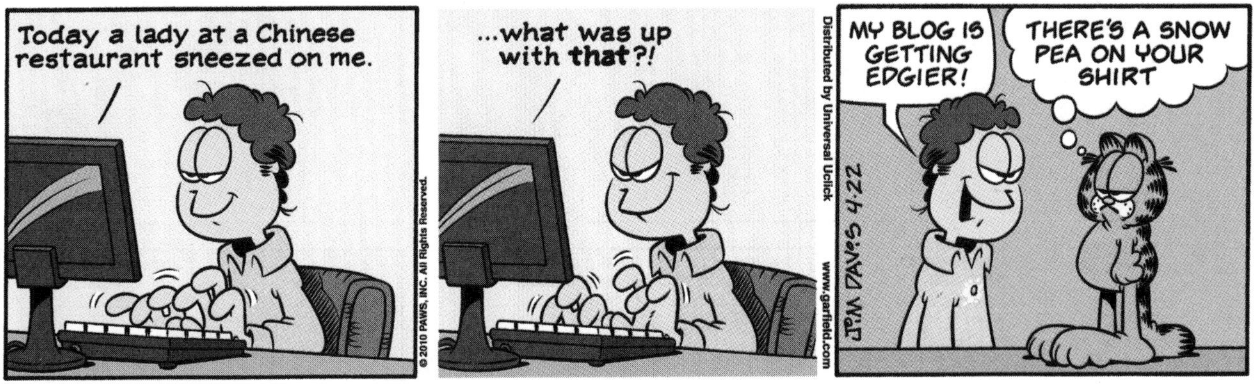
Today a lady at a Chinese restaurant sneezed on me.
© 2010 PAWS, INC. All Rights Reserved.
...what was up with **that**?!
Distributed by Universal Uclick
www.garfield.com
JIM DAVIS 4-22
MY BLOG IS GETTING EDGIER!
THERE'S A SNOW PEA ON YOUR SHIRT

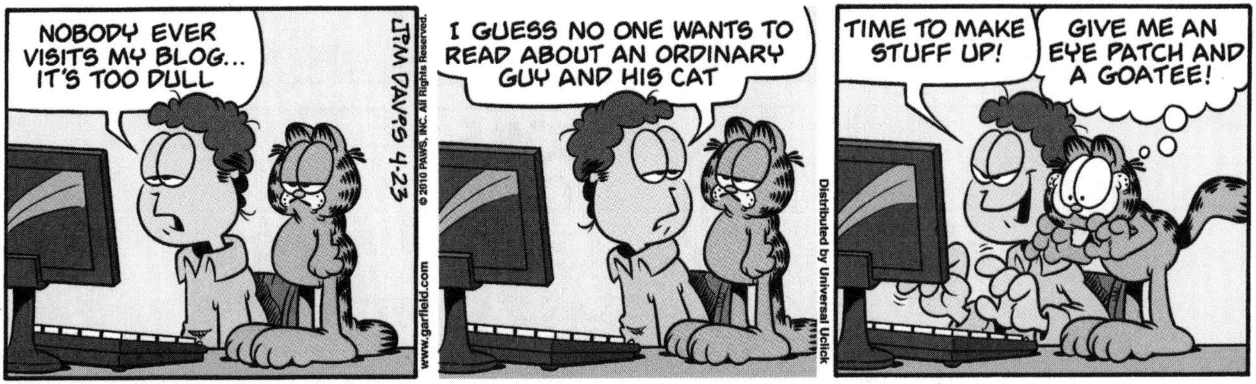
NOBODY EVER VISITS MY BLOG... IT'S TOO DULL
JIM DAVIS 4-23
© 2010 PAWS, INC. All Rights Reserved.
www.garfield.com
I GUESS NO ONE WANTS TO READ ABOUT AN ORDINARY GUY AND HIS CAT
Distributed by Universal Uclick
TIME TO MAKE STUFF UP!
GIVE ME AN EYE PATCH AND A GOATEE!

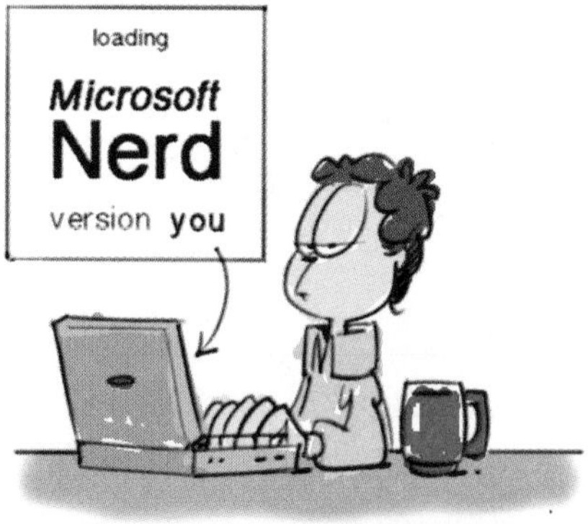
loading
Microsoft
Nerd
version you

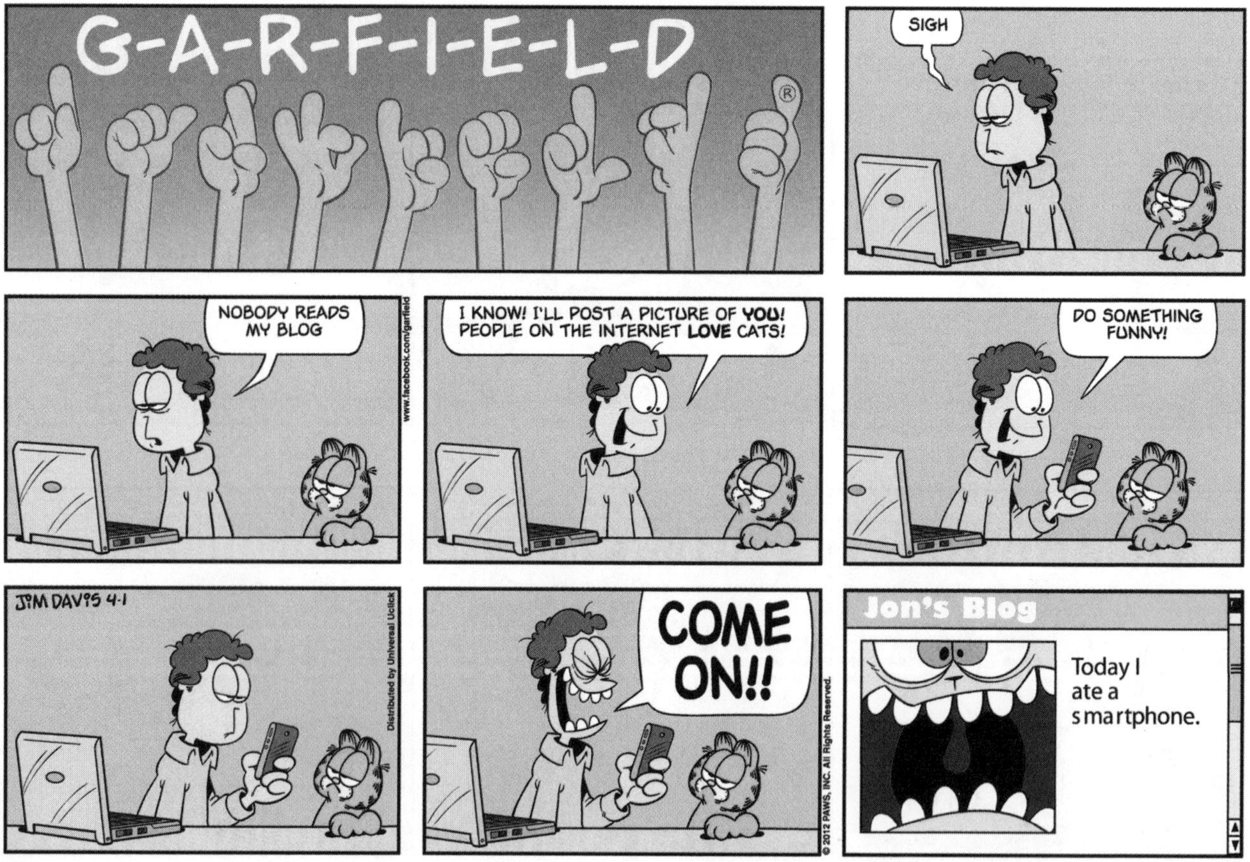
G-A-R-F-I-E-L-D
SIGH
NOBODY READS MY BLOG
www.facebook.com/garfield
I KNOW! I'LL POST A PICTURE OF YOU! PEOPLE ON THE INTERNET LOVE CATS!
DO SOMETHING FUNNY!
JIM DAVIS 4-1
Distributed by Universal Uclick
COME ON!!
© 2012 PAWS, INC. All Rights Reserved.
Jon's Blog
Today I ate a smartphone.

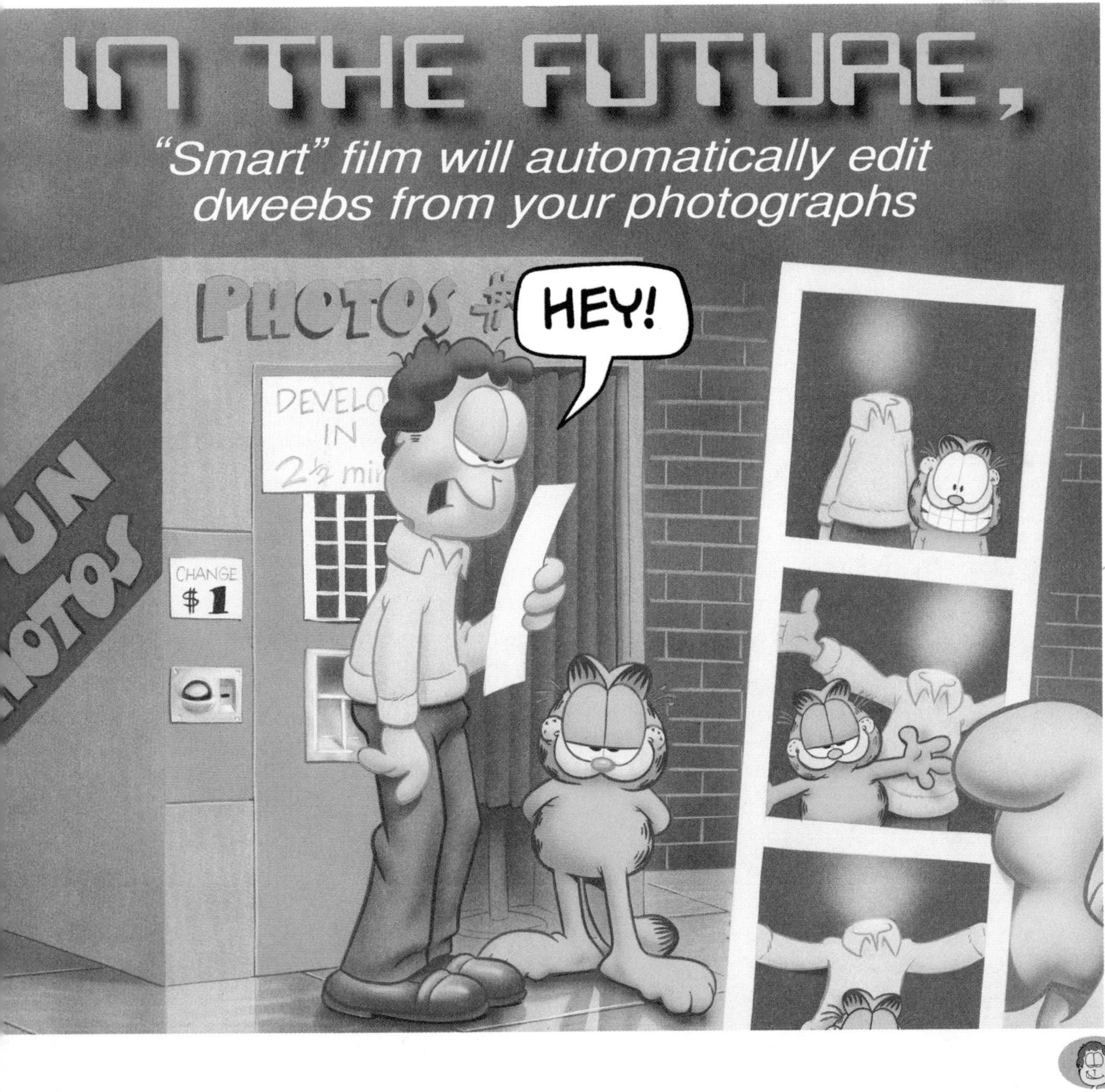
IN THE FUTURE,
"Smart" film will automatically edit dweebs from your photographs
PHOTOS
HEY!
CHANGE $1

THE DORKY DOZEN

You can only write what you know. . . .

I'm Jon Arbuckle.

When I write for Jon, all I have to do is conjure up my college dating days. I was the fraternity strikeout king! It's hard to say why I had so much trouble getting dates; primarily because there were so many reasons. I always waited until the last minute to call anyone. Who knew when there would be a hot game of double-deck euchre starting in the card room? I could never afford to take a girl out on a real date (like one with food). In a day of bell-bottoms, I still sported jeans with a six-inch peg. Accessorize that with a bright red Ban Lon shirt and matching Hush Puppies (avec red socks), and well, you get a reputation. . . . But, darn it, you gotta love Jon/me because I/Jon always look on the bright side of things. Don Quixote said it best, "Tomorrow will be a new day."

Jon is an eternal optimist. . .even when he's getting stood up by yet another blind date or hung up on for the hundredth time. That optimism is why fans love Jon. So much so that they started feeling sorry for him and his endless bad luck with women. They said, "Can you give Jon a life, please?" I was happy to oblige. After all, there's only so much abuse one guy can take (and I'd certainly given him enough over the years).

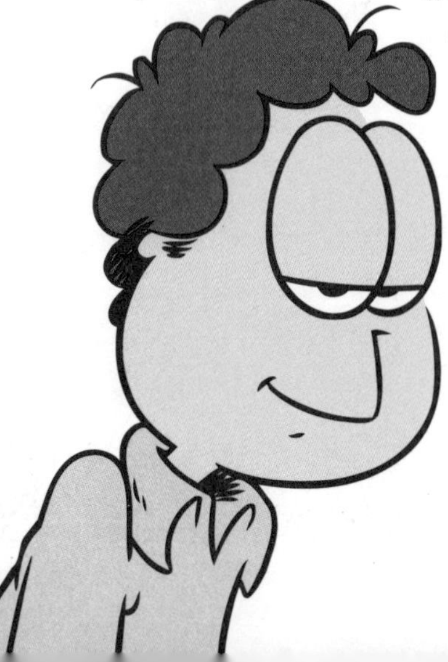

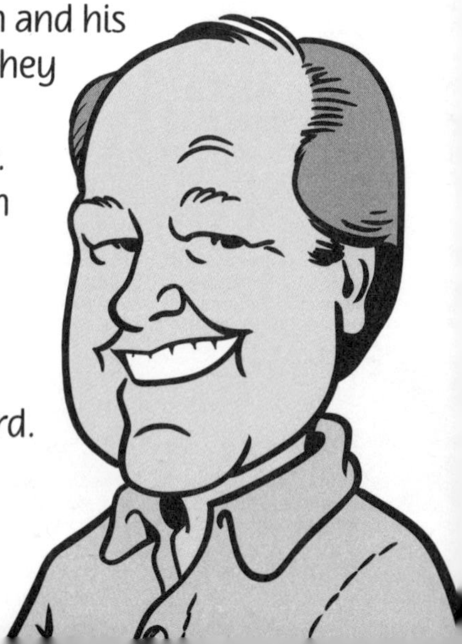

But don't worry; Jon is still a nerd. He's just a nerd who now has a girlfriend. A very, very, very, VERY patient girlfriend.

Looking over the Jon strips from the past thirty-plus years, it was hard to pick just twelve. I had to include the very first strip, as that established the relationship for the reader and set the tone for the comic. And the March 8, 1991, strip has it all: a silly premise, funny words, and hilarious visuals (and who among us hasn't had a little "fun with tape"?).

Enjoy!

JIM DAVIS

HI, THERE... I'M JON ARBUCKLE. I'M A CARTOONIST, AND THIS IS MY CAT, GARFIELD.
JIM DAVIS 6-19
© 1978 PAWS, INC. All Rights Reserved.
HI, THERE. I'M GARFIELD. I'M A CAT, AND THIS IS MY CARTOONIST, JON.
OUR ONLY THOUGHT IS TO ENTERTAIN YOU.
FEED ME.

YESSIREEBOB
JIM DAVIS 3-8
© 1991 PAWS, INC. All Rights Reserved.
WHAT AN EXCITING FRIDAY NIGHT...
SNAP!
FUN WITH TAPE

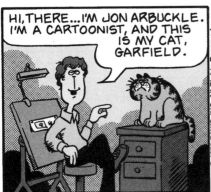

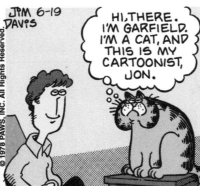

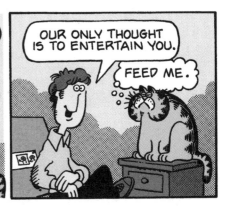

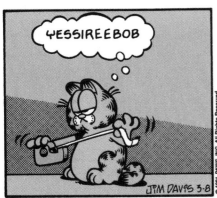

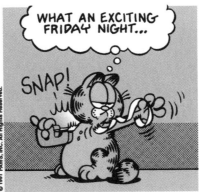

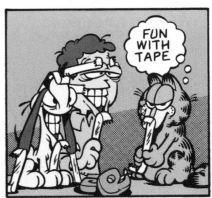

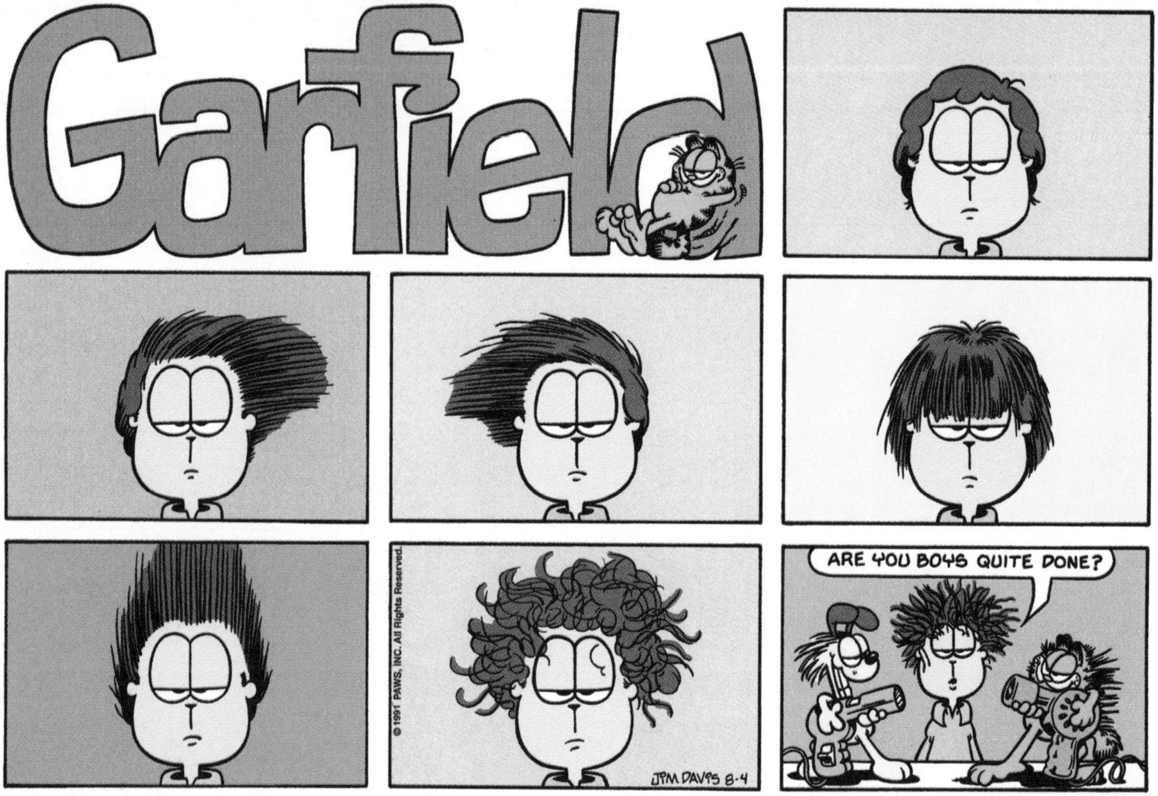
Garfield
© 1991 PAWS, INC. All Rights Reserved.
ARE YOU BOYS QUITE DONE?
JIM DAVIS 8-4

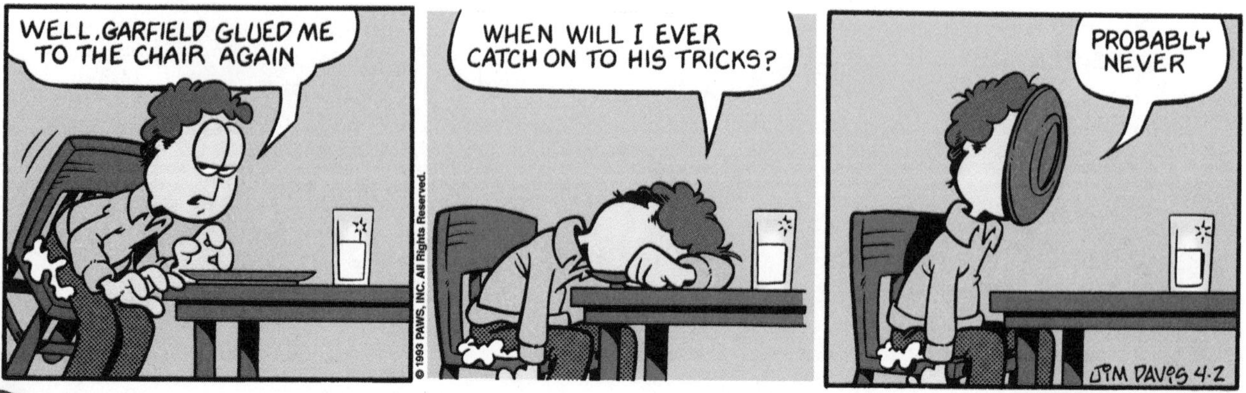
WELL, GARFIELD GLUED ME TO THE CHAIR AGAIN
© 1993 PAWS, INC. All Rights Reserved.
WHEN WILL I EVER CATCH ON TO HIS TRICKS?
PROBABLY NEVER
JIM DAVIS 4-2

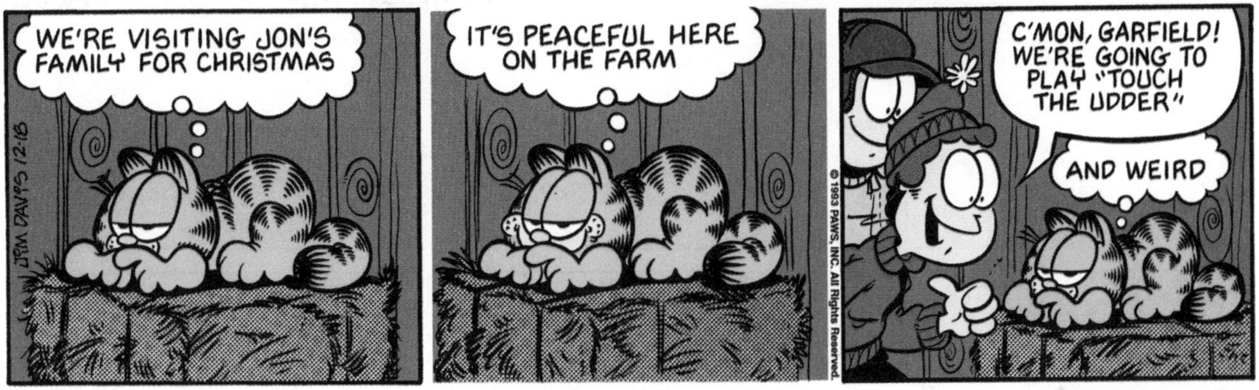
WE'RE VISITING JON'S FAMILY FOR CHRISTMAS
JIM DAVIS 12-18
IT'S PEACEFUL HERE ON THE FARM
C'MON, GARFIELD! WE'RE GOING TO PLAY "TOUCH THE UDDER"
AND WEIRD

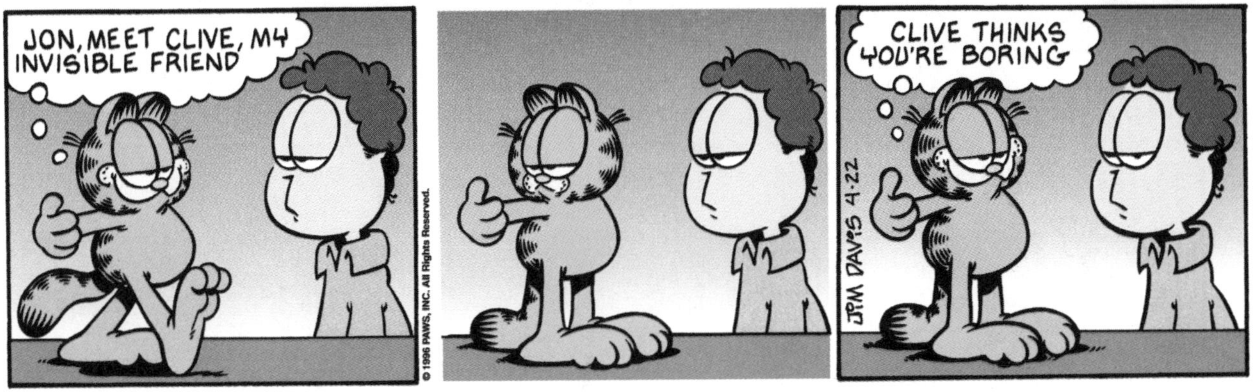
JON, MEET CLIVE, MY INVISIBLE FRIEND
CLIVE THINKS YOU'RE BORING
JIM DAVIS 4-22

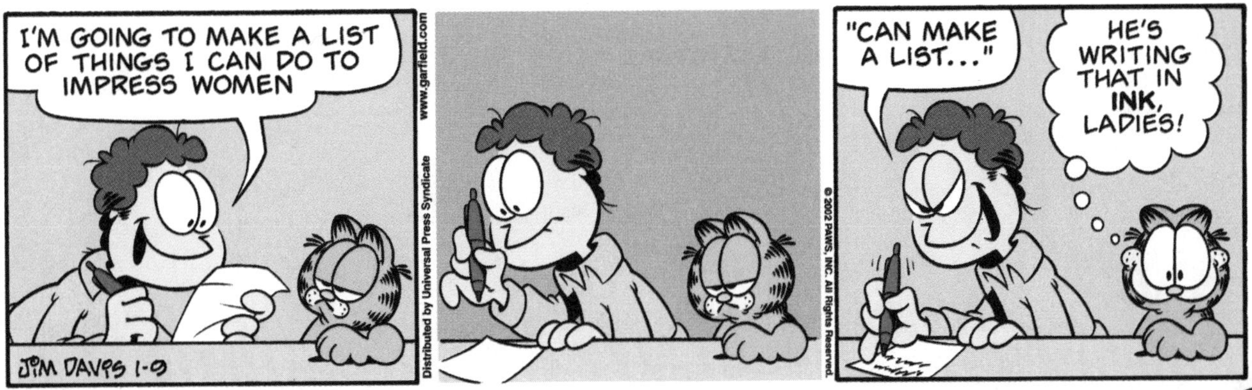
I'M GOING TO MAKE A LIST OF THINGS I CAN DO TO IMPRESS WOMEN
JIM DAVIS 1-9
"CAN MAKE A LIST..."
HE'S WRITING THAT IN INK, LADIES!

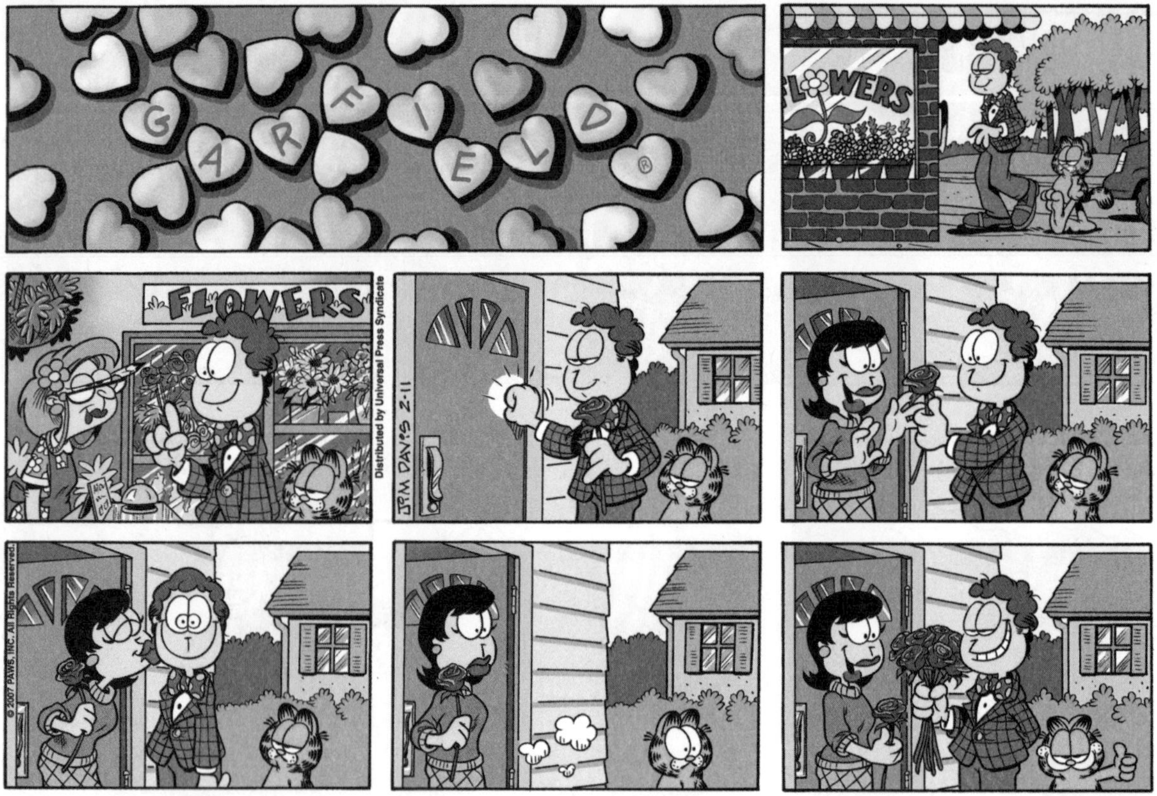
GARFIELD®
FLOWERS
FLOWERS
JIM DAVIS 2-11
Distributed by Universal Press Syndicate
© 2007 PAWS, INC. All Rights Reserved.

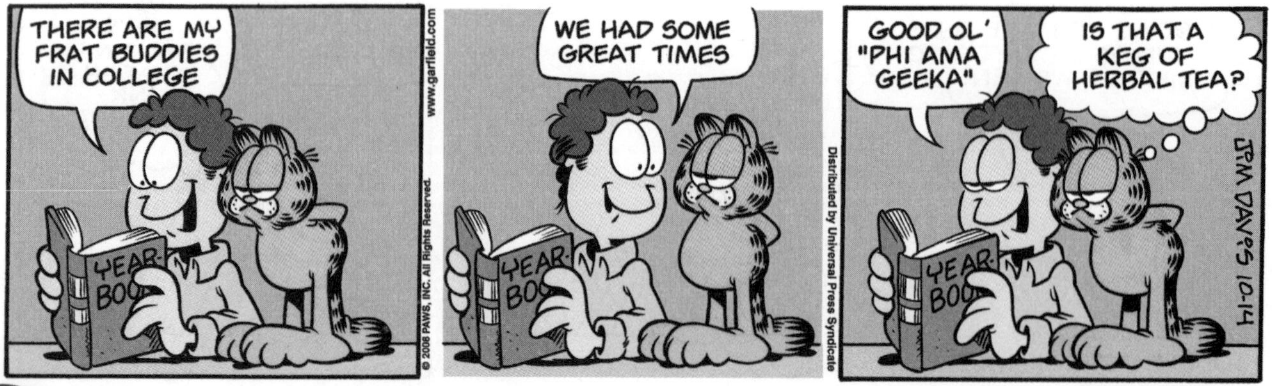
THERE ARE MY FRAT BUDDIES IN COLLEGE
YEARBOOK
© 2006 PAWS, INC. All Rights Reserved.
www.garfield.com
WE HAD SOME GREAT TIMES
GOOD OL' "PHI AMA GEEKA"
IS THAT A KEG OF HERBAL TEA?
Distributed by Universal Press Syndicate
JIM DAVIS 10-14

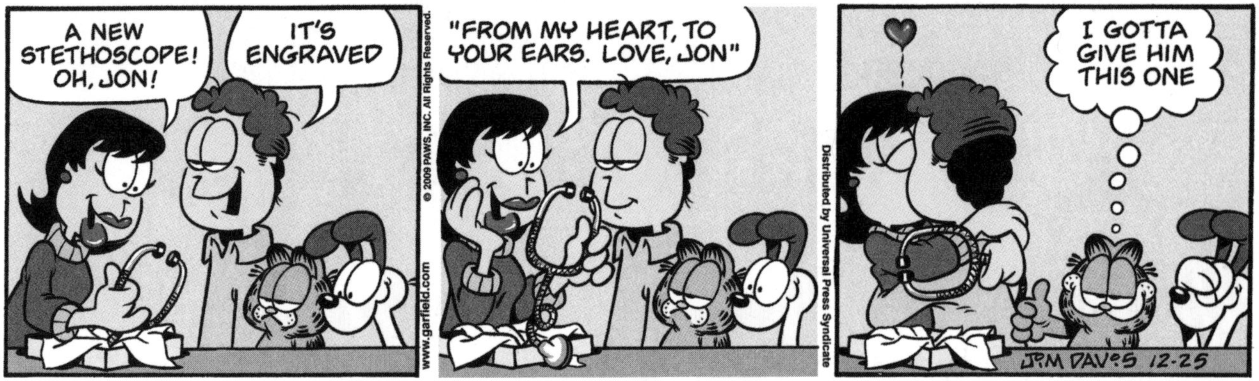
A NEW STETHOSCOPE! OH, JON!
IT'S ENGRAVED
© 2009 PAWS, INC. All Rights Reserved. www.garfield.com
"FROM MY HEART, TO YOUR EARS. LOVE, JON"
Distributed by Universal Press Syndicate
I GOTTA GIVE HIM THIS ONE
JIM DAVIS 12-25

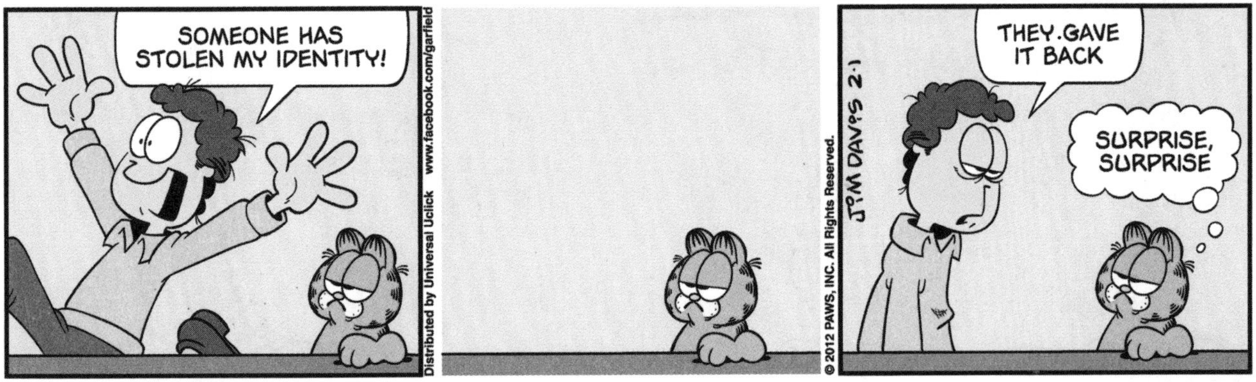
SOMEONE HAS STOLEN MY IDENTITY!
Distributed by Universal Uclick www.facebook.com/garfield
© 2012 PAWS, INC. All Rights Reserved.
JIM DAVIS 2-1
THEY GAVE IT BACK
SURPRISE, SURPRISE

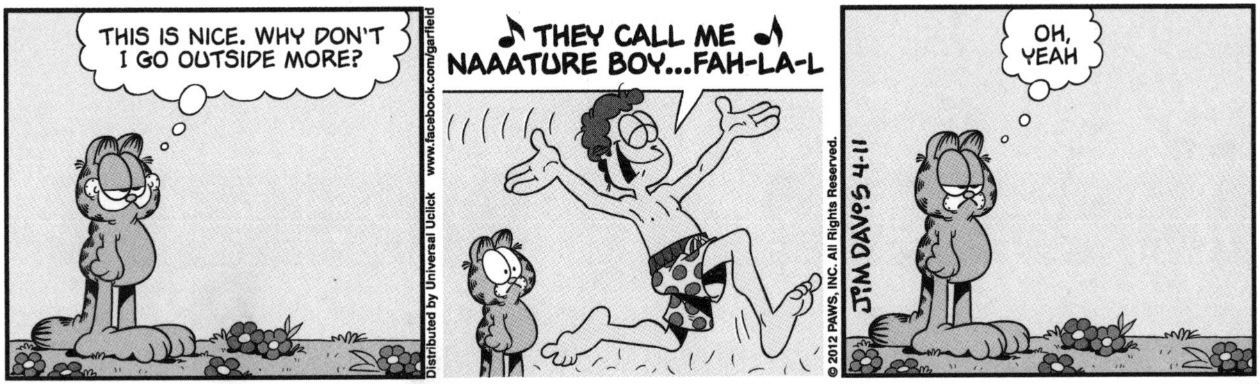
THIS IS NICE. WHY DON'T I GO OUTSIDE MORE?
Distributed by Universal Uclick www.facebook.com/garfield
♪ THEY CALL ME ♪ NAAATURE BOY...FAH-LA-L
© 2012 PAWS, INC. All Rights Reserved.
JIM DAVIS 4-11
OH, YEAH

A behind-the-scenes peek at Jon's weird, wacky world.

Watch Your Step!

NERLET
(LARVAL STAGE)

THE TUX SHIRT THAT ATE MUNCIE

ÜBER NERD

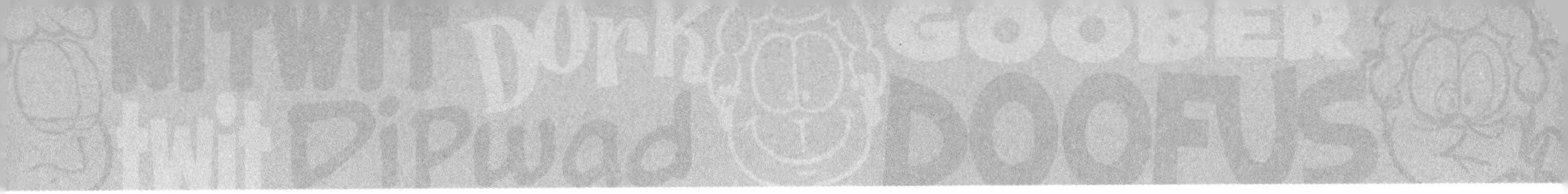
NITWIT Dork GOOBER
twit DiPwad DOOFUS

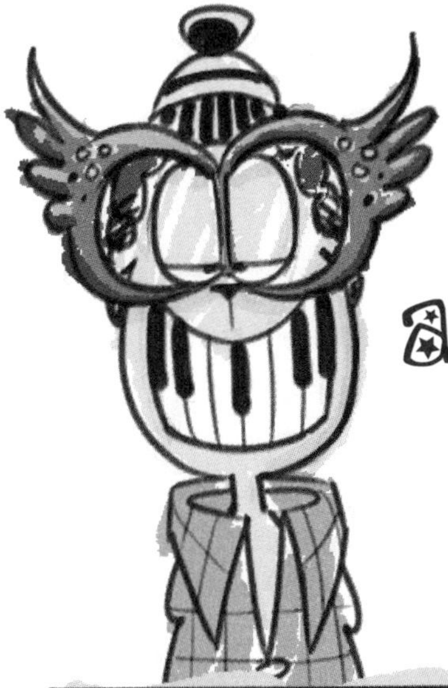

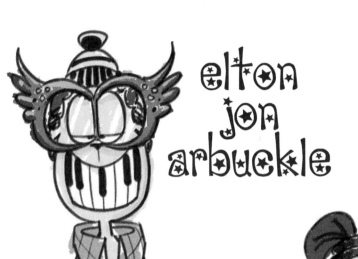

elton
jon
arbuckle

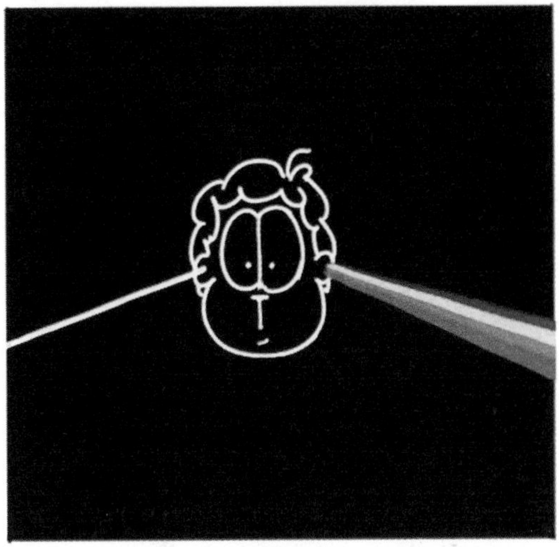

THE DORK SIDE OF THE MOON

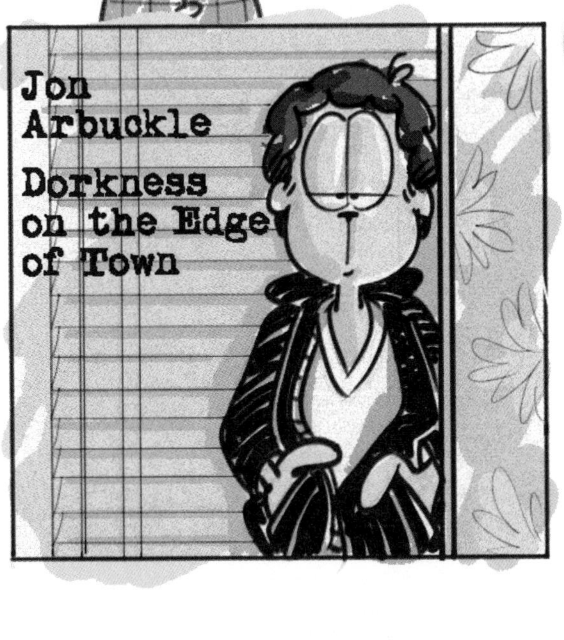
Jon
Arbuckle
Dorkness
on the Edge
of Town

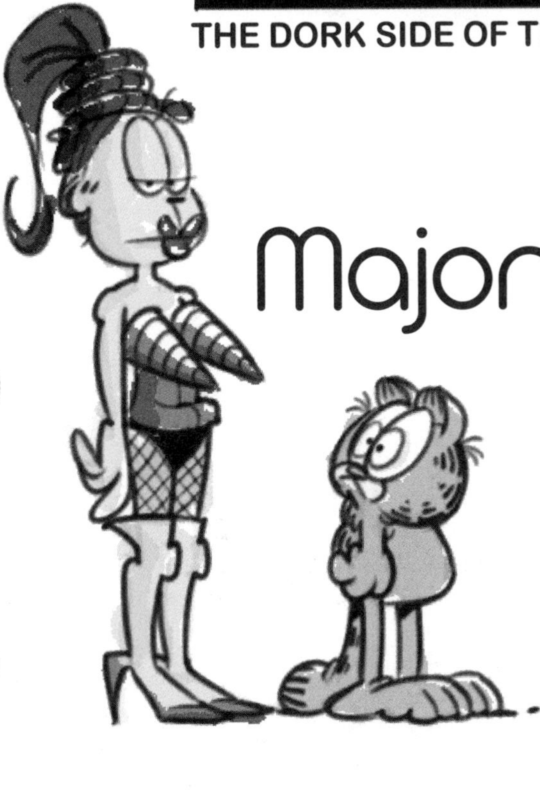

Majonna

REJECTED COVERS

MISTER WONDERFUL
THE JON ARBUCKLE CHRONICLES
REJECTED

RAW AND EXPOSED
REJECTED
The Jon Arbuckle Chronicles

JON OF ARC
REJECTED
the Jon Arbuckle chronicles

Straight Man
REJECTED
The Jon Arbuckle Chronicles

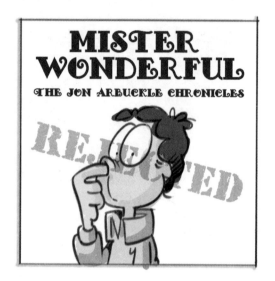

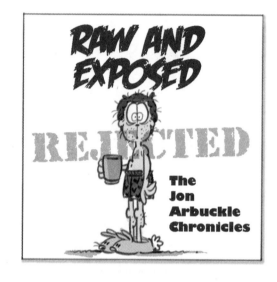

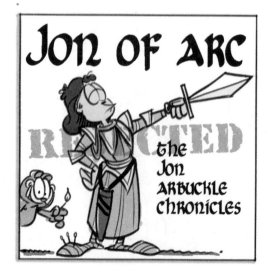

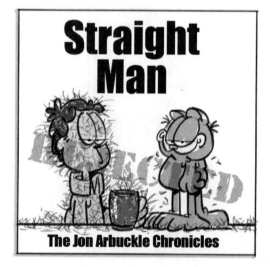

SARTORIAL GOD
THE JON ARBUCKLE CHRONICLES
REJECTED

WHY ME?
THE JON ARBUCKLE CHRONICLES
GARFIELD
REJECTED

The Joy of Socks
REJECTED
The Jon Arbuckle Chronicles

Arbuckle's Ashes
REJECTED
The Jon Arbuckle Chronicles

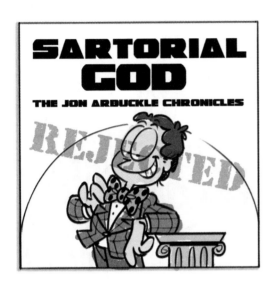

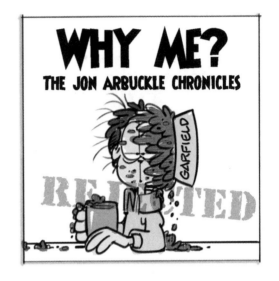

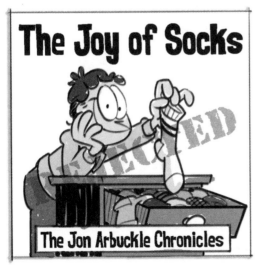

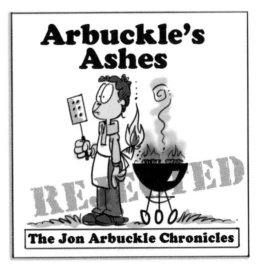

V.I.P.
Very
Irritating
Person

the BOY with the
DACHSHUND
TATTOO

BATTERED PET
OWNER SYNDROME

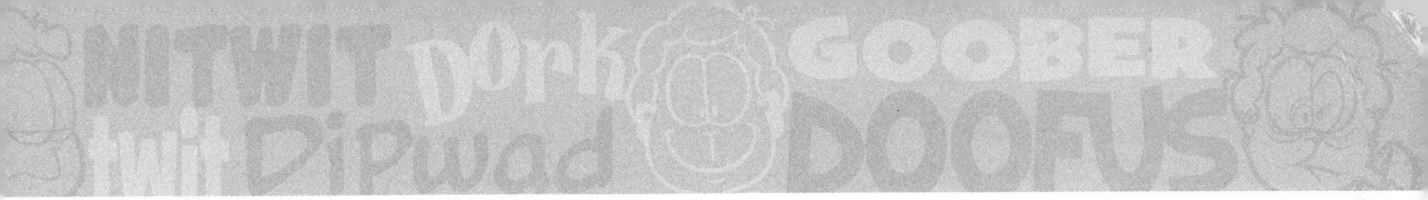
NITWIT
Dork
GOOBER
twit
DipWad
DOOFUS

Author! Author!

Other Books by Jon Arbuckle

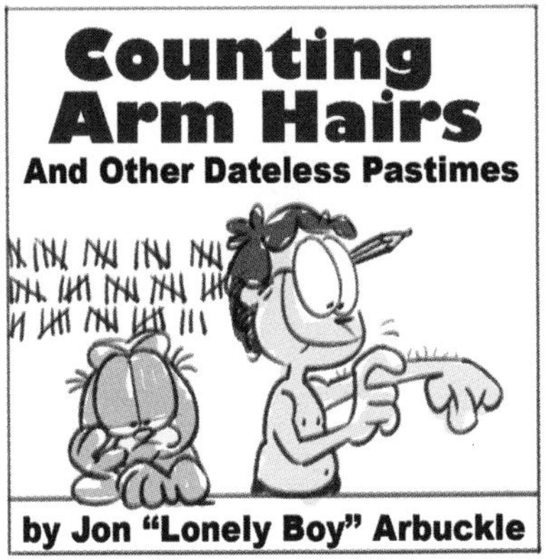
Counting Arm Hairs
And Other Dateless Pastimes
by Jon "Lonely Boy" Arbuckle

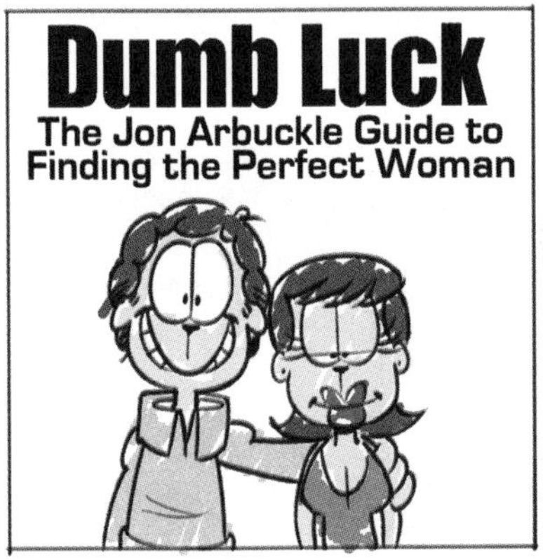
Dumb Luck
The Jon Arbuckle Guide to Finding the Perfect Woman

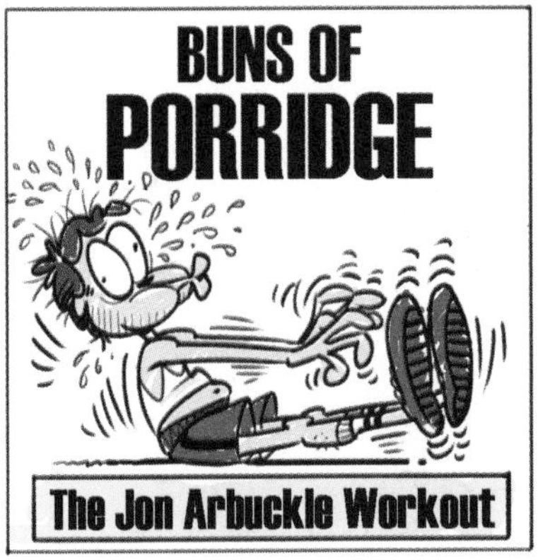
BUNS OF PORRIDGE
The Jon Arbuckle Workout

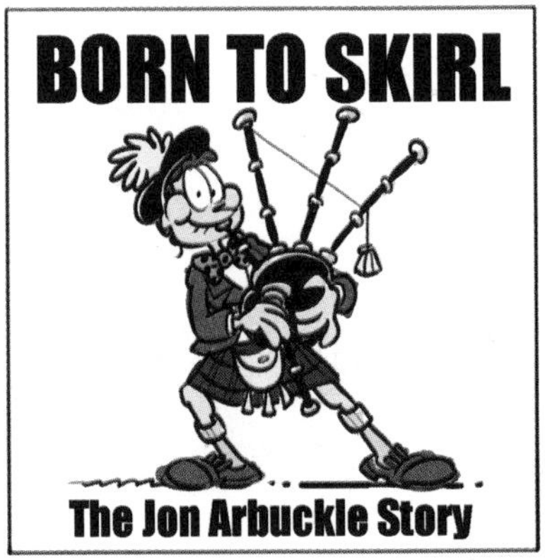
BORN TO SKIRL
The Jon Arbuckle Story

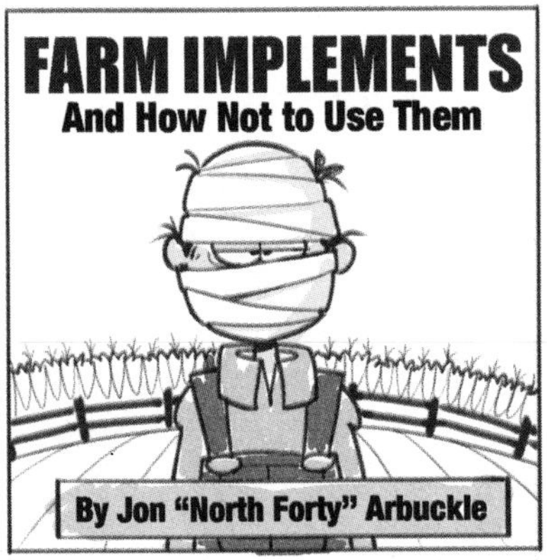
FARM IMPLEMENTS
And How Not to Use Them
By Jon "North Forty" Arbuckle

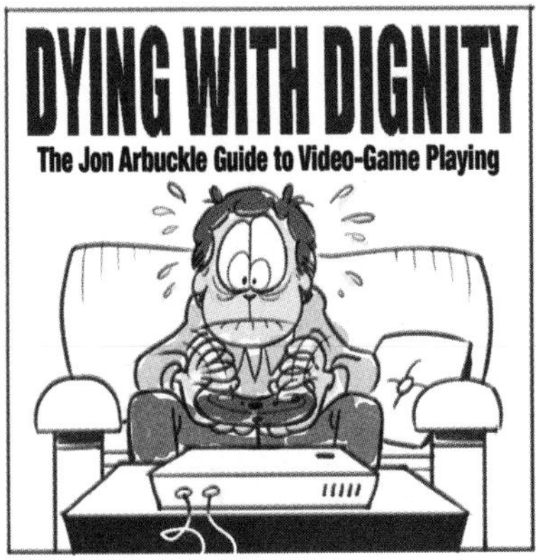
DYING WITH DIGNITY
The Jon Arbuckle Guide to Video-Game Playing

HURR

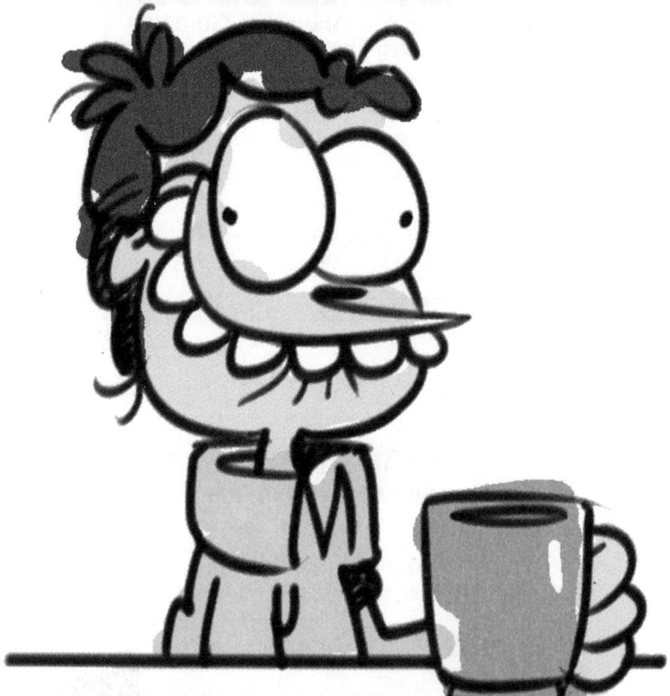

DERP